T0134075

Enterprise Cloud Computing
for Non-Engineers

Enterprise Cloud Computing for Non-Engineers

Edited by
Frank M. Groom and Stephan S. Jones
Ball State University

CRC Press
Taylor & Francis Group
Boca Raton London New York

CRC Press is an imprint of the
Taylor & Francis Group, an **informa** business

AN AUERBACH BOOK

CRC Press
Taylor & Francis Group
6000 Broken Sound Parkway NW, Suite 300
Boca Raton, FL 33487-2742

© 2018 by Taylor & Francis Group, LLC
CRC Press is an imprint of Taylor & Francis Group

No claim to original U.S. Government works
Printed in the United States of America on acid-free paper
10 9 8 7 6 5 4 3 2 1

International Standard Book Number-13: 978-1-138-10621-5 (hardback)

Library of Congress Cataloging-in-Publication Data

Names: Jones, Steve (Virtual computer systems specialist), editor. | Groom, Frank M., editor.
Title: Enterprise cloud computing for non-engineers / [edited by] Steve Jones, Frank M. Groom.
Description: Boca Raton, FL : CRC Press/Taylor & Francis Group, 2018. | "A CRC title, part of the Taylor & Francis imprint, a member of the Taylor & Francis Group, the academic division of T&F Informa plc." | Includes bibliographical references and index.
Identifiers: LCCN 2017054592 | ISBN 9781138106215 (hbk. : acid-free paper) | ISBN 9781351049221 (ebook)
Subjects: LCSH: Cloud computing--Popular works. | Business enterprises--Data processing--Popular works.
Classification: LCC QA76.585 .E57 2018 | DDC 004.67/82--dc23
LC record available at https://lccn.loc.gov/2017054592

Visit the Taylor & Francis Web site at
http://www.taylorandfrancis.com

and the CRC Press Web site at
http://www.crcpress.com

Contents

Acknowledgements

We would like to thank the many contributors of this book, as well as the research they have presented from their industry.

In addition, thank you to Victoria Bishop and Sophie Guetzko, Associate Editors of the Compilation of Cloud Studies.

About the Editors

Frank M. Groom is a professor of information and communication sciences at the Center for Information and Communication Sciences at Ball State University. He conducts research into high-bandwidth networking and the storage and transmission of multimedia objects. Dr. Groom has conducted research into multiprotocol label switching (MPLS)-driven fiber networks, intelligent agents, network-based data deployment, and firewall-based security. He has conducted a number of national research projects using surveys, focus groups, personal interviews, and student research culminating in two of his published books. Furthermore, he has conducted many specialized statistical research studies for AT&T, McDonalds Corp., and Nth Dimension Software. In addition to his graduate level networking, information systems, network security, and advanced database courses at Ball State, Dr. Groom annually conducts a graduate research methods course for Ball State graduate students where he teaches many of the methods he has employed in his own research. His research has been conducted both in industry and at the university, studying both big data problems as well as smaller situations. Dr. Groom has presented networking and data processing courses to major American corporations, including PricewaterhouseCoopers, IBM, AT&T and its various units, Motorola, Digital Equipment Corp. (now HP), Unisys, Ford Motor, Hillenbran Industries, and McDonalds.

AT&T has twice sponsored Dr. Groom to present advanced data processing and networking courses to the graduate students and faculty of Beijing University of Posts and Telecommunications (BUPT) and the People's Republic of China Government Office of Telecommunications. He was honored with having two of his papers presented at the Plenary Session of the 1996 International Conference on Information Infrastructure (ICII'96) in Beijing, China, and another paper presented as the Plenary Session for the Broadband 2000 conference in Tokyo. Furthermore, in 1996, 1998, and 2006, Dr. Groom presented papers on ATM networking, Multimedia, and Voice over Internet Protocol (VoIP) at the leading French Graduate School of Telecommunications (Ecole Nationale Superiore des Telecommunications [ENST]) while consulting with research professors and reviewing the PhD dissertation research of current candidates.

In addition to publishing over 120 technical papers concerning networking, systems design, corporate reengineering, and object-oriented storage, Dr. Groom has published a number of books, including *The Future of ATM and Broadband Networking, The Future of IP and Packet Networking, The ATM Handbook, The Basics of Voice over Internet Protocol, The Basics of 802.11 Wireless LANs,* and *Multimedia over the Broadband Network.* Further, he has authored two chapters in other books: *Network Manager's Handbook* and *Knowledge Management.* He is the coeditor of the four-volume 2006 Annual Review of Communications, and is one of the coauthors of the second edition of *The Fundamentals of Communication for Non-Engineers* with Stephan S. Jones and Ronald J. Kovac for Taylor & Francis.

Dr. Groom has a PhD in management information systems from the University of Wisconsin, was division manager in charge of the Information Systems Division of Wisconsin Bell, and is the retired senior director of information systems for Ameritech (now once again part of AT&T).

Stephan S. Jones spent over 16 and a half years in the communication technology industry while operating his own teleconnect company, providing high-end commercial voice and data networks to a broad range of end users. Later, Dr. Jones was district sales manager for the Panasonic Communications and Systems Company, providing application engineering and product support to distributors in a five-state area.

Since joining Ball State as a professor of information and communication sciences, Dr. Jones has served as the codirector of the Center for Information and Communication Sciences Applied Research Institute and has conducted research in the development of broadband delivery systems, unified communications, and healthcare information technologies, and he has written/edited 15 books and authored numerous book chapters. In his current role as the director of the Center for Information and Communication Sciences, he is charged with external funding development, student career development and placement, the pursuit of new curriculum ideas, graduate student recruiting, and the out-of-classroom learning experience for the Student Social Learning Program.

Dr. Jones received his PhD from Bowling Green State University, where he also served as the dean of continuing education, developing a distance learning program for the College of Technology's undergraduate Technology Education program.

Contributors

Chris Ardeel
Butler University

Victoria Bishop
Burwood Group Inc.

Nick Chandler
ClearObject

Joe Ciuffo
Gensys

Cheer Dheeradhada
Telecom Peers, Inc.

Jake Ellis
Ford Motor Company

Rob Faix
Impact Advisors, LLC

Eric Gerard
Impact Advisors, LLC

Eric Germann

Frank Groom
Ball State University

Kevin M. Groom
AT&T

Sophie Guetzko
Accenture PLC

Tucker Hale
Accenture LLP

Rob Hartman
Butler University

Tom Janke
Butler University

Dan Jones
Ball State University

Kevin Keathley
Ontario Systems LLC

Jared Linder
State of Indiana Family and Social
    Services Administration

Austin McClelland
Accenture Federal Services

Alonso Miller
Adapt Telephony Services

Cameron Schmidt
Ford Motor Company

Ruth Schwer
Butler University

Peter Williams
Butler University

Zach Skidmore
Butler University

Kirk Young
Butler University

Chapter 1

The Basics of Cloud Computing

Frank M. Groom

Ball State University

Contents

Cloud Computing Services

Introduction

The enormous cost of constructing, operating, maintaining, upgrading, and growing a corporate data center has led to the desire to create cheaper and more flexible shared processing centers that can provide on-demand services that meet dynamically changing (elastic) user requirements. This concept emerged with the outsourcing of corporate data center operations to companies such as IBM and the building of disaster recovery data centers for shared use by companies such as SUN. This concept of outsourcing corporate data processing of applications followed by the ability to isolate their operation in a shared usage environment has grown rapidly across the United States and globally, allowing major corporations, sections of the federal and state governments, and individuals to move their processing to virtualized data centers (VDCs) that can host the processing of a large number of clients. Furthermore, the enormous growth in social media and pervasive use of portable devices to interconnect people with each other and their personal and business data has further pressured data center providers to rapidly implement a more affordable model for processing, storage, networking, and even desktop application usage on less expensive, commodity rack-mounted X86-based Xeon servers. This new model of data center operation is termed cloud computing since the user has very little idea where and how their data is stored and processed—thus it is in the "cloud."

To provide cloud computing services requires a process of abstracting the computing through the process of virtualization. A new layer of software sits between each operating system (OS), its supported applications, and the computer hardware. That new software is called a hypervisor which allows multiple applications and the OSs that run them to be placed on a shared use computer. That set of applications and their OS are packaged as a unit which is termed a Virtual Machine (VM). Each VM's applications and their OS have access to the hosting computer's hardware by means of the overall manager of this environment, the hypervisor, which acts as the overall OS for the hardware. All hosted VMs must execute through the hypervisor's Kernel to use the hardware of the physical computer that hosts them.

Furthermore, in our mobile world, cloud computing also enables a standard desktop computing service and application to be extracted from the user's device and placed in a cloud computing data center where other workers and social friends with portable devices can access them. This process allows users with their smart mobile phones and tablets to have the power of an office computer while maintaining the small size, mobility, and portability of that intelligent mobile device. Pools of data storage can be created at the cloud data centers to provide on-demand storage services, which can grow and shrink as the moment-by-moment needs of the user occur.

Before discussing the complete cloud infrastructure and service management, it is important to understand the concept of cloud computing in more detail, including its characteristics, benefits, services, and deployment models (NIST, 2011).

Operating these virtual data centers (VDC) provides flexibility, improved resource utilization, and ease of management compared to the operation of traditional data centers, enabling them to operate more effectively (Wu, 2015).

An example of such cloud computing is Amazon's EC2 Cloud Services offering. Where in the past an organization might have grown its requirements and costs beyond standard large mainframe processing and begin to consider distributing processing over a large number of midrange or smaller servers, they can now purchase the equivalent of up to 1,000 instances of such servers from Amazon to run their mission-critical business applications. Amazon provides service agreements guaranteeing their service offering will meet the required service levels necessary to support the client-company operations and meet the customer expectations of that client–company purchasing these cloud processing services.

Drivers, Characteristics, and Benefits of Cloud Computing

The conversion of traditional computing environments to virtualized environments has also enabled the movement of various organizations to offer cloud computing services to government agencies, large and small businesses, and even special services to individuals. Virtualizing a computing environment means that the various hardware and the software resources are managed as a pool, providing improved utilization of resources. The objectives of virtualization are to centralize management; provide services on standard, lower cost, commodity equipment (processors, network switches, and storage); optimize resources by over-subscribing customer requirements to them; and then managing the available computing and storage capacity so efficiently among the users and their applications that the ebbs and flows of individual requirements offset each other and conserve total overall requirements (IBM, 2017b).

The companies' desire to reduce their capital expenditures while controlling their expenses has triggered a number of companies to offer remote cloud computing services on a pay-as-you-use basis which is accessed over a network, usually the public Internet. Service oriented architecture is a popular service business that processes client application software and stores client data. Cloud computing centers provide a collection of services on a for-use basis. These can include running a set of pre-packaged applications and operating the clients own private applications. The available packaged applications can be offered across many business domains as a set of services and may also be shared by many clients (Zaigham & Puttini, 2013).

The following sections cover the fundamentals, service management, migration strategy, and security aspects of cloud computing.

The Essential Characteristics of Cloud Computing

The infrastructure for cloud computing has six essential characteristics.

1. **On-Demand Services**: Customers of cloud computing can request services on-demand, arrange those services as they need them, and expand or contract them as the business needs evolve.
2. **Services Catalog**: Customers can pick required services from a prearranged catalog of such services. The selected offerings from a cloud data center are then accessed by means of the Internet from an array of devices including desktops, laptops, tablets, iPads, or smartphones.
3. **Internet Access**: Traditionally, users have to install software packages, such as Microsoft Word or Microsoft PowerPoint, in order to use them. If the user is away from the computer where the software is installed this software is no longer available for usage. However, now much of the required software used can be accessed over the Internet. Free Internet versions of common software such as web-based Google Docs allows users to access and edit documents from any device which has Internet connection, thus eliminating the need to have access to a particular office-based computer device.
4. **Dynamic Allocation**: Cloud-based resources, both processing and storage, can be automatically and dynamically allocated, expanded, and contracted quickly and efficiently without interruption of service. When users experience large fluctuations in their required capacity, they can request that the cloud center temporarily increase the number of application servers and storage arrays for the duration of a specific task or for a specified period of time, and

then contract when the demand subsides. The customer only pays for the actual capacity as it is used and not for any standby capacity that might be reserved in case of temporary need.

5. **Metered Service**: The cloud computing services providers keep track of the actual customer usage with a metered service system. They then provide billing and chargeback information for the Cloud resource used by each consumer with a detailed usage file available for customer inquiry. The metering software continuously monitors used CPU time, bandwidth, and storage capacity and regularly provides reports concerning that usage to the consumer along with the billing. Thus, the users avoid the large capital expenditures and operating expenses associated with running their own data center and pay only usage expenses for the services delivered by the cloud computing provider.

6. **Rapid Elasticity**: When organizations need to rapidly expand their business and computing capacity to support those increased operations, cloud computing services quickly accommodates such requirements without the need to raise capital and purchase additional equipment. The customer merely needs to request expanded facilities and the cloud vendor allocates those facilities from their pool of resources and monitors and bills accordingly.

The Advantages of Employing Cloud Services

Cloud computing offers a number of advantages to a customer when compared to the cost of operating their own data center or data centers, staffing the operation, purchasing and deploying the equipment, maintaining that equipment, and then powering, cooling, and protecting it. In contrast, contracting for cloud computing services provides the following advantages (Hamdaqa, 2012):

1. **Reduced IT Cost**: Cloud services can be purchased on an as-used basis. Consumers can avoid the large amount of up-front capital costs and associated operating expenses with no capital expenditure for equipment required. Consumers of cloud services can leverage the cloud service provider's infrastructure while avoiding the ongoing expenses for running a data center; these include the cost of power, cooling, management, construction of buildings, and purchasing of real estate. Consumers pay only for that portion of the costs that they actually consume.

2. **Business Agility Support**: The speed at which new computing capacity can be provisioned is a vital element of cloud computing. These providers can reduce the time required to provision equipment and deploy new applications and services from months to minutes for the consumer. Cloud computing allows organizations to react more quickly to market conditions and enables the cloud operators to scale up and scale down the provided resources as required by individual customers.

3. **Flexible Scaling**: A cloud can be easily and quickly scaled up and scaled down based on individual customer demand. This appears to the customers as if the cloud computing resources are infinitely expandable. Consequently, cloud service users can independently and automatically scale their computing capabilities without any interaction with the cloud service providers.

4. **Increased Availability**: Cloud computing can provide a variety of application availability levels that depends on individual customer policy and the priority of each application. Redundant servers, network resources, and storage equipment, coupled with clustered and redundant software enables fault tolerance for the entire cloud infrastructure. The technique of spreading processing over multiple data centers in different geographic regions which have identical resource configurations and applications diminishes the potential of data unavailability due to individual data center or regional failures.

5. **Less Energy Consumption**: For those organizations concerned with energy and environmental issues, cloud computing enables organizations to reduce power consumption and space usage. Cloud computing further provides services from areas where power outages, tornados and hurricanes, and water shortages are minimized and energy costs are at the lowest possible levels.

Contracting for Cloud Services

Cloud computing services are supplied along three basic models—Infrastructure-as-a-Service (IaaS), Platform-as-a-Service (PaaS), and Software-as-a-Service (SaaS). These three models may also be offered publicly, privately, or in a combination of both, which is commonly termed hybrid (IDC, 2010).

Services Offerings

IaaS

IaaS is the base form of a cloud computing service offering and serves as the foundation for the other two offerings (SaaS and PaaS). The cloud infrastructure consisting of servers, routers, storage, and networking components is provided by the IaaS cloud infrastructure provider. The customer hires these resources on an as-needed basis, paying only for their actual usage. The customer is able to deploy and run their own OS and application software on the provided computers. The customer does not manage or control the underlying cloud infrastructure but does exercise control over the OSs and the deployed applications. However, the customer does need to know the resource requirements for each application to exploit IaaS service to its maximum potential. In this situation, where only the infrastructure components are provided (on an as-needed basis), correct estimation of the required resources and the elasticity of their moment-to-moment usage are the responsibilities of the consumer, not the provider. Thus, IaaS is a bare-bones cloud data center service where the infrastructure is provided, but the customer must configure the required resources (servers and storage) to provide the desired processing level required. Therefore, major responsibility falls to the customers with this level of service as they use it to meet their own customer expectations.

One of the leading IaaS models is provided by Amazon, named the Elastic Compute Cloud (Amazon EC2 and Amazon S2). This is an IaaS model that provides scalable computing capacity on demand. Amazon's EC2 service enables consumers to leverage Amazon's massive infrastructure without expending any up-front capital investment. Furthermore, Amazon's EC2 reduces the time required to obtain and boot new server instances to minutes, thereby allowing consumers to quickly scale capacity—both up and down—as their computing requirements change (Amazon).

Larger customers are experienced with undertaking these responsibilities. However, until now small consumers did not have the capital to acquire massive computer resources that also ensured they had the capacity to handle unexpected spikes in load. The level of service assistance small users demand from a cloud provider are thus much more intensive than the larger companies might require.

PaaS

PaaS is the service that provides the capability to deploy the customer's own created or acquired applications directly into the cloud infrastructure. PaaS offers both an application development environment as well as a production operating environment. These platforms typically have an Integrated Development Environment that includes an editor, a compiler, a builder, and a deployment mechanism to assist the customer in developing and then operating their own applications. After developing and testing an application, the customer proceeds to deploying that application on the infrastructure offered by the cloud provider. When consumers create and install their own applications to run over the PaaS provider's platform, elasticity and scalability are transparently provided by the cloud vendor. The consumer does not manage or control the underlying cloud infrastructure, such as network, servers, OSs, and storage. Instead, the customer controls the deployed applications and the application-hosting environment configurations. For PaaS service, consumers pay extra for usage of the platform software components such as databases, OS instances, any middleware software, and other associated infrastructure costs (Jones, 2016).

Once again, some prominent companies have offered PaaS cloud computing. For instance, Google's App Engine is a PaaS offering that allows consumers to build Web applications using a set of Application Programming Interfaces (APIs) and to then run those applications on Google's infrastructure. With App Engine, there are no servers which the customer is required to maintain, as they would have to undertake in their own data centers. They merely need an application that is ready to serve the customer. Google's App Engine provides a provisioned and managed platform that allows customers to install a completed application or to build a new application that operates reliably, even under heavy load, with large and varying amounts of data. The customer's applications can run in standard C programmed environments or in web-oriented Java or Python programmed environments (Google, 2017). Each environment provides the standard protocols and common technologies that web application developers are accustomed to having at their disposal to employ. The App Engine software development kits (SDKs) for Java and Python include a Web server application that emulates all of the App Engine services on the consumer's local computer. Each SDK kit includes all of the APIs and libraries available on Google's App Engine service platform. Each SDK kit also includes the required tools to enable the customer to upload the consumer's application to Goggle's App Engine platform in Google's data centers. After the consumer has developed the application code and constructed the appropriate configuration files, the customer can then run the provided upload tool from Google to upload the application to Google's data center (Finn, 2012).

Microsoft also has a PaaS offering, the Azure Platform. Microsoft's Azure Platform supplies a broad range of tools, resources, and other functionalities to allow customers to build, host, and scale applications which will then be operated in Microsoft data centers. Customer application developers have available familiar Microsoft tools, such as visual studio and .NET Framework, to use in developing applications. Microsoft's Azure software contains a cloud-based OS that enables the development, hosting, and service management environments for the overall Azure platform which is offered as a service to Microsoft's customers (Microsoft, 2018).

SaaS—Software-as-a-Service

SaaS is the most complete service offering of the cloud computing stack. It offers the capability to the consumer to use the cloud service provider's applications, which are installed and running on the cloud service provider's cloud infrastructure. These provided applications can be accessed from many client devices by means of a thin client interface, such as a standard web browser. Customer-built, customer-operated, and customer-hosted applications are quite expensive to develop, run, and maintain. In a SaaS model, the applications of customer billing, accounts receivable, customer relationship management (CRM), sales management, email, and instant messaging can all be pre-built by the vendor and offered as a packaged commodity application service by the cloud service provider. The customer only uses the applications they need and they pay a subscription fee for that usage. The cloud service provider hosts and manages the required infrastructure, provides the management and control of the application tools to support these services, and supplies a set of pre-built and packaged application suites of services which the customer requires (CIO).

The SaaS providers can perform much of the software maintenance, testing, upgrades, and problem repair for the employed software, significantly reducing the amount of customer effort.

There are also a number of vendors who have begun offering SaaS services. Some examples are provided by EMC and Salesforce.com. Among these are

1. EMC provides the Mozy software product as a SaaS backup and recovery solution for individuals and corporations which utilize EMC's scalable back-end storage architecture. Consumers can use their own devices or can use the Mozy console to perform automatic and secured online backup and recovery of their data. MozyHome and MozyPro are two variations of the Mozy product. MozyHome is for the individual consumer who wants a cost-effective way to backup and store their data, photos, music, and documents. Alternatively, MozyPro is intended for organizations looking for a cost-effective way to back-up their end user's data. Both of these software services are available for a monthly subscription fee. Using EMC's Mozy backup service, consumers can avoid purchasing their own backup storage and processing resources. They need only minimal resources to manage such storage from either the provided console or from their own devices (EMC, 2016).

2. Salesforce.com provides a SaaS-based set of CRM products for managing a company's interactions with both current and future customers. Organizations can use CRM applications to access the tools and services required to build improved relationships with their customers. These CRM applications run in the provider's cloud computing data centers. They enable the consumer to access the application from anywhere through an Internet-enabled interface to the provider's cloud-based computer systems. Customers pay on a subscription basis for using these CRM applications from Salesforce.com and manage their operation as their own virtual infrastructure.

Some Deployment Models for Offering Those Cloud Services

Three broad deployment models have been used to provide cloud computing services. These deployment models offer Platform as a Service (PaaS), Software as a Service (SaaS), or IaaS in a specialized fashion, and may even offer all three Service levels simultaneously in a given cloud data center facility.

Public Cloud Service Offerings

IT resources are made available to the general public or organizations and are owned by the cloud service provider. The cloud services are accessible to everyone via standard Internet connections. In a public cloud, a service provider makes IT resources, such as applications, storage capacity, or server compute cycles available to any contracting consumer. This model can be thought of as an on-demand and a pay-as-you-go environment, where there are no on-site infrastructure or management requirements of the customer. However, for organizations these benefits come with certain risks. The customer has no control over the resources in the cloud data center, the security of confidential data, basic network performance, and little control over the interoperability between applications. Popular examples of public clouds include Amazon's Elastic Compute Cloud (EC2), Google Apps, and Salesforce.com's Cloud Service.

The public cloud infrastructure is shared by several organizations and supports a specific community of users that share certain concerns about the operation of such a processing center—its mission, high level of security requirements, common policy, and strict compliance considerations. An example where a community cloud could be useful is in a state government setting. If various agencies within the state government operate under similar guidelines, they could all share the same infrastructure and spread the cost among themselves.

In addition, a community cloud might be managed by the organizations or by a third party with the costs spread over fewer users than a public cloud. Although the community cloud option is more expensive than a public cloud offering, it offers a potential of a higher level of privacy, security, and policy compliance as well as access to a larger pool of resources than would be available in a private cloud offering.

Private Cloud Service Offerings

Private cloud service offerings are where the cloud infrastructure is operated solely for one organization's utilization and is not shared with other organizations. This cloud model offers the greatest level of security and control but significantly weakens the customer's ability to reduce costs through sharing resources across a number of companies' computing requirements.

There are two variations to a private cloud:

1. Cloud services offered in an on-premise private cloud: On-premise private clouds, also known as internal clouds, are hosted by an organization within their own data centers. This model provides a more standardized process and the customary protection, but is limited in terms of size and scalability. Organizations also need to incur the capital and operational costs for the physical resources. This is best suited for applications which require complete customer control and configurability of the infrastructure and security (IBM, 2017a).

2. Externally-hosted private cloud: This type of private cloud is hosted externally with a cloud provider, where the provider hosts an exclusive cloud environment for a specific customer organization with full guarantee of privacy or confidentiality. This is best suited for organizations that do not prefer a public

cloud due to data privacy/security concerns but also wish to avoid the burden of financing and operating their own data centers.

Like a public cloud, a private cloud enables provisioning through an automated service request rather than by means of a manual task processed by an on-site IT technician. In the case of on-premise private cloud service, organizations that chose this type of cloud service will have to run their own hardware, storage, networking, hypervisor, and cloud software. Many enterprises, including EMC, Cisco, IBM, Microsoft, Oracle, and VMware, now offer such private cloud service platforms and the services, tools, and procedures to build and manage a private cloud (Oracle, 2017).

A Hybrid Approach

Virtualization in private cloud service allows companies to maintain service levels in the face of rapid workload fluctuations. Organizations use their computing resources in a private cloud computing center for normal usage, but access the public cloud for less risky, high/peak load requirements. This ensures that a sudden increase in computing requirement is handled gracefully. An organization might use a public cloud service, such as Amazon's Simple Storage Service for archiving data, but continue to maintain in-house storage for important operational customer data. Ideally, the hybrid approach allows a business to take advantage of the scalability and cost-effectiveness that a public cloud computing environment offers without exposing mission-critical applications and data to third-party vulnerabilities (Santana, 2014).

Changing the Cost Incurred for Providing Data Processing

Enormous capital expenditure is required to build a corporate data center infrastructure and sizable operational expenditure (OPEX) is needed to run and maintain such centers. When companies can contract with a reliable cloud service provider to provision and operate such centers they can convert their expenditures to operational expenses. They thus gain the tax advantages of OPEX while avoiding the requirement of acquiring the capital to create, grow, and modernize their own data centers. Contracting for cloud computing services provide the following cost savings:

1. **Data Center Creation Costs**: To build a large-scale data center system, a company needs to acquire the real estate and construct a data center building. Following the construction of that building, electricity, water sources, sewerage, and telephone company facilities are ordered and connected to the major infrastructure within the data center. These resources connect to

the necessary electric transformers, distributors, and uninterruptible power system for the data center operation. Also installed are a number of diesel generators that operate should public power fail. Furthermore, the data center operator must purchase a number of computer servers, data storage devices, routers and switches, and the Fiber Channel networks to interconnect these components. Then, they need to license, install, upgrade, and maintain the software which operates these computers, storage, and networks. With cloud computing contracts, such investment in the data center infrastructure is off-loaded to the cloud computing vendor and allocated to the usage cost per unit of time billed to the customer.

2. **Operational Management Cost**: Operating a corporate data center also involves employing and training a variety of technical personnel. Among these are operational personnel for running the applications, supporting the networks, and proving help desk support to end-user customers who access the data center to make use of the offered computing services. Furthermore, a number of technical support personnel are required to plan, order, configure, install, troubleshoot, and upgrade the set of computers, storage networks, power equipment, and associated software. Particularly scarce are the hardware technicians knowledgeable in deploying and managing data storage and the allocation of space to user applications. This array of specialized people is a critical component of the operation of cloud data centers and they are significantly in demand by the IT industry. Including end user help and support personnel as an allocated part of the cost of using the contracted services and avoiding the direct cost of those specialized people significantly reduces the cost of operating the client company's day-to-day operation (Jayaswal, 2006).

3. **Managing Power, Energy, and Cooling Costs**: Power consumption has become a concern for most organizations because energy costs continue to rise. Constructing a data center involves a sizable capital expenditure of that infrastructure. The cloud service provider organization must employ specialized monitoring and control software to minimize the energy use of the infrastructure equipment and the applications that require usage of those resources. Managing energy efficiency is a major aspect of delivering cloud data center services at a reduced cost to the customer, while providing a profit to the supplying company.

The Required Cloud Computing Infrastructure

The aggregated resource components to provide cloud computing services to create the virtual infrastructure are the applications and platform software, the cloud computing service creation tools, and the infrastructure management programs and procedures, as well as the hardware, building, technical, and management personnel and supporting systems.

The physical infrastructure for cloud computing service offerings consists of an array of computer servers, a pool of intelligent storage systems, and a Fiber Channel network which connects all components within the data center. Using that network, servers are collected into an interconnected pool that also includes a pool of intelligent storage systems. These within-center facilities are then connected to external networks for regional, national, and global data center communication. Connection is also made to the public Internet enabling customer access and as a means of providing connectivity for management and tech support personnel.

Cloud computing services collect resources from one or more data centers in order to provide their offered pay-as-you-use services. Interconnectivity among the cloud data centers enables the pooled resources across the data centers to be managed as a single large virtual data center and facilitates provisioning across the array of pooled resources. The provider must balance offered customer processing load on a dynamic basis across those resources located in the multiple cloud data centers while provisioning, expanding, and maintaining those resources on a transparent basis that remains hidden from customer view and does not affect customer operations.

The managed virtual infrastructure within these cloud data centers contain CPU pools, memory pools, network bandwidth pools, and intelligent storage pools. In addition, identity information pools such as Virtual Local Area Network ID (VLAN ID) pools, Virtual Storage Area Network (VSAN ID) pools, and Media Access Control (MAC) address pools are present. These pools are managed as VMs, virtual volumes, and virtual networks with virtual switches and virtual NICs (InfoWorld, 2016). CPU cycles, memory, network bandwidth, and storage space are allocated from these resource pools for use by VMs.

Customer-provided business applications and shared-use platform-provided business applications used by the clients, as well as a variety of OSs and database management systems, are run on VMs hosted on physical machines. The shared-use platform software applications are delivered by the cloud services vendor as pay-for-usage SaaS or as PaaS offerings.

For SaaS, applications and platform software are provided by the cloud service providers. For PaaS, only the platform software is provided by the cloud service providers while consumers export their applications to cloud computing resources. In IaaS, consumers upload both applications and platform software to the cloud data center. Cloud service providers supply migration tools to consumers, enabling deployment of their applications and platform software to the Cloud.

Cloud infrastructure management and service creation tools are responsible for managing physical and virtual infrastructures. Cloud infrastructure management and service creation tools automate consumer requests, processing, and creation of cloud services. These tools enable consumers to request cloud services and allow operators to provide cloud services based on consumer requests so that consumers can have access to and use of the cloud services. They also provide administrators a single management interface to manage resources distributed in multiple VDCs (Hamdaqa, 2012).

Cloud management tools are classified in three categories. First is the virtual infrastructure management software which enables the management of both the physical and virtual infrastructure resources. Second, there is the unified management software which is employed for the creation of cloud services. Third, there is the user access management software which enables consumers to issue requests for the cloud services that they require. These various software components interact to automate the overall provisioning of cloud services.

Virtual infrastructure management software provides tools to construct the virtual infrastructure that represent the underlying physical infrastructure. It enables the communication components, such as hypervisors, to enable the processors to be partitioned into VMs. It allows the control of physical switches interconnecting components in the data center to be abstracted to operational control centers. Furthermore, this software enables the configuration of pools of virtual storage resources by means of these infrastructure management tools.

In a VDC, computers, storage, and network resources of both the physical and virtual infrastructure are independently configured using a variety of virtual infrastructure management software. For example, a storage array has its own management software. Similarly, network and physical servers are managed independently using specialized network and computer management software respectively.

Systems That Make the Cloud Work

Vendor Virtualization Software

As an example of available virtualization software, Dell/EMC, EMC's subsidiary VMWare, and Cisco have delivered an integrated set of products under the label Vblock which help companies build virtualized cloud data centers. This set of prebuilt infrastructure components quickly can be put into operation forming the core computers, storage, and networking components of a cloud data center.

Furthermore, VMware, along with a number of other companies, provides a cloud user access management system (vCloud Director) which enables cloud service consumers to create VM service offerings and then request a service through a Web-based user interface. VMware further supplies authentication routines for verifying consumer identities as they request and access cloud services.

VMware also offers a chargeback system that performs the monitoring of usage and the measurement of the costs for providing those services. Fixed costs, allocated VM costs, actual usage of resources cost, and a reporting system for charging are included.

EMC offers Unified Infrastructure Manager for configuring resources and activating services through a single, dashboard-like, user interface. Through this interface the customer can manage multiple Vblock-based services from one management system which eliminates the need for separate systems and tools to manage separate computer, network, and storage resources and services in a cloud data center.

Employing Automation, User Portals, and Racks of Commodity Components

On the surface it is difficult to see how a provider can operate a multi-tenant data center, with the added difficulty of individually satisfying each client, compared to each company providing their own data processing operation under their own control. The answer is due to a number of factors, which are as follows:

1. Everything is automated – service offerings, ordering services, managing services, changing services, processing, connecting, and storing (Lowe, 2016).
2. Customers and data center managers operate by means of preestablished service portals.
3. All equipment is off-the-shelf – inexpensive commodity computers, switches, and disk storage. This is contrasted with the large specialized mainframe and mid-range computer servers; large, specialized disk units; and specialized interconnectivity populating traditional data centers.
4. Finally, everything in the data center is virtualized so that it can be placed on an initial device, then expanded, contracted, moved, and reconnected at will by the data center operators by means of their orchestrating management portal.

The following discusses each of these components which allow improved quality of processing at a significantly reduced price and reliability through shared use cloud data centers.

Automate Everything

The secret to the profitable delivery of large-scale, global cloud computing is that all aspects of running such a data center operation have been computerized such that only minor monitoring of ongoing operations require professional personnel. The installation and maintenance of equipment, software, and applications are performed by a specialized team entering, performing the task, and then exiting the data centers. In many cases those activities can be performed remotely.

Additionally, all offered services are standardized and stacked as Gold (with top scale storage, computing, and online turn-around performance), Silver (with medium levels of these components), and Bronze (with lesser levels of such components). Each of these levels of service is priced and a contract is presented for completion.

A customer portal is presented to the remote customer with access by a browser over the Internet through which they can select the broad category level of service required. The customer can then choose small augmentations to enhance the service level, with each of these enhancements priced individually.

The Customer Portal

The customer portal is offered by the cloud provider as the single, unified interface for the customer to communicate with the cloud provider in the process of purchasing, enhancing, modifying, and extending their cloud service. The customer can access the portal from any location using any intelligent device. Through the customer portal they can chose their OS, desired Database Management System, the number of CPUs and performance, the amount of internal computer memory, the amount of external storage, and the number of additional features and services. They can also find an explanation of the technology, features, and services as well as the pricing of all items at various levels of usage. Finally, a standard Service Level Agreement (SLA) is presented for the customer to endorse. An example of some of these items on such a portal is displayed in Figure 1.1.

Information about the infrastructure resources available to the customer are presented for selection by the customer through the user portal. These include:

1. Computer systems including the number of blade servers, CPU speed, memory capacity, CPU and memory pools, and mapping between virtual and physical compute systems.
2. Network components, including the switch models, network adapters, VLAN IDs, VSAN IDs, physical-to-virtual network mapping, Quality of Service (QoS), physical network topology structure, and separate zones into which those networks may be subdivided.

A catalogue of services available to the user
available database, processor
and storage and pricing example

	Alternate 1	Alternate 2
Database	Oracle object	SQL server
CPU	1 Virtual CPU expandable to 4 V-CPUs	1 Virtual CPU expandable to 4 V-CPUs
Storage	100 GB expandable to 400 GB	100 GB expandable to 400 GB
Pricing arrangement	Prorated by amount selected and deployed	Prorated by amount selected and deployed
Netcost	$1,500/week to $5,000/week	$900/week to $4,000/week

Figure 1.1 Example of a customer portal for service level selection.

3. Storage systems, including the type of storage systems available, the drive types in each, the total capacity in each, and of that total capacity the usage breakdown including the free portion of capacity available and the used capacity, the RAID level (Levels 0–6), the storage pools, and the individual physical-to-virtual storage mappings.

Note: RAID (redundant array of independent disks) is a data storage virtualization technology that combines multiple physical disk drive components into a single logical unit for the purposes of data redundancy and performance improvement. The standard RAID levels (Levels 0–6) comprise a basic set of RAID configurations that employ the techniques of striping, mirroring, or parity to create large reliable data stores from multiple general-purpose computer hard disk drives (HDDs).

Further choices to be selected by the consumer include three categorized service pools offered through that user portal. These have scaled levels of pricing associated with the service quality guaranteed based on predefined criteria. Multiple grade levels, such as Gold, Silver, and Bronze, may be defined for each type of service pool including processor pools and storage pools. Costs and prices of resource pools will differ depending on the grade level (Figure 1.2).

Through the customer portal, customers are presented with an outline of the available services to choose from, as displayed in Figure 1.3. In addition to CPU, memory, storage, and OS, a whole catalog of available services are presented, each with pricing and any extra charges that might be incurred and some sample SLAs to be used as a possible template for their own SLA.

Furthermore, cloud providers such as Amazon will provide to the customer a list of all Web services that are available to the customer.

Choosable grades of service levels offered

Grade 'Gold': Includes flash, FC, and SATA drives, supports automated storage tiering, capacity 3 TB (Flash 1TB, FC 1TB, SATA 1TB), and RAID level 5

Grade 'Silver': Includes flash, FC, and SATA drives, supports automated storage tiering, capacity 3 TB (Flash 0.5TB, FC 1TB, SATA 1.5TB), and RAID level 1+0

Grade 'Bronze': Includes FC drives, capacity 2TB, RAID level 5, and does not support automated storage tiering

Figure 1.2   Service level grade pools are offered to the customer.

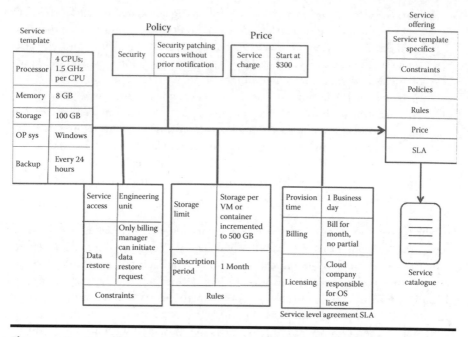

Figure 1.3 An example of the service offering components that can be customized.

The Cloud Data Center Management Portal

In a similar fashion to the customer portal, the minimal operations personnel in the data center perform their surveillance and operations management activities through their own portal. This is presented to them as a layered dashboard with lists of important items with green, yellow, and red lights indicating the status and warning levels with buttons to open up detailed information about current and historical events (Figure 1.4).

Working through an overall management system, sometimes referred to as the "Orchestrator," operations personnel can access all data center service elements and dynamically allocate, de-allocate, or rearrange them as necessary. Operations can also bring online, by means of a set of Service Management Tools, newly installed or rearranged equipment, features, and services as they become available (Figure 1.5).

The customer's portal is directly interfaced to the data center operations dashboard and orchestrator system so that a quick activation of customer needs and concerns can be accomplished as soon as requested. Surveillance and management soon follow. This sequence from the customer to the portal and to the operations personnel, all by means of the direct interconnection to the orchestrator, is presented in Figure 1.6.

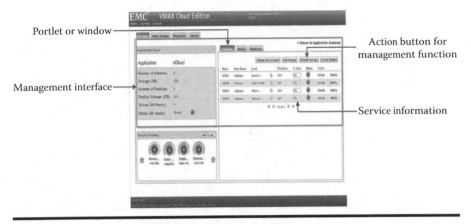

Portlet or window

Management interface

Action button for
management function

Service information

Figure 1.4   The management dashboard.

Reducing Costs by Employing Inexpensive Commodity Equipment

Commodity Computers, Disks, and Operating Systems

In the 1990s, data centers contained expensive IBM Mainframe computers priced in the range of $5 million and arrays of disk storage each costing from $100,000 to $500,000. Furthermore, the annual cost of the OSs (MVS and VM) and the database management system (MIS, DB2, Ingress, Informix, or Oracle's DB) was an additional burden. In the first decade of the twenty-first century, inexpensive RAID storage arrays became commonplace, directly connected to midrange computers in the $500,000–$1,000,000 range.

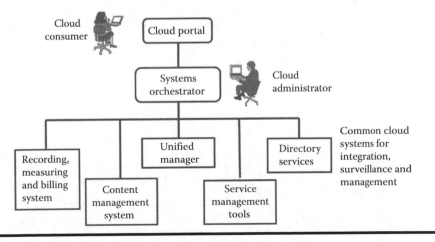

Figure 1.5   The overall structure of the data center management system.

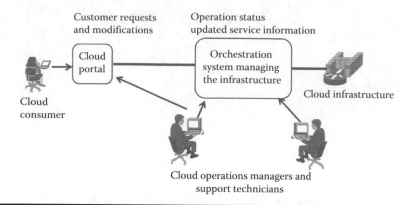

Cloud consumer

Cloud operations managers and support technicians

Figure 1.6 Direct connection of customer portal, operation dashboard, and orchestrator system.

For cloud computing data centers to offer significant savings to their customers, these hardware and software costs needed to be drastically reduced. In order to make such processing effective at a dramatically reduced cost, a large array of rack-based commodity computers were employed and placed in a string of holding racks. These computers were stripped of standard unnecessary components, including

Intel Xeon E5-2670 specifications
General information
Type   CPU/Microprocessor

Market segment   Server
Family   Intel Xeon E5-2600

Model number E5-2670

CPU part numbers   CM8062101082713 is an OEM/tray microprocessor
      BX80621E52670 is a boxed microprocessor
Frequency 2600 MHz
Turbo frequency   3300 MHz (1 or 2 cores)
3200 MHz (3 or 4 cores)
3100 MHz (5 or 6 cores)
3000 MHz (7 or 8 cores)
Bus speed ?
8 GT/s QPI (4000 MHz)
5 GT/s DMI
Clock multiplier 26
Package   2011-land Flip-Chip Land Grid Array
Socket   Socket 2011/LGA2011
Size   2.07" × 1.77"/5.25 cm × 4.5 cm
Introduction date March 6, 2012

Price at introduction $1552 (OEM) $1556 (box)

Figure 1.7 A commonly employed Intel Xeon E5-2670 computer specification.

video cards and internal disk storage. The following Figures 1.7 and 1.8 present specifications for a common Intel Xeon computer (one of the set of a number of Xeon versions with increasing power that are commonly employed) and a picture of a rack which contains a number of such computers.

Additionally, a commonly employed open OS, Linux, is installed to execute applications on the Xeon processors. Linux is frequently available at a small price from companies such as Red Hat.

Such Xeon processors are stripped of unnecessary components, such as advanced video cards, a mouse, and keyboard ports and mounted in racks similar to the rack in Figure 1.8.

Figure 1.9 presents a standard 50K square foot data center with extensive rows of rack-mounted Xeon computers and arrays of RAID disk storage.

A small operations team surveilles the operation and the components of the data center from a central operations control facility through the orchestrator display module.

Storage

Rows of inexpensive RAID disks are employed under the control of a set of computerized RAID controllers, whereby application data can be stored in a striped fashion across the array of disks as shown in Figure 1.10.

Commodity Network Switches and Routers within Data Center Switching

Standard switches and routers from companies such as Cisco are employed in cloud data centers to connect a cluster of rack mounted computers to a bank of RAID

Figure 1.8   An array of Xeon computers enclosed in a rack.

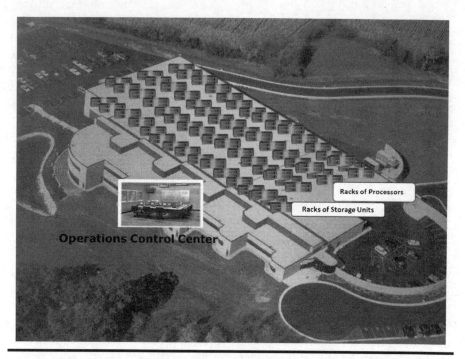

Figure 1.9 A cloud data center with racks of Xeon computers and RAID storage arrays.

disk arrays. With fiber as the physical connecting links, Gigabit Ethernet, Fiber Channel, and Fiber Channel over Ethernet are standard transmission protocols which can be switched by commodity Ethernet and Fiber Channel switches and routers to alternate destinations in the cloud data center. That common network can then be further connected to external carrier facilities which employ Carrier

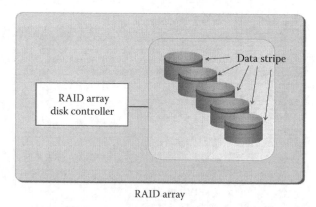

Figure 1.10 An array of inexpensive RAID disk units under the control of a local processor.

Ethernet and MPLS over fiber links to other cloud data centers which also employ Ethernet and IP packets for standardized framing of data for transmission.

Virtualizing of All Aspects of the Cloud Data Center for Cost Effective Cloud Service Delivery

Virtualized Computing

Computer virtualization is a technique of separating (masking or abstracting) the physical hardware from the OS that runs the sets of applications. This process enables multiple OSs (and their individual sets of applications) to be individually ported to and installed on a cloud computer/server and each set (OS and its applications) to be installed on and executed on a single machine. These OSs can be a mixture of Windows 10, UNIX, Linux, or Mac OS10.

A separate overall OS, usually Linux, runs the machine hardware and interfaces for all with the computer hardware and plug-in modules, such as Ethernet Networking cards.

This process can be extended further to a cluster of machines running many OSs and giving the impression to each OS that it has the complete physical machine or cluster of machines to itself. Each OS can then manage and allocate shared resources, without knowledge that such sharing extends way beyond the set of applications that each OS serves. This virtualization thus encapsulates an OS and a set of applications into a logical entity termed a VM. Each VM is further enabled with the capability of portability where it can be moved and operated on other physical machines or clusters of machines—thus creating a portable VM.

Placing a Processing Unit in a Cloud Data Center

Figure 1.11 presents a laptop computer with its stored and functioning OS, probably Windows 10, and a set of applications which are represented as App1, App2, and App3. The intent is to move this set of an OS, its supported Apps, and their

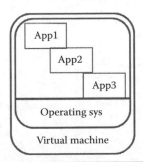

Figure 1.11 Laptop items now identified as a virtual machine with OS and 3 Apps.

stored data to a cloud data center. As an illustration, the following outlines this process of porting the OS and a set of applications from a laptop to a cloud data center and demonstrates the flexibility such a movement creates for the customer.

From that laptop, the OS (Linux, UNIX, Windows 10, or MAC OS10), the set of applications, and the data for each application can be extracted and packaged as a unit. We will call that package of items a VM. When placed on a processor in the cloud data center, this package operates as if it were still operating virtually on the original laptop. It is virtually on its own original machine. That VM unit is now viewed as presented in Figure 1.10.

Such VMs tend to be run by a single OS (say Windows 10, Linux, or UNIX) with the common preference being Linux. This is packaged as a single portable processing entity—a portable VM—that is transferable from the original processor and to be placed as a combined, packaged VM on a computer in a cloud data center. That VM processing unit (OS, applications, and data) was originally on a laptop, desktop, server, tablet, or possibly even on a smartphone (Figure 1.12).

Now take that same processing module VM from the laptop (with its enclosed OS and set of Apps and their data) and move it to a cloud data center and install it on one of the available cloud computers and you now are ready to be a client of a cloud data center.

Virtualizing Cloud Data Center Computers: The Heart of Cloud Computing

First Virtualize the Computing Compute virtualization is a technique of separating (masking or abstracting) the physical hardware from the OS. This then enables multiple OSs to run at the same time on a single machine. Moreover, this

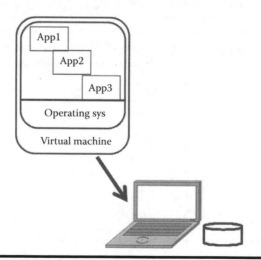

Figure 1.12 A virtual machine on a laptop.

process can further be extended to a cluster of machines running many OSs and giving the impression to each OS that it has the complete physical machine or cluster of machine to itself. Each OS can then manage and allocate shared resources without the knowledge that such sharing extends way beyond the set of application that each OS serves. This virtualization thus encapsulates an OS and a set of applications into a logical entity termed a VM. Each VM is further enabled with the capability of portability where it can be moved and operated on other physical singular machines or clusters of machines—thus creating a portable VM.

Each Cloud Data Center Computer Has a Super Operating System: The Hypervisor

The Hypervisor

To overcome the limitations of inefficiently running a small number of applications in time-share fashion on a large physical machine, a hypervisor software package has been created which allows many OSs, each with their own applications, to run on a single physical machine. This improves computer utilization by the sharing of computing resources while also reducing and delaying the cost of additional hardware acquisition.

To enable computer sharing among OSs and their applications, a hypervisor serves as an intermediary between the hosted OSs and the applications that run over them. The hypervisor interacts directly with the physical resources of a computer system— frequently an x86 based computer. Because the hypervisor enables the sharing of the available computing resource among more applications and OSs, it is the key component of data center consolidation efforts allowing multiple OSs and applications to reside and be executed simultaneously on a common physical machine.

The two key components of the hypervisor are the kernel module and a virtual machine monitor. The kernel module acts as an interface to the physical hardware for the hosted OSs and their applications. This is one of the prime functions performed by an OS itself. Now with the addition of the hypervisor as the interface to the computer hardware, many OSs can be simultaneously hosted on the computer, each one supporting its own set of application programs. The result is that by employing the hypervisor kernel module, we have the opportunity to more completely use the full capacity of the computer hardware resources. The hypervisor's kernel module provides process creation and scheduling as well as the file system management. A process is the official term for a loaded program including its code, identity information, preliminary page table, queue entries, and the stack information used by the hosting OS. Since a hypervisor is designed to support multiple VMs, including a set of OSs and their applications, it provides a core OS to hardware functionalities for all installed VMs, such as hardware resource scheduling, and Input/Output (I/O) stacks for reading and writing to external devices and networks.

The hypervisor's virtual machine monitor actually executes each OS and their hosted application's commands on the CPUs. The virtual machine monitor module also performs binary translation for software such as Java encoded programs, which might contain some instructions that are not directly supported by the hosting computer's hardware. The virtual machine monitor allows the shared hardware to appear to the OSs and their applications as an unshared physical machine with its own CPU, memory, and I/O devices. Each VM is assigned to the virtual machine monitor which is allocated a portion of the usage of the CPU, memory, and I/O devices on the physical computer. When a VM starts running, the control is transferred to the virtual machine monitor, which subsequently begins executing instructions from both the application and hosting OS assigned to a VM processing through the hypervisor on a real physical computer.

Hypervisors are generally provided in one of two ways, either as a bare-metal hypervisor or as a hosted hypervisor. A bare-metal hypervisor is directly installed on the computer hardware and has direct access to all the hardware's resources. This hypervisor approach is the most common approach for virtualized cloud computing data centers. On the other hand, the hosted hypervisor is installed and runs as an application on top of an OS with that OS interfacing for the hypervisor to execute instructions on the computer hardware. Since the hypervisor is running on an OS, it supports the broadest range of possible hardware configurations that the OS can handle.

The hypervisor has two major components:

1. A kernel module which talks to the computer hardware for the entire set of running guest OSs and their Applications (Apps).
2. A main OS processing component called a Virtual Machine Manager (VMM) which manages the guest OSs that it hosts on the serving computer (Figure 1.13).

Currently, some of the most popular hypervisors are Dell/EMC's VMware ESX and ESXi, which requires a licensing fee has been extensively employed for a number of years; Microsoft's Hyper-V, which is tightly integrated with Microsoft's Windows OS but lacks many of VMware's advanced features; Citrix's XenServer, which has been widely deployed and is free but lacking advanced features; and Oracle's OracleVM which is based upon the open source version of Xen. Some other frequently employed open source hypervisors are OpenStack, VirtualBox, and KVM (Citrix, 2017).

Docker Containers: A Streamlined Alternative to VM Hypervisor Virtualization

Virtualization by means of the elaborate mechanisms of constructing VM modules, each with their own guest OSs and all run by a hypervisor and host OS for the serving computer, is an effective method for migrating large portions of an enterprise's data

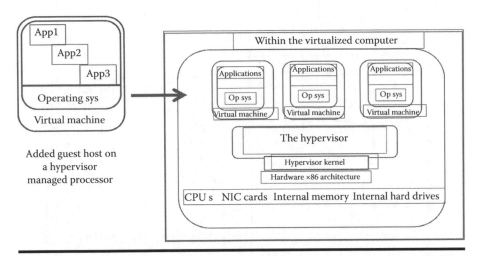

Figure 1.13   Installing customer's ported virtual machine on a cloud computer with other hosted VMs.

processing to a cloud center. However, a more streamlined alternative was sought for bringing single applications to a cloud data center. This would also offer faster expansion and contraction of capacity and quick movement of applications to other processors when necessary. The Linux OS community created such a streamlined approach— Linux LXC. Following that, the Docker Company created a more commercial version of this approach. The resulting Docker Container is a packaged approach whereby one application can be packaged with the libraries and bins it will use. No OS is packaged with that application. The Docker Container comes with its own installation routines for placing the container on the processor. Containers only work with the open-source Linux OS, which is separately installed on the serving computer. In place of the elaborate hypervisor as the intermediary between each installed container (and its application) and the Linux OS and the hardware it uses for execution is a streamlined container or Docker Engine. Figure 1.14 presents a visual summary of the similarities and differences between the more elaborate VM with the required hypervisor and the more streamlined container approach (each with only one application and no OS of its own) to virtualizing the application execution environment.

Containers decouple applications from OSs. Users can have a clean and minimal Linux OS running a processor and install a number of guest applications. Each application is packaged into a separate isolated Container or Sandbox. All containers expect a common, shared Linux OS to run the hardware. Each container employs its own bins and libraries for use with that common Linux OS.

Also, because the OS is separated from the containers, a container can be quickly and simply moved to any other processor/server which is running Linux and has installed an enabling container engine (which can be thought of as a mini-hypervisor).

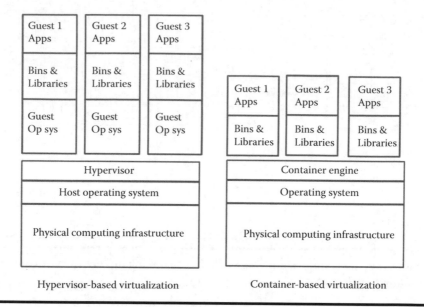

Figure 1.14 Hypervisor-based processor virtualization versus container-based virtualization.

Initially Linux had its own single-application LXC containers. Docker then introduced a change to Linux LXC that makes containers more portable and flexible to use. Using the more advanced Docker Containers, you can initially deploy containers, replicate them, move them to other processors and data centers, and back up their workload more quickly and easily than you can do so using standard VM environments where each guest has their own OS and a Super-OS. The hypervisor allows all the processing to occur over a common machine OS whose kernel interfaces with the hardware and any virtual inter-guest communication. Instead of the VM hypervisor, Docker Containers employ a Docker Engine which is a lightweight container runtime and robust tooling that builds and runs your container. The Docker Engine runs on both Linux and Windows OSs on any infrastructure to create the operating environment for applications. From a single container on a single host to a multi-container application networked across a cluster of hosts, the Docker Engine delivers powerful tooling with a very simple user interface. Docker allows packaging of application code and dependencies together in an isolated container that shares the OS kernel on the host computer system. The in-host daemon communicates with the Docker Client to execute commands to build, ship, and run containers.

The concept of Virtualization through VMs or containers is to separate applications from the underlying hardware. However, containers additionally decouple applications from their OS allowing for fast scaling and portability.

As the interest in containers has grown, Microsoft has begun offering its own version of containers with the Microsoft Windows Server OS. The first is a pure container – the Windows Server Container. The second, the Hyper-V Container, runs as a highly optimized VM working with Microsoft's Hyper-V Hypervisor. Both will be offered as options with Microsoft's own Azure cloud computing offering.

Virtualizing the Hypervisor's and Cloud Data Center's Networking

If one of the applications on their newly moved and installed VM processing unit wants to send messages or use a processing subroutine on another VM on the same computer, there is a packaged connection pre-built into that cloud computer which is supplied by the hypervisor.

That inter-VM connectivity within the computer is a Virtual Ethernet. It is really just some table entries in a hypervisor file. However, to the Apps and Guest OSs the Virtual Ethernet looks to them like a real Ethernet and they send traffic to each other within the computer over the Virtual Ethernet just like they would over a real Ethernet. There are even Virtual NICs (network interface cards) (not real ones, table entries), one which is used by the sending guest VM and one which is used by the receiving VM. Logically between them lies a Virtual Ethernet Switch (which is a table entry as well). All of these transfers and virtual switching are performed by the hypervisor as if it is physically happening over a physical Ethernet between two distant VMs and their Apps.

Therefore, if any of the Apps on the newly moved and installed VM processing unit wants to send messages or use a processing subroutine on another VM on the same computer where it has been installed, there is a packaged connection pre-built into that cloud computer provided by the hypervisor.

Of course, that connectivity is not by means of a real Ethernet, but a Virtual Ethernet. In reality, the connectivity is by means of a set of table entries in a file used by the hypervisor. But to the Apps and Guest OSs it looks and acts like they are transmitting over a real Ethernet to a distant VM on another computer. There are even Virtual NIC cards (not real ones, table entries) that include one for the sending guest VM, one for the receiving VM, and a Virtual Ethernet Switch (Figure 1.15).

The Virtual NICs for each VM and Virtual Ethernet Switch cross connecting them are just table entries in the hypervisor's Virtual Management files. You might ask—why do that virtual operation? Why go to all that trouble of creating a table version of a real Ethernet network inside a computer with virtual (table entry) hardware—NICs and Switches? This is so that VMs and their Apps can quickly be moved to other machines and even other data centers with no change to the VM itself.

If a set of VMs have been loaded into a cloud computer hosted by the hypervisor and the machine's OS, a virtual connection of the Apps in one VM can be created across the computer through a logical, virtual Ethernet Switched Network using virtual NICs for each VM.

Within the virtualized computer

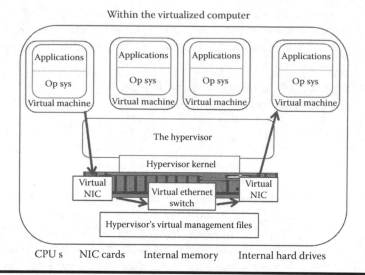

Figure 1.15   Interconnecting VM Apps by a virtual Ethernet to other VM apps on the same computer.

That virtual switching environment in each switch exists so we can connect within the switch and can also move any VM processing module anywhere else in a cloud data center (or to any other cloud data center) should the cloud provider find the need. A VM can be installed on a computer and then moved to any of the cloud computers (each run by their own hypervisor) which have the capacity to host this moved VM and operate it along with the other VMs already hosted. Everything looks the same to the moved VM processing module after the move as before. If that moved VM needs to connect to the other VM on the original hypervisor-run computer across the cloud data center, it transmits the same way over an Ethernet, but in this case out over a real Ethernet. It all looks the same to the moved VM and its applications.

Because of the high bandwidth required for interconnection in cloud data centers they connect their computers, network components, and storage devices by fiber and employ Fiber Channel (or Fiber Channel over Ethernet) protocol and use Fiber Channel NICs and ports. The Ethernets that the VMs see are operated on top of the underlying Fiber Channel and physical fiber network (Figure 1.16).

The hypervisors on the various cloud computers share their hosted VM information on a commonly shared native hypervisor file system. This allows for quick movement of hosted customer VM packages to other computers whose hypervisor knows about them from the common hypervisor file system (Figure 1.17).

The two computers (the one where the VM was originally installed and the one to which the VM was moved) share a common virtual processing file system listing all of the VMs with their specifications and locations. This shared file system also stores all the specifications of the virtual networks and the virtual storage systems,

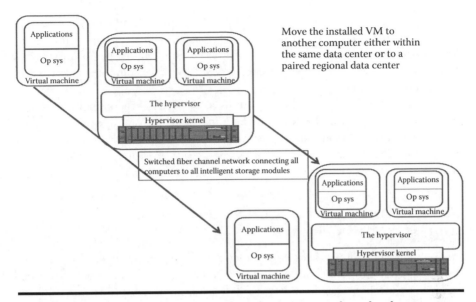

Figure 1.16 Porting a VM with its OS and Apps to another cloud computer—same data center.

as well as the lists of links to the real physical components that are used by all the computer systems, the VMs, and their Apps. Furthermore, we can run Ethernet traffic from the Virtual Ethernet inside the computer out over the real intra-Data Center Fiber Channel Network or Gigabit Ethernet to connect to Apps on all the other Computers in the Data Center.

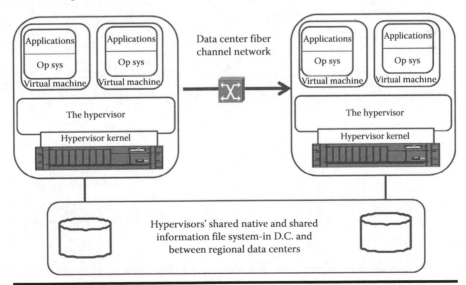

Figure 1.17 The shared hypervisor file system.

Nothing changes when we move the VM processing module from one computer to another. When the host computer changes, the virtual machine has no knowledge of the migration. It thought it was communicating across an Ethernet that was across a real data center Ethernet LAN to a distant computer, possibly even in a distant data center.

The hypervisor fooled it into thinking the Virtual Ethernet inside a computer was a real Ethernet LAN so that later it enabled transfer to occur over a real Ethernet (over the cloud data center's real Fiber Channel network). And it can extend that Ethernet connectivity out over a Carrier Wide Area Network (WAN) between cloud data centers.

Software Defined Network Connection with Cloud Data Centers

As traditional networking became dominated by large, expensive switches and routers empowered by installed software, cloud computing with its focus on off-the shelf hardware (switches) and open software moved towards what is termed software defined networking. In this approach, the control of the software and tables driving switches and routers is elevated to a centralized control center. This operations control center contains all the Policy Components that inform the switches. Such items as device type (of the End Unit), type of traffic that can flow through the device and from whom and to whom, and what each tenant (processor or storage device) can do are all maintained by the central control center with information downloaded to the switches and routers of the data center. This is portrayed in Figure 1.18.

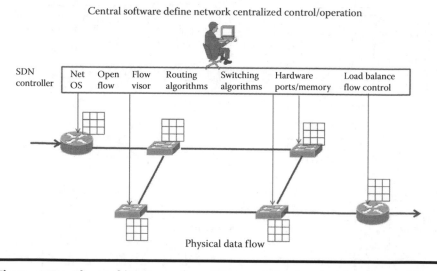

Figure 1.18 The architecture of a software defined network managed by a central control center.

Furthermore, following the move towards utilizing off-the-shelf hardware and opensoftware, the three-layered architecture of more expensive commercial large switches is being replaced with a two-layered approach. This architecture is termed a Spine and Leaf architecture. Here each processor or storage device is attached to an inexpensive Leaf Switch. The leaf switches do all the work of interconnecting the processors to each other, to storage, and to leaf switches connecting the outside world to the cloud data center, while the spine switches provide the backbone cross connection. Each leaf switch is only one hop away from any other leaf switch. And thus, each processor is only one hop away from any other processor or storage device. This provides a very efficient means of connection. Such a spine and leaf architecture providing connection within a cloud data center is portrayed in Figure 1.19.

With the employment of these commodity switches, there has been an emphasis on employing the fast 10 Gigabit Ethernet protocol to replace Fiber Channel and other switching protocols. This may eventually be enhanced or replaced by 40 Gigabit and even 100 Gigabit Ethernet in the future as the need arises.

Interconnecting VMs and Containers across Distant Data Centers

The national carriers, such as AT&T and Verizon, offer a number of connection services that allow for the creation of high speed circuits across distance so that a

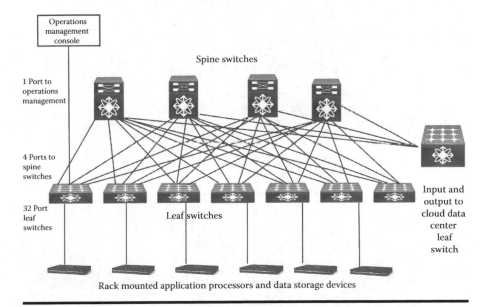

Figure 1.19   The Spine and Leaf Architecture interconnecting processing and storage units.

set of a cloud vendor's data centers can be interconnected to form either a tightly connected regional nest of data centers operating as a single virtual data center, or a separate but interconnected set of data centers. Since the common protocols used inside the data center are Ethernet and Fiber Channel, carriers currently have a set of facilities to carry such traffic on national high-speed fiber links. A number of such facilities are Carrier Ethernet and MPLS. Cloud data centers already use high-speed Ethernet networks to carry IP traffic from computers to data storage units and to VMs on other computers within the data center. That traffic can be merely switched to an external Carrier Ethernet or MPLS service to be transported to another cloud data center (Figure 1.20).

Mobile customers can access the cloud data center portal and its presentation of available services by means of the public Internet. Furthermore, when these customers are present in offices they can access the cloud data center by means of the array of carrier-provided wide-area high-speed services such as Carrier Ethernet and MPLS.

Computer-using customers can access the cloud data centers by means of traditional browser-based web access over the Internet or once again by means of carrier

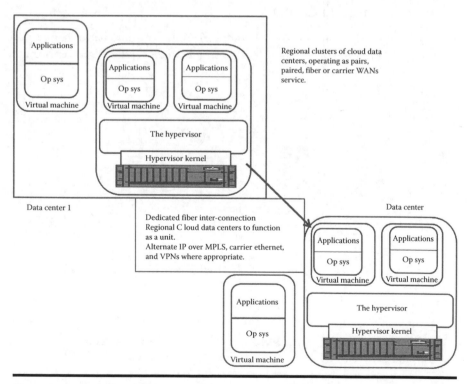

Figure 1.20   Carrier-wide area services—carrier Ethernet and MPLS to interconnect data centers.

provided wide-area services such as Carrier Ethernet, MPLS, or MPLS Virtual Private Networks with encryption capabilities.

Increasingly customers with volume traffic, especially those who seek to bring traffic to multiple cloud data centers, deliver their traffic to a network consolidator (such as Equinix in the United States and Huawei in Europe) (Equinix, 2017). That consolidator then forwards that customer's traffic along with mixture of data streams from other customers over a set of leased fiber cables each connected to the appropriate data center location of a vendor (such as Amazon). Or the consolidator may split the traffic and transmit some, for example, to a Microsoft Center and other traffic to an IBM Center. For a volume transmitter this approach provides flexibility, while it also off-loads to the consolidator the responsibility for dealing with the carriers, monitoring and managing the traffic flows, and addressing routing and rerouting issues. These alternatives are portrayed in Figure 1.21.

An App in the customer's VM processing module doesn't know whether it is communicating within the same computer or to another computer across the data center floor when it attempts to send packets over an Ethernet LAN. A VM and its applications can be processed on its initial computer or moved to any other computer on the floor with sufficient resources to satisfy the customer's service requirement of the moment. The VM may also be moved once again if further increased resources are subsequently required.

As a result, one App may now be communicating across the cloud data center to an App still residing on the initial computer in DC 1 or to an App on any other computer in another regional, national, or global cloud data center. In our virtual

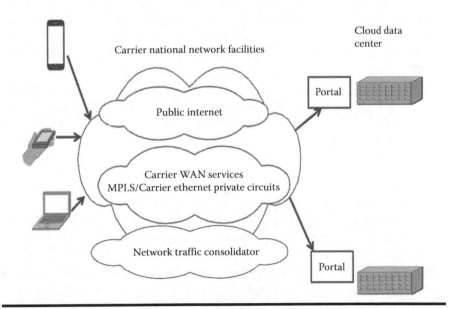

Figure 1.21   Customer traffic is also connected by similar carrier services.

world, any App and its whole VM can be at one place today and offered somewhere else tomorrow. And its destination storage can be moved around as well. Either can be moved and still connect to the component that has the right capacity and performance. This way processing capacity can be elastic and grow and shrink as quickly as needed. The guest OS and its Apps (a VM) don't need to be aware that any change has occurred.

Moreover, the same flexibility exists for both our networks and storage capacities. Virtual files of our networks and storage specs are maintained and used by the systems (and through them by the cloud operations personnel) to manage real capacity by employing the virtual specification tables for networks and storage similarly to how they manage the virtual processing capability. They only need to manage tables of information defining where components are placed. The virtual table information is mapped to the real physical network, storage components, and their capacity. Through software, the system and the operators can effectuate that required allocation of those physical network and storage capabilities where they are needed.

The network inside the computer internally connecting VMs and their applications is a Virtualized Ethernet with virtual NICs and a virtual Ethernet switch (a logical switch with logical components). External to the computer exists a real physical network of real Fiber Channel NICs, Fiber cable, Fiber Channel Switches, and Fiber Channel Routers interconnecting all computers and data storage devices.

A WAN, possibly employing Multiprotocol Label Switching (MPLS) to carry IP packets, can connect traffic from customer Apps in one VM to other Apps located in another VM which exists in another cloud data center.

Utilizing a shared file of Virtual Network specs along with similar virtual computer and virtual storage specifications, the networks virtually can be similarly employed, whether they connect within the computers, physically across a data center, or when they carry communication between data centers. As an example, such virtualized networking can be employed so that

1. A VM 1 processing module can be installed on Computer 1 in Cloud DC 1.
2. Later the VM can be moved (unknown to the customer or the VM itself) to another Computer 2 in the same Cloud DC1.
3. Or that same VM 1 processing module could be moved to Computer 1 in Cloud Data Center 2 across the country.
4. This is enabled by logically updating the hypervisor master files of virtual information (with its mapping to the real components).
5. The VM processing module must be moved from the computer in Cloud DC 1 across the country (likely at night) to a Computer in DC2.

The special "sauce" that makes a cloud data center operate and provide elastic capacity on demand for customers is the hypervisor, the shared hypervisor master files of virtual information with its mapping to the real components, and the control software that makes whatever is commanded to happen in the virtual world to actually happen in the real world on the real computers, networks, and storage components. The software that makes this virtual to physical process occur is proprietary to each cloud computing provider and distinguishes one vendor's performance against another (Shrivasttava, 2011).

Virtualizing Storage

In the office or home, every PC has its own disk drive for storage and usually employs the OS's simple flat file storage system. Mid-range computers may do the same, but usually employ external storage devices, most frequently RAID-based units of disk arrays.

In the cloud data center, logical subsets (termed Logical Units or LUNs) of arrays of disk drives are carved out. The LUN is just a file entry of assignable units of tracks and even full disks from the storage systems that the hypervisors share through their shared virtual file system. For RAID storage, records are striped across a set of disk drives, as shown in Figure 1.22 and frequently striped again across a second back-up set of disks.

Then, a virtual storage space (a set of logical storage LUNs) can be assigned to each App for that App to connect to its data. For the App, nothing has changed from storing on a local drive on the PC or to the locally connected drive on a larger computer. This cloud storage is all logical, so the storage can be assigned to any storage array placed anywhere among the cloud facilities.

The hypervisors have access to all this information, as do the operational people who supervise and control the cloud data centers with their files describing the physical provisioning functionality, tables that indicate the physical disks to which the logical storage refers, the files describing the physical provisioning functionality, and tables that indicate the physical disks to which the logical storage refers (Figure 1.23).

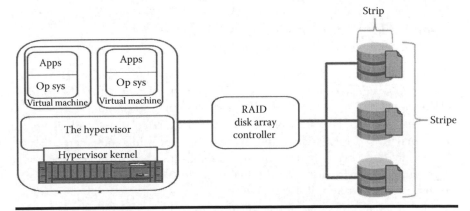

Figure 1.22   Records striped across a set of RAID disk drives.

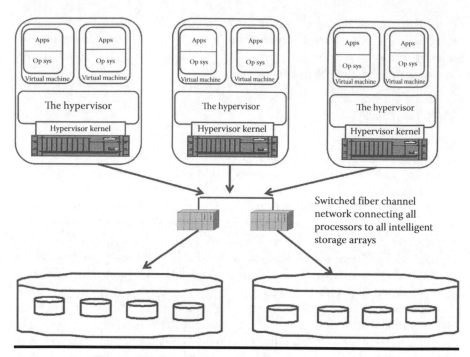

Figure 1.23   Switched fiber connection from virtual processors to virtual storage pools.

The App on our initial VM processing unit still thinks it is storing on its local PC storage. However, it is actually storing on virtual capacity across the data center in one of the intelligent storage unit's disk arrays (Figure 1.24).

Connection can be made to a distant cloud data center for backup storage or expanded storage capacity is made over dedicated fiber links provided by the carriers such as AT&T, Verizon, and their competitors, as portrayed in Figure 1.25.

Using Hadoop and MapReduce to Analyze Big Data across Multiple Processors

Hadoop and its two primary routines, MapReduce and HDFS (Hadoop Distributed File System), is the core for processing Big Data in cloud data centers. MapReduce allows for processing code to be broken up into small portions and distributed to hundreds, and even thousands, of inexpensive rack-based computers, all distributed by and controlled by a Master and treating the processing computers as slaves. Furthermore, the HDFS file system allows the data to be distributed over a very large number of inexpensive RAID disk arrays for effective massive parallel processing. This is portrayed in Figure 1.26.

Such parallel processing which emerges from the Big Data analysis requirement appears to be a considerable portion of future data center operation. As

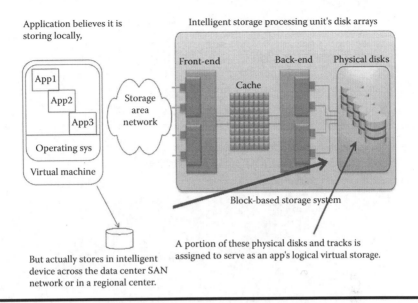

Figure 1.24 Disk arrays controlled by an embedded intelligent storage processor.

programmers absorb and experiment with the various features of Hadoop, and as Google brings to the market their own versions of the Google File System and their more powerful version of MapReduce parallel programming architecture and distributed process, we can expect this to be shared through open source offerings.

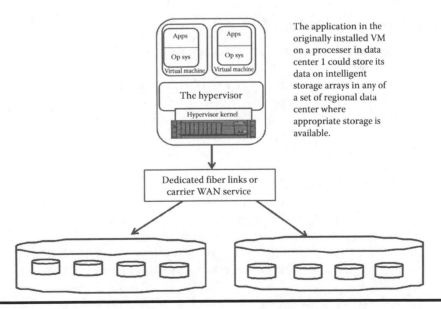

Figure 1.25 Virtual processors connected to remote storage by carrier services.

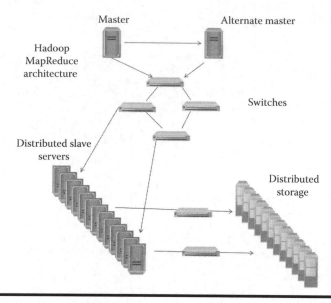

Figure 1.26   Hadoop distributed processing and file system for massive parallel processing.

These are available from such sites as GitHub (a popular open software web site) improving the capability of cloud computing (White, 2015).

Factors Contributing to Cost Effectiveness

Cloud data center services are thus cost effective due to the following factors.

1. Customers perform their own selection of services and equipment levels through the customer portal.
2. Minimal operation personnel can perform surveillance and operation activities through a management dashboard.
3. Large inexpensive racks and arrays of commodity equipment perform the processing, switching, and storage activities. Open OSs and database management systems tend to be utilized.
4. All computing, networking, and storage are virtualized allowing the quick service initiation, modification, movement, and performance without the requirement of service technicians to be dispatched.
5. Technicians are only utilized when required and then temporarily dispatched.
6. A number of cloud data centers can be nested and operate as a virtual data center.
7. National and international alternative cloud data centers can operate as backup and load-sharing alternatives.

8. Virtually all activities have been coded into software and Learning Artificial Intelligence systems are rapidly anticipating and activated to algorithmically perform desired services without the need for operations personnel activation.

These aspects are all blended into an inexpensive set of components which enables cloud providers to significantly reduce the cost of service delivery while simultaneously improving performance and reliability that customers could not achieve on their own.

Conclusion

Cloud computing offers companies an alternative to constructing, staffing, operating, growing, and maintaining their own data centers for processing their corporate records, supporting business functions and personnel, and offering services to the company's customers. By means of cloud service offerings, companies can now off-load the costs and responsibilities of data center operations while paying for the usage of cloud data center services on a pay-as-you-go basis. With adequate service level agreements and a track record of performance by cloud vendors, companies can assure themselves of a near term QoSs. However, companies grow successful for a while and then retreat. Moreover, new technology emerges which obviates the value of existing technology. Furthermore, the very operation and behavior of company personnel changes over time. Thus, the advantages to be reaped from cloud computing should be in the plan of companies while they remain ever vigilant that change will occur and plans should be laid for a variety of possible approaches for corporate processing in the future.

References

Amazon. Amazon Web Services (AWS), https://Amazon.aws.amazon.com.

CIO Magazine. Software as a Service (SaaS) Definition and Solutions, http://www.cio.com/article/109704.

Citrix. Citrix XenServer, https://www.citrix.com/products/xenserver/ March 7, 2017.

EMC. Cloud Infrastructure and Services, EMC Academic Alliance, 2016, https://education.emc.com/academic alliance/default.aspx.

Erl, Zaigham and Puttini. *Cloud Computing—Concepts, Technology, &Architecture.* Prentice Hall, Upper Saddle River, NJ, 2013.

Equinix. Equinix Cloud Exchange, http://www.equinix.com/services/interconnection-connectivity/cloud-exchange/, March 7, 2017.

Finn, Aidan et al. *Microsoft Private Cloud Computing.* Wiles, 2012, Comparing Amazon's and Google's Platform-as-a-Service (PaaS) Offerings, Enterprise Web 2.0 ZDNet.com, http://www.zdnet.com/article/comparing-amazons-and-googles-platform-as-a-service-paas-offerings/.

Google. Google Cloud Platform Documentation, https://cloud.google.com/docs/, March 6, 2017.

Hamdaqa, Mohammad. *Cloud Computing Uncovered: A Research Landscape*. Elsevier Press, Amsterdam, Netherlands, 2012.

IBM. IBM Cloud Documentation, http://www.ibm.com/cloud/ March 6, 2017a.

IBM. Softlayer Cloud Computing Service, http://www.softlayer.com/, March 6, 2017b.

IDC. Defining 'Cloud Services' and "Cloud Computing". IDC. 2008-09-23. Retrieved August 22, 2010.

InfoWorld. Linux containers and Docker explained, www.infoworld.com/.../linux/containers-101-linux-containers-and-docker-explained/ May 26, 2016.

Jayaswal, Kailash. *Administering Data Centers: Servers, Storage, and Voice over IP*, Wiley, Indianapolis, IN, 2006.

Jones, Kovac and Groom. *Introduction to Communications Technology*, 3rd ed. CRC Press, Taylor & Francis Group, New York, 2016.

Lowe, Scott, David M. Davis, and James Green. *Building a Modern Data Center: Principles and Strategies of Design*, ActualTech Media, Bluffton, SC, January 14, 2016.

Microsoft. Microsoft Azure Cloud Platform, https://azure.microsoft.com/en-us/?b=17.05.

NIST. *The NIST Definition of Cloud Computing*. National Institute of Standards and Technology. July 24, 2011.

Oracle. Oracle Cloud Documentation, https://docs.oracle.com/en/cloud/ March 6, 2017.

Santana, Gustavo. *Data Center Virtualization Fundamentals*, Cisco Press, Indianapolis, IN, 2014.

Shrivasttava, Alok. *Cloud Infrastructure and Services Course*, EMC, 2011.

White, Tom. *Hadoop: The Definitive Guide*, 4th ed. O'Reilly, Champagne, IL, 2015.

Wu, Caesar and Rajkumar Buyya. *Cloud Data Centers and Cost Modeling: A Complete Guide to Planning, Design, and Building a Cloud Data Center*. Morgan Kaufmann, March 16, 2015.

Chapter 2

Carrier Role in Cloud Computing Connectivity

Kevin M. Groom

AT&T

Contents

Businesses have standardized the employment of Transmission Control Protocol/ Internet Protocol (TCP/IP) over Ethernet for their business operations in offices, buildings, and campus environments. However, their inter-building communication has historically been limited by telephone service offerings which were themselves limited by the underlying telephone facilities. Connection from a building on one side of a city to another is generally provisioned by contracting for a telephone company private line service including T-1 (1.5 Mbps), DS-3 (45 Mbps), or a variety of fiber connection services. Metropolitan Ethernet service can be provisioned over the fiber connections and then across the metropolitan backbone network (Figure 2.1).

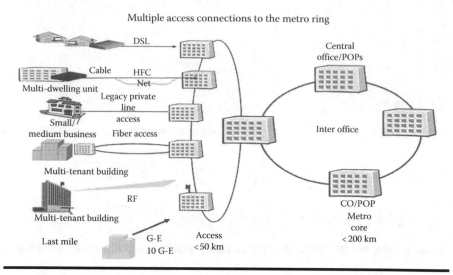

Figure 2.1   Alternative access services to the Metropolitan Network services employed.

These alternate access facilities were historically interconnected over the telephone metropolitan backbone network which was most frequently a Synchronized Optical Network (SONET) fiber ring facility.

This telephone network architecture was created as a set of hierarchical service planes. The addressing scheme used for this hierarchical structure mimicked that structure. It starts with an individual customer line number (4175), served by a Central Office (865) in a specific area or metropolitan area (765) which is located in a particular country (+1 for the United States). This is presented in Figure 2.2.

The first level was the central office switching centers, which could serve up to 50,000 customers and was placed in the center of a circle initially covering a diameter of 15 miles. Over time, it then extended to well beyond 30 miles.

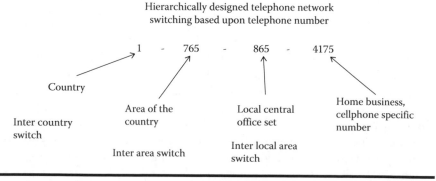

Figure 2.2   Hierarchical telephone numbering scheme.

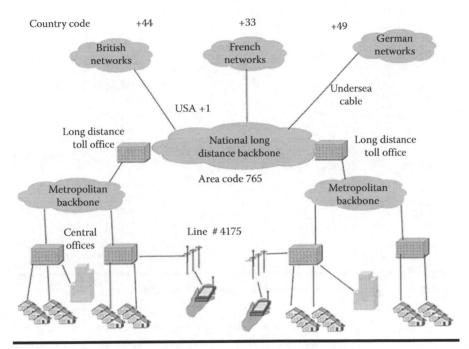

Figure 2.3   The hierarchical structure of the telephone network.

The second service layer was an interconnecting layer which was upgraded to set optical SONET rings in the 1990s, which cross-connected each of the central offices in a metropolitan area. That metropolitan interconnection network was then connected to the national backbone network by a long-distance toll switching office. The national backbone was connected globally to the rest of the world by means of undersea fiber cables. These service layers are presented in Figure 2.3.

However, over the past decade, the leading U.S. carriers have architected this network as a flat structure employing end to end a common IP numbering scheme for switching and routing all types of traffic from source to destination. Such an IP address is presented in Figure 2.4.

The national network is now principally structured as a flat, interconnected IP network containing the original components but relies increasingly on routing/switching based upon the destination IP address. This flat structure is pictured in Figure 2.5.

Flat IP-based address

176-285-212-115

Route/switch based upon unique IP addresses (permanent or temporary)

Figure 2.4   An example of the well-known IP address.

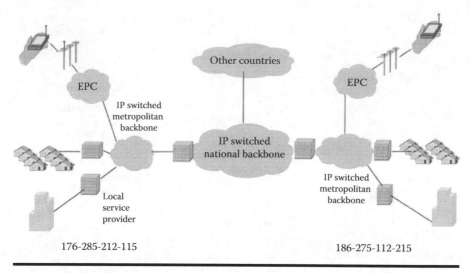

176-285-212-115   186-275-112-215

Figure 2.5   The flat IP switched/routed network structure.

Part of the impetus for the architecting of the national network is the transformation of customer access from landlines to wireless. The devices used wirelessly include IP-based smartphones, tablets, and laptops. These devices have evolved to deliver a plethora of media which streams to the user. The physical network has since evolved to meet that customer and device demand through employment of fiber in its various connections including access, backbones, and the employment of advanced switched and routing protocols.

The Evolved Packet Core Flat IP Network

To meet the mobile connection needs of customers, the former cellular network has been upgraded to a 4th-generation (and 5th-generation in the not too distant future) of high-speed, high-bandwidth IP packet transmission with exceedingly smart tower access points (termed evolved nodes [eNodeBs]), each with its own built-in computer center. A base station antenna had minimum functionality and was controlled by a separately located Radio Network Controller (RNC). Traditionally, a Node B has minimum functionality and is controlled by an RNC. However, with the new evolved base station antenna (eNodeB), there is no separate controller element. This functionality is provided by the attached computer which is colocated with the receiving antenna. The tower and its computer communicate wirelessly with mobile handsets and transmit downstream over cable or fiber through the 4th-generation evolved packet network. This simplifies the architecture and allows lower response times. The smart tower and attached computer are portrayed in Figure 2.6.

Figure 2.6 The 4th-generation smart eNodeB cellular tower with built-in processor.

The collection of access towers is then connected by cable or fiber to a set of downstream servers, as portrayed in Figure 2.7. The towers connect to a nested set of information servers and packet gateway devices located in a telephone facility. The smart antennas and the connected set of serving servers form what is now termed an Evolved Packet Core (EPC) access network.

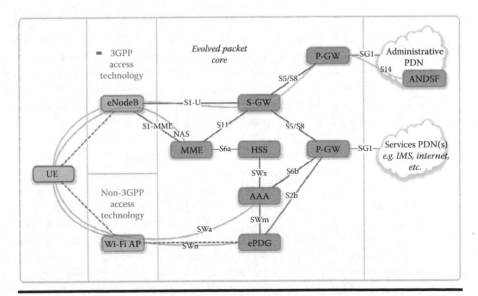

Figure 2.7   The IP network connecting the Smart eNodeB towers to the flat area, national, and international networks.

The functional services of each of these servers in the EPC are as follows:

1. The user equipment (UE) is the user's smartphone and the eNodeB is the smart, computerized access tower.
2. Mobility management entity (MME) is the key control node for the 4th-generation access network. The MME is responsible for UE paging, tagging, and retransmissions. It is involved in the bearer activation and deactivation and in choosing the Serving Gateway (SGW) for a UE smartphone at the time of the initial attach and at the time of intra-long-term evolution (LTE) handover involving Core Network node relocation. It is also responsible for authenticating the user by interacting with the Home Subscriber Server (HSS). The MME also provides the control plane function for mobility between mature 4th-generation mobile networks, LTE early 4th-generation mobile networks, and still earlier 3rd- and 2nd-generation access networks where they continue to be employed.
3. HSS provides authentication at a central database that contains user-related and subscription-related information such as mobility management, call and session establishment support, user authentication, and access authorization. The HSS is based on an earlier pre-4th-generation version of the home location register and authentication center.
4. The SGW routes and forwards user data packets, while also acting as the mobility anchor for the user plane during inter-eNodeB antenna handovers and as the anchor for mobility between LTE and other 3rd Generation Partnership Project (3GPP) technologies (terminating S4 interface and relaying the traffic between 2G/3G systems and Pocket Data Network Gateway (PGW). For idle state UEs, the SGW terminates the downlink data path and triggers paging when downlink data arrives for the UE. It manages and stores UE contexts (e.g., parameters of the IP bearer service and network internal routing information). It also performs replication of the user traffic in case of lawful interception.
5. PGW provides connectivity from the smartphone (UE) to external packet data networks by being the point of exit from the EPC mobile network to local and national networks and the entry for traffic directed to the UE mobile device. A UE may have simultaneous connectivity with more than one PGW for accessing multiple PDNs. The PGW performs policy enforcement, packet filtering for each user, charging support, lawful interception, and packet screening. Another key role of the PGW is to act as the anchor for mobility between 3GPP and non-3GPP technologies such as World Wide Interoperability for Microwave Access (WiMAX) and 3GPP, code division multiple access, and Evolution-Data Optimized. All are telecommunications standards for the wireless transmission of data through radio signals, typically for broadband Internet access. The 3GPP is a collaboration between groups of telecommunications associations, known as the Organizational Partners.

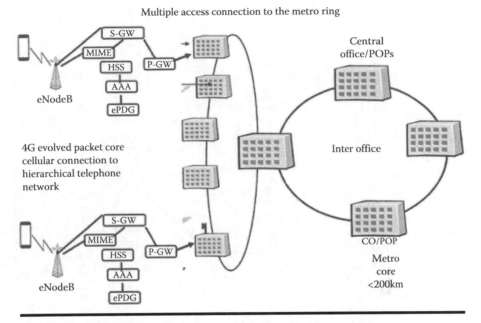

Figure 2.8   Connection of the EPC to the metro backbone rings.

As presented in Figure 2.8, the wireless EPC is connected to the metropolitan backbone networks and to the national backbone network by means of the previous ring service.

This metropolitan interconnecting backbone has been upgraded as a switched IP packet-interconnecting facility and connects downstream to the national backbone network by means of a point-of-presence center (termed a POP). This center provides a gateway to the long-distance network and contains a large number of switches and routers. These devices provide a range of distance transmission services including Carrier Ethernet, MultiProtocol Label Switching (MPLS), as well as traditional telephone transmission facilities (Figure 2.9).

Figure 2.10 portrays the full connection potential for transmitting mobile IP traffic across a flatly architected network.

Some of the rationalization for creating the switched metropolitan backbone follows in the next section.

Metropolitan Backbone Networks—Rings and Mesh

Early metropolitan Ethernet services were offered but required adjustments to accommodate the differences between the local transmission and the SONET transmission, particularly speed matching and packaging. Additionally, pricing was

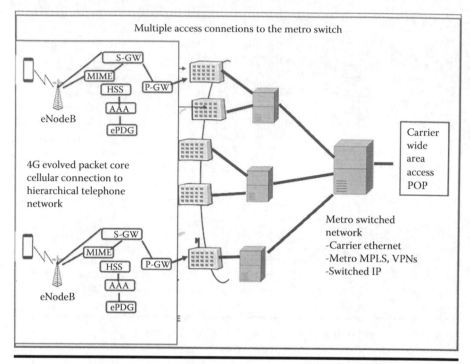

Figure 2.9   Connection of the EPC to the metro IP-switched backbone.

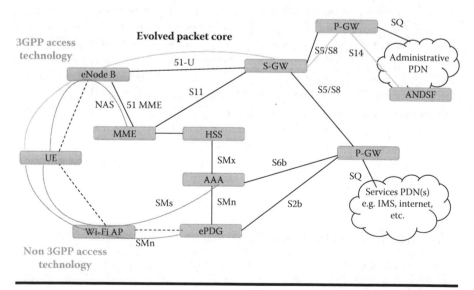

Figure 2.10   The connection of wireless traffic across the various backbone facilities.

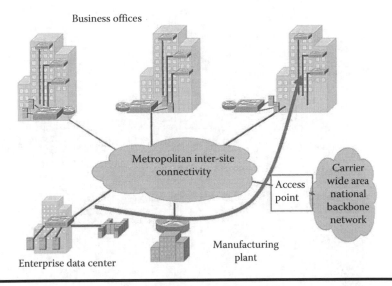

Business offices

Metropolitan inter-site connectivity

Access point

Carrier wide area national backbone network

Enterprise data center

Manufacturing plant

Figure 2.11 Metropolitan connectivity to businesses and the carrier WAN networks.

high since the Ethernet transmissions tended to dominate and sometimes exhaust the SONET ring capacity (Figure 2.11).

The solution to the capacity limitation was the creation of a parallel switched mesh fiber network, which is used for high-bandwidth connection for businesses across city connections. Metropolitan Ethernet traffic is frequently carried to other local business sites and to other cities. Access to the wide area facilities are gained through a carrier POP office for wide area (regional and national) network access (Figure 2.12).

Connection to a special access point to telephone wide area network was also established. Companies will frequently purchase virtual private network (VPN) service which encrypts the transmitted information. They then purchase metropolitan Ethernet service (sometimes termed Carrier Ethernet service) to connect from their building across the city by means of the mesh fiber switched backbone to the edge of the wide area telephone backbone network. At that location, they will deliver their Ethernet traffic to a distance transmission service. For slower speed traffic, this may be either a point-to-point connection or a frame relay service for T-1 (1.5 Mbps) service. Some faster traffic may use the older asynchronous transmission mode (ATM) service. The companies may even connect to a wide area Ethernet (or more appropriately termed Carrier Ethernet) service which employs end to end Ethernet connectivity. However, the most popular wide area connection service is MPLS. This service carries the Ethernet traffic across a country to a destination city where the process is reversed. MPLS traffic is converted back to metropolitan Ethernet traffic, which is then forwarded to a destination building. At that destination building, the traffic is then locally delivered by the company's own TCP/IP over Ethernet network facilities.

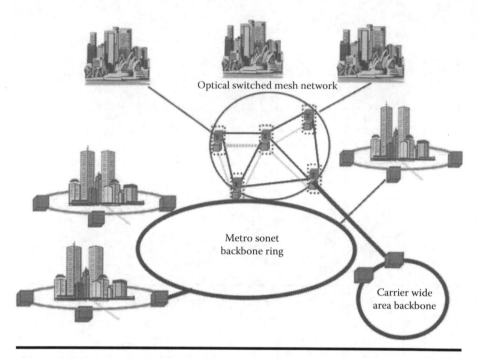

Figure 2.12 Metro SONET backbone and optical switched mesh network alternatives.

Metropolitan Carrier Ethernet

In a Carrier Ethernet network, data is transported across point-to-point and multipoint-to-multipoint Ethernet virtual connections (EVCs) according to a set of attributes and definitions. Each EVC carries data in the form of Carrier Ethernet service frames from a source demarcation point at the source building to a destination demarcation point at the destination site.

Each EVC, or virtual circuit, can be configured with a rich set of attributes, bandwidth profiles, multiple classes of service, application-oriented performance objectives, traffic management requirements, and forwarding rules. These are chosen in conjunction with one of the following four service offerings of metropolitan (also called carrier) Ethernet transmission service to which one can subscribe. Metropolitan Ethernet Forum defined services are as follows:

A. **CE 2.0 Ethernet-Line Services** provides point-to-point services including service multiplexing and bundling. These services enable the support of multiple, separate EVCs at the source and destination. CE 2.0 Ethernet-Line services also provide the mapping of more than one virtual local area network (VLAN) ID for transmission across the metro area as if it were an extension of the transmission originating building's local area network. EVCs define a layer 2 bridging architecture. An EVC is defined by the Metropolitan Ethernet Forum (MEF) as an association between two or more user–network interfaces that identifies a point-to-point or a multipoint-to-multipoint path within the service provider network. An EVC is a conceptual service pipe within the service provider network. A bridge domain is a local broadcast domain that exists separately from VLANs.

B. **CE 2.0 E-LAN Services** provide multipoint-to-multipoint services with a high degree of transparency such that the transported service frames are identical at both the source and destination. This minimizes the coordination between the subscriber to the metro Ethernet service and the service provider of the service. Most importantly, this concerns the definition and ID of the virtual extension (VLAN) across the metro area of both the transmitting source local area network and the receiving destination local area network.

C. **CE 2.0 E-Tree Services** provide a broad range of rooted, multipoint services using a dedicated root and leaf, like with a tree, and a high degree of transparency. The transmitted service frames are identical at both the source and destination sites. This approach minimizes the coordination between the subscriber and the service provider on the definition VLAN IDs.

D. **CE 2.0 E-Access Services** provide a broad range of access services that can support multiple service instances and a high degree of transparency. Service frames are delivered unchanged at the destination with the addition of special virtual local area network tags (S VLAN tags) and the use of special frames that are delivered unchanged at the destination with the removal of the specialized additional S-VLAN tags.

These sets of services defined by the MEF are just the early set of such defined services. As high-speed Ethernet pervades the metro and wide areas, many more specialized services that enable the support of quality-of-service guarantees will emerge.

Carrier Wide Area Backbone Networks

The telephone carrier's wide area network facilities are structured to carry all types of information. Initially, these were voice telephone calls which later developed into a variety of data transmissions including video transmissions, cellular wireless communication, public and private Internet traffic, and now social media communication which can be transmitted over the wide area backbone. These varieties of communication are each differently formatted and framed. Fortunately, they can be placed in IP packets, which helps standardize much of the information to be transmitted at least at Level 3 of the standard transmission model.

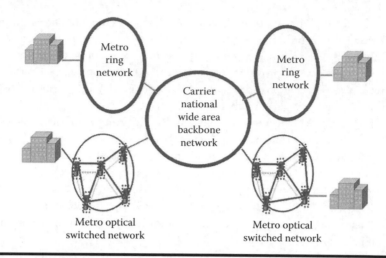

Figure 2.13 Metro ring and optically switched nets cross connected by carrier WAN.

The carrier's wide area network facilities begin at an access point in each city across the country. That access point contains a variety of switching and routing facilities. Traffic is received from the metropolitan backbone SONET rings (carrying voice and data packets and private line data transmissions) and from the switched mesh fiber network usually carrying metropolitan Ethernet traffic (Figure 2.13).

The carrier's wide area backbone network is constructed as a set of alternate fiber paths from city to city across the nation. There are direct paths as well as alternate via (from Italian, meaning "way") paths. At switching points along the network, optical switches are deployed. They may be provisioned as an optical switch or pure optical switches with input being optical, switching being optical, and output remaining optical with no electrical conversion in the middle and thus no delay in switching. Or they may be provisioned as OEO switching, with optical input signals converted to electric signals for switching and then converted back to optical signals for output with the resultant delay in the switching due to the step-down and back to the traditional electronic switch fabric at the heart of the switch.

ATM carries the traffic which usually is in the form of IP packets. Or Ethernet frames carrying IP packets can be carried in ATM cells. These cells are then transmitted by means of a SONET protocol over a fiber facility. Furthermore, MPLS service may offer label switching as an overlay switching component and likely will become the eventual replacement of the SONET component (Figure 2.14).

MPLS is one of the principal technologies for providing delivery of IP-based traffic which guarantees the quality of that service by transmitting through prearranged carved out paths of an underlying layer 1 and layer 2 facility.

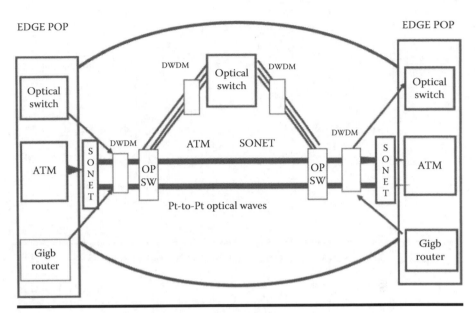

EDGE POP

EDGE POP

Figure 2.14   Carrier wide area backbone network carrying various local protocol traffic.

MPLS is a vehicle for carrying all forms of traffic and functions by applying a set of labels to the carried traffic. These labels identify a best path for that traffic over fundamental connection-oriented networks. Such an MPLS overlay network to the carrier backbone facilities is displayed in Figure 2.15.

Carriers provide specialized regional and national high-speed and IP-based connections by attaching switches and routers at various points along the national backbone network, frequently in the point-of-presence metro access points. This is portrayed in Figure 2.16.

An MPLS-enabled network can also transport traffic of many other protocols delivered to it. Figure 2.17 portrays MPLS's ability to carry just a few of them: ATM, Frame Relay, Ethernet, and Carrier Ethernet.

Additionally, MPLS also enables the creation of a VPN for private data delivery over public carrier facilities. This is portrayed in Figure 2.17.

Furthermore, MPLS-TE (Traffic Engineering) allows, among other services, the ability to create primary and alternate secondary routes to redirect traffic around network delivery issues and rerouting traffic when necessary. This is portrayed in Figure 2.18.

In today's world, businesses cannot be too cautious in protecting their data. Thus, when they transport critical information from cell phones, iPads, laptops, or desktop computers those transmissions are often encrypted using encryption keys and authentication to secure the data. This is usually performed with an

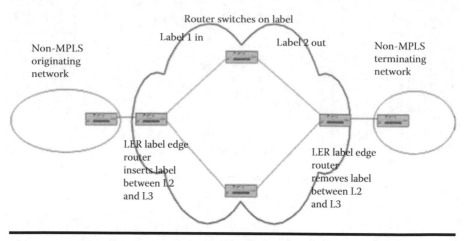

Figure 2.15   The structure of a label-switched MPLS network.

Internet Protocol Security (IPSEC) encryption package provided by their company. For transmission, the encrypted packets are placed inside an additional unencrypted packet for transmission over the public or a private internet, and then the encrypted packet is unencrypted at the other end. In some situations, the sender must first access a special service to acquire an encryption key and

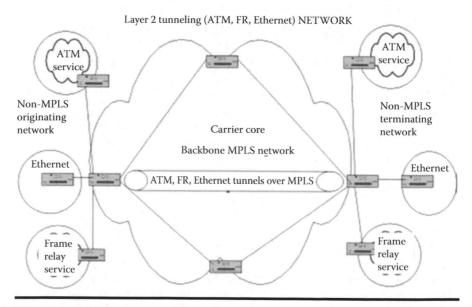

Figure 2.16   ATM, Frame Relay and Ethernet, and Carrier Ethernet carried by MPLS.

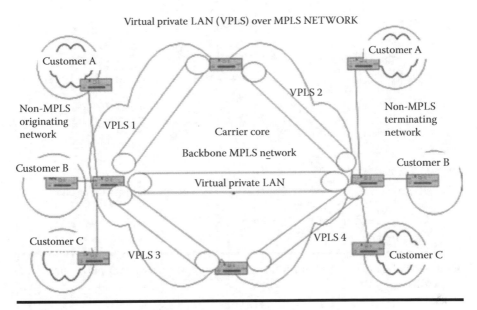

Figure 2.17 Carving a VPN over public facilities by MPLS.

authorization prior to proceeding through the encryption and transmission processes. The most popular of such authorization services employs the RADIUS authorization system where both source and destination keys are provided upon request with an authorization component to be attached to the transmission.

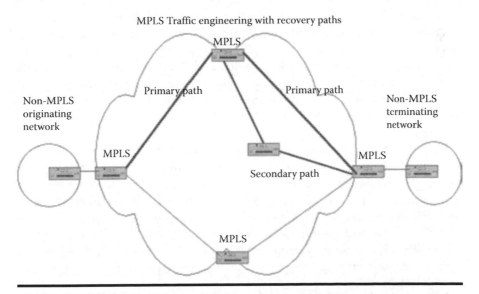

Figure 2.18 MPLS's facility for alternate routing and delivery of recovery paths.

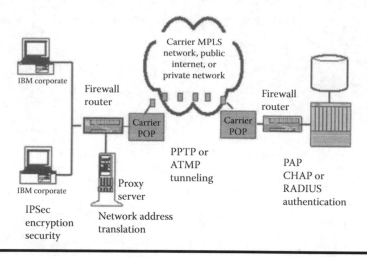

Figure 2.19   Encrypted VPN traffic authorized and carried over public or private networks.

MPLS is uniquely capable of delivering such VPN encrypted traffic. This is portrayed in Figure 2.19.

Cloud Center Placement

Cloud providers such as Amazon Web Services (AWS) construct their data centers in locations that can handle the traffic loads and avoid possible problems associated with certain areas. For instance, Amazon Virginia Data Center is locally connected to a set of regional data centers which operate as an interconnected unit. This cluster of data centers might then be connected across the country with the Oregon data center. If storms, electric problems, or other area-specific issues arise, the alternate data center in Oregon can take over the traffic from the Virginia data center. This establishment of cloud data centers around the globe is portrayed in Figure 2.20.

In 2016, one of Amazon's domain name service (DNS) providers experienced a massive distributed denial-of-service (DDoS) attack. Such an attack occurs when a hacker infects a set of geographically dispersed set of computers, cell phones, and even home monitors. Then when triggered, these dispersed devices simultaneously send messages to the DNS server and overload it, thus effectively disabling it. Fortunately, Amazon had one of its alternate DNS providers switch the traffic destined for its Virginia center over to its globally paired Ireland data center with only minimal outage and delay for its served customers. This is portrayed in Figure 2.21.

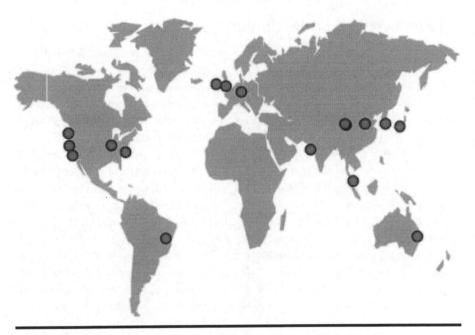

Figure 2.20   The global placement of Amazon Cloud Data Centers.

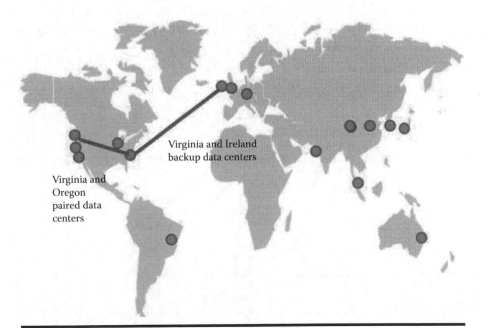

Figure 2.21   Amazon pairing nationally and internationally.

Cloud Access Connection as a Service

Cloud Access Connection as a Service (CACaaS) is sometimes referred to as OutSource and OutBoard Network Clustering. This is a popular service offered to large customers who have placed critical applications and data in cloud data centers, such as Amazon's AWS service; it establishes links to a network consolidator's site. At that site, such services as DNS are provided with tools to minimize hacking attacks. Filtering for DDoS and other hacking attack filtering is offered.

This network clustering center maintains a large number of fiber links to the various data centers of the major cloud providers. These established fiber links can offer network sharing and virtual channeling, load balancing and rerouting, and management and connection monitoring of all offered traffic as well as trouble ticketing, trouble tracking, fixing, and facility and service restoration. Figure 2.22 portrays such a consolidated network service.

A principle power of cloud computing is that a widely dispersed cluster of cloud data centers can be operated at one large center. Since multi-gigabit Ethernet and fiber channel over Ethernet are the predominant transmission protocol used within a cloud data center, inter-cloud connectivity can be constructed as Carrier Ethernet and MPLS links between these data centers. This allows them to function as one virtual data center as shown in Figure 2.23.

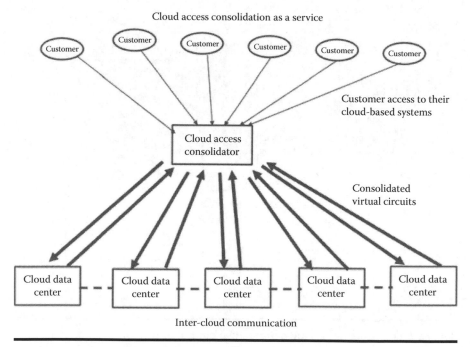

Figure 2.22 Consolidate network service.

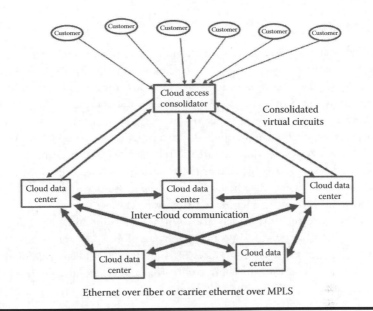

Figure 2.23   Cloud data centers interconnected by carrier facilities to operate as a unit.

An additional advantage when customers employ a connection consolidator is that they can employ multiple cloud vendors. Each cloud vendor might provide unique capabilities for processing particular applications. This interconnection to multiple cloud vender data centers, using IBM and Amazon as examples, is shown in Figure 2.24.

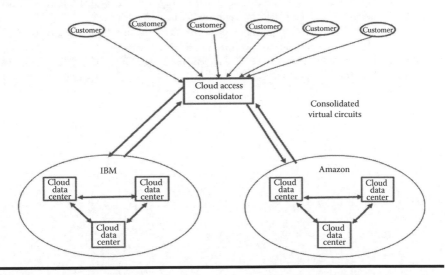

Figure 2.24   Consolidating traffic destined for diverse cloud data centers.

Conclusion

Businesses employ a variety of transmission facilities to transmit their packet-based transmissions. The first step is deciding if they need to encrypt their transmission. Then businesses contract for an access facility to the metro and national telephone backbone networks. Once this is completed, businesses decide if they need to further contract for a specialized transmission service, such as Carrier Ethernet. If they wish to further transmit to offices in distant cities, they might then contract to employ MPLS service over the wide area or rely on the public Internet for transmission. The carriers will usually package these options as various levels of service and increasing pricing levels. The choice is left to the customer to define their requirements and an affordable budget for transmission services.

The cloud data center providers also contract for front-end connection services and procure high-bandwidth links between their global data centers. This series of connection links are the core products of the national and international carriers which provide the network of connectivity that allows cloud computing to exist and to prosper.

References

Alwayn, Vivek, *Advanced MPLS Design and Implementation* (CCIE Professional Development), Cisco Press, Indianapolis, IN, Sept. 25, 2001.

Bedell, Paul, *Gigabit Ethernet for Metro Area Networks*, McGraw-Hill, New York, Dec. 24, 2002.

Fordham, Stuart, MPLS for Cisco Networks: A CCIE v5 Guide to Multiprotocol Label Switching (Cisco CCIE Routing and Switching v5.0) (Volume 2), CreateSpace Independent Publishing Platform, Sept. 26, 2014.

Groom, Kevin M., Carrier Metropolitan Connection to Customers, *Optical Networking in the MAN Conference*, Chicago, IL, Jun. 14, 2001.

Held, Gilbert, *Carrier Ethernet; Providing the Need for Speed*, CRC Press, Boca Raton, FL, Mar. 11, 2008.

Chapter 3

Healthcare Industry

Rob Faix and Eric Gerard
Impact Advisors, LLC

Contents

Introduction

"It's in the cloud" continues to be an increasing common response as businesses and vendors discuss how a particular application or service is provided to users these day. While businesses and individual consumers alike have come to embrace the idea of cloud-based delivery of information services, the underlying technologies and types of cloud-based solutions may not be as clearly understood. Within the healthcare industry specifically, adoption of cloud computing technologies have made significant inroads in recent years. While adoption of such solutions may lag behind other industries, healthcare vendors (software, hardware, and services) are devoting significant portions of their research and development budget to defining and enhancing their delivery capability vis-a-vis the cloud. Notable uses of cloud services have included vendor solutions aimed at storing large amounts of data for purposes of clinical trial research and business analytics, disaster recovery of mission critical systems, and significantly reducing the overall space within a hospital which is occupied by a physical data center.

Brief Overview of Traditional Enterprise Computing Considerations

To understand what cloud computing is, perhaps it is best to compare that model to a more traditional data center environment. Traditionally, if an organization wanted to implement and deliver an application to their employees several investments and activities were necessary to ensure the application functioned as expected. The following summarizes some of the common considerations an organization would evaluate as it prepared to install the new application enterprise-wide:

Define the compute requirements for servers physically installed in an organization's data center to properly host the application (i.e., processing power, storage, and memory); procure appropriately sized physical server(s) and storage hardware; physically install the servers and storage hardware into a designated location within a data center; install and configuring an Operating System; install and configure the desired application; provision access to designated users of the application.

Depending upon the complexity of the system being implemented, these tasks could take days, weeks, or months to complete and represent a significant capital spend in addition to the time and skilled technical expertise for a successful implementation. From the perspective of the business, only the last activity of providing access to the application is what really mattered. Every step leading up to providing end users access to the application may be considered a "necessary evil" to achieve the goal. Further adding to the costs and complexity of providing access to the application, organizations must account for sufficient power and cooling in the data center, retaining qualified staff to maintain each constituent component of this system (data center environment, physical server and storage hardware, Operating System, and the application itself), and address issues which inevitability arise and potentially result in an interruption of service to the user community. Needless to say, this approach can become costly and complex to the organization and still doesn't include other critical activities such as backup and archiving of systems and data, maintaining an alternate disaster recovery location, or performing major upgrades to newer versions of the application.

Strategic Benefits of Cloud Computing

With a baseline of understanding for the "old" way of thinking about the delivery of services and applications, we can now turn our attention toward the highly scalable, rapidly deployable, and cost-effective model known as cloud computing. Cloud computing as a concept and strategy can trace its roots back several decades in various forms, but it wasn't until the late 1990s and early 2000s that the technology evolved to a point where businesses and consumers would embrace the vision and benefits of this new delivery method for applications and services. Key to the adoption of cloud computing solutions has been the ubiquitous nature of high-speed, highly reliable, and relatively inexpensive network connectivity to a variety of device types. The National Institute of Standards and Technology's definition of cloud computing identifies "five essential characteristics" [1]:

On-demand self-service – A consumer can unilaterally provision computing capabilities, such as server time and network storage, as needed automatically without requiring human interaction with each service provider.

Broad network access – Capabilities are available over the network and accessed through standard mechanisms that promote use by heterogeneous thin or thick client platforms (e.g., mobile phones, tablets, laptops, and workstations).

Resource pooling – The provider's computing resources are pooled to serve multiple consumers using a multi-tenant model, with different physical and virtual resources dynamically assigned and reassigned according to consumer demand.

Rapid elasticity – Capabilities can be elastically provisioned and released, in some cases automatically, to scale rapidly outward and inward commensurate with demand. To the consumer, the capabilities available for provisioning often appear unlimited and can be appropriated in any quantity at any time.

Measured service – Cloud systems automatically control and optimize resource use by leveraging a metering capability at some level of abstraction appropriate to the type of service (e.g., storage, processing, bandwidth, and active user accounts). Resource usage can be monitored, controlled, and reported, providing transparency for both the provider and consumer of the utilized service.

Why Embrace a Cloud Computing Strategy?

Cloud computing, as a strategy, significantly streamlines the process of implementing an application or service and extending its functionality to end users. Organizations that choose to implement cloud-based applications and services will likely see value in transferring the day-to-day operational activities associated with maintaining the application or service to the hosting vendor. With Service Level Agreements and corresponding penalties for non-performance defined as part of most enterprise-grade cloud solutions, organizations are able to hold vendors accountable for the delivery of services and potentially seek monetary or other recompense should services encounter an interruption which exceed a particular service level. Moreover, organizations are not saddled with high operating costs associated with service contracts, employing skilled support staff, and the recurring costs associated with routine maintenance, planned upgrades, and resolution of unplanned downtimes, much less the high initial investment of equipment. Finally, the fundamental shift for organizations embracing cloud solutions involves the transfer of Capital Expenditures to Operating Expenditures on the balance sheet. Given that cloud services are typically subscription based, organizations need not incur significant capital outlay to implement the underlying infrastructure to deliver the service. These costs, along with other routine maintenance and potentially future upgrades, are typically incorporated into the subscription fee for simply accessing the service.

Robert Eardley, CIO at Houston Methodist noted

> There are different definitions of the cloud that are used in healthcare. For me, the best definition of a cloud service is one where it offers device synchronization. Think Kindle, think iTunes—the kind of application that allows device synchronization via the cloud. But people also use the term cloud to describe a remote-hosted software application. And then there's software as a service (SaaS), which is kind of in between those two, which goes beyond remote hosting of an application on somebody else's servers and adds ancillary solutions as a service. I think a lot of healthcare organizations are using the cloud for different parts of their IT programs. But a lot of these offerings need to mature before we think about using them with PHI, so we can make sure the security we need is there [2].

The ability to scale on demand, in near real-time, is a great advantage. This allows organizations to scale up when needed, or scale down when resources are not being used. This typically takes place during month-end and year-end activities.

Limitations of Cloud Computing

Cloud computing, like any technology, does have some limitations or tradeoffs. Organizations embracing a cloud computing strategy may be forced to accept functional and operational limitations as imposed by the vendor providing the service. It is the vendor, and not the customer, who controls the back end infrastructure and management policies.

A recent Cloud Academy blog noted the following six disadvantages of cloud computing:

Downtime – This may be one of the worst disadvantages of cloud computing. No cloud provider, even the very best, would claim immunity to service outages. Cloud computing systems are Internet based, which means your access is fully dependent on your Internet connection. And, like any hardware, cloud platforms themselves can fail for any one of a thousand reasons.

Security and Privacy – Any discussion involving data must address security and privacy, especially when it comes to managing sensitive data. We mustn't forget Code Space and what happened to it after its AWS [Amazon Web Services] EC2 console was hacked and its data eventually deleted, forcing the company to close doors forever. By leveraging a remote cloud based infrastructure, a company basically outsources everything it has.

Of course, your cloud service provider is expected to manage and safeguard the underlying hardware infrastructure of a deployment; however, remote access is your responsibility and, in any case, no system is perfectly secure. You'll have to carefully weigh all the risk scenarios.

Vulnerability to Attack – In cloud computing, every component is potentially accessible from the Internet. Of course, nothing connected to the Internet is perfectly secure and even the best teams suffer severe attacks and security breaches. But since cloud computing is built as a public service it can be easy to run before you learn to walk. No one at AWS checks your administration skills before granting you an account: all it takes to get started is a valid credit card.

Limited Control and Flexibility – To varying degrees (depending on the particular service) cloud users have limited control over the function and execution of their hosting infrastructure. Cloud provider end user license agreements (EULAs) and management policies might impose limits on what customers can do with their deployments. Customers are also limited to the control and management of their applications, data, and services, but not the back-end infrastructure. Of course, none of this will normally be a problem, but it should be taken into account.

Cloud Computing Platform Dependencies – Implicit dependency, also known as "vendor lock-in" is another of the disadvantages of cloud computing. Deep-rooted differences between vendor systems can sometimes make it impossible to migrate from one cloud platform to another. Not only can it be complex and expensive to reconfigure your applications to meet the requirements of a new host, but migration could also expose your data to additional security and privacy vulnerabilities.

Cloud Computing Costs – Cloud computing – especially on a small scale and for short term projects – can be pricey. Though it can allow you to reduce staff and hardware costs, the overall price tag could end up higher than you expected. Until you're sure of what will work best for you, it's a good idea to experiment with a variety of offerings. You might also make use of the cost calculators made available by providers like Amazon's AWS (http://calculator.s3.amazonaws.com/index.html) and Google's GCP (https://cloud.google.com/products/calculator/).

(http://cloudacademy.com/blog/disadvantages-of-cloud-computing/ posted March 17, 2015.)

Types of Cloud Solutions

Three primary strategies for cloud computing functionality are:

External Cloud – Probably the most common cloud-based solution. External cloud solutions typically involve a single vendor hosting an application or service which customers may enter into a subscription model for the ability to access the hosted solution. External cloud services are provided over a network that is open for public use (e.g., the Internet). While technically there may be little differences between external and internal cloud architectures, there is a big difference when it comes to security considerations when providing services over a public, non-trusted network.

Internal Cloud – Also known as a Private cloud, this is a hosting model where the infrastructure is entirely managed by a single organization. Implementing and managing an internal cloud solution is a complex and challenging endeavor typically reserved for very large organization with access to robust information technology staff. Undertaking a private cloud project requires a significant level of technical sophistication and business engagement to virtualize the environment while reevaluating roles and responsibilities of existing resources.

Hybrid Cloud – As the name may imply, a hybrid solution is a combination of an external and internal cloud environment. Organizations with sensitive data may elect to implement a hybrid cloud environment whereby the core application and infrastructure are managed and hosted by a vendor; however, the customer implements an infrastructure environment locally which integrates to the vendor's cloud solution. For example, an organization can host sensitive data on their private cloud but connect that data to an external, cloud-based application.

To fully appreciate the promise of cloud computing, it's necessary to define specific terminology related to types of cloud based solutions:

Infrastructure as a Service (IaaS) – IaaS is the most basic cloud service model offering basic computing infrastructure: computer processing, servers, and storage. These are provided on-demand from large pools of equipment installed in data centers. The cloud user installs and maintains the operating system (OS) and applications. The cloud provider typically charges based on resources that have been allocated or consumed.

Platform as a Service (PaaS) – PaaS cloud providers offer a computing platform that generally includes operating system, programming-language execution environment, database, and web server. These are typically used as a development environment for applications with the computing and storage resources scaling automatically based on demand so that the cloud users do not have to allocate resources manually. PaaS provides a development environment enabling customers to host, develop, and run their own applications. Unlike SaaS, customers essentially "own" the application used in the PaaS environment and may maintain full control and ability to customize the application as they see fit.

Software as a Service (SaaS) – With SaaS, users access applications over the Internet. The cloud provider installs and maintains everything up to and include the application. These are usually priced on a pay-per-use basis or using a subscription fee. Users access a specific piece of software, typically a business or clinical application used by one or more end users.

While several other "X as a Service" type solutions exist, the three previously noted are the most common. Additionally, the cloud computing space has numerous vendors offering a wide array of solutions. The following charts identify the market leading companies offering cloud-based infrastructure services as of mid-2016 as a percentage of market share, year-over-year growth, and revenues (Figures 3.1 and 3.2):

How Do Organizations Access Cloud-Based Solutions?

Access to cloud-based solutions is typically accomplished in one of two ways: establishing a permanent network connection between the customer organization and service vendor or accessing the solution via a standard Internet connection and often leveraging a web browser or dedicated mobile device app to display the application. This allows for device independence since users can access an application in the cloud from a Windows PC, an Apple Mac, or mobile device. Once connectivity

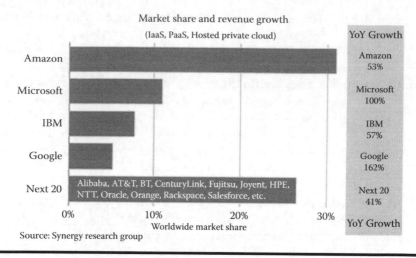

Figure 3.1   Cloud infrastructure services – Q2 2016.

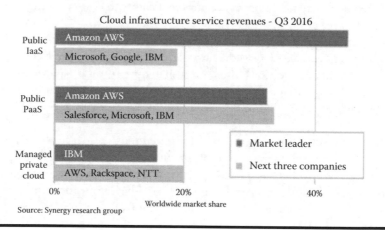

Figure 3.2   Cloud market leadership.

between the organization and service provider has been established, vendors may require subscribers to perform additional configuration activities such as defining users of the cloud solution and integrating the solution to any other enterprise applications for the purpose of sharing data between the cloud solution and another application. Functioning more like a utility, consumers of an application are able to quickly gain access, increase or decrease user accounts, and never worry about the ongoing maintenance of the hardware and software being used to support the application itself.

Cloud Computing and Information Security Considerations in Healthcare

One question that always comes up about cloud computing is security. "Is my data really safe in the cloud?" More often than not, security is as good or better when using cloud-based solutions. Most all major cloud solution vendors have dedicated experts focused solely on maintaining the highest levels of information security and privacy whereas small and mid-size organizations often may not have the means to justify or afford a comparable level of internal expertise. However, cloud computing does make security a more challenging proposition since data can be distributed across a wide area or over a larger number of devices. There may also be the additional challenge of accessing security audit logs as organizations may only disclose a subset of the information to customers upon request.

When asked about information security, Robert Eardley, CIO at Houston Methodist replied:

> We have a number of remote-hosted and cloud solutions in our IT environment. And the cloud makes a lot of sense when you are talking about email tools, video distribution services, and learning management systems...The cloud makes a lot of sense when you are talking about a solution that largely stands by itself and can be sold and serviced as a solution. It makes less sense when it's highly interfaced and has a lot of PHI [Protected Health Information], because there are a lot of potential security concerns. That's why we still tend to store PHI on premise at this point [2].

External Cloud in Healthcare

One of the most important applications for healthcare organizations is their electronic health record (EHR) or electronic medical record solution. These are very complex applications which often provide comprehensive suites of functionality to address most or all of the clinical and business needs involved in patient care [3]. These systems often have many touch points throughout inpatient and outpatient workflows and may be integrated with various other clinical or business applications. In response to market demands for EHR vendors to offer hosted solutions, many of the leading software vendors have expanded their portfolio of services to include hosting their own application and occasionally other third-party applications in a SaaS model. Among the leading EHR vendors offering hosted solutions for their own application, the following may be considered market leaders: Epic, Cerner, Allscripts, NextGen, athenahealth, GE Healthcare, eClinicalWorks, and McKesson.

Many healthcare organizations also leverage SaaS for a number of key applications besides their EHR. These often include back-office applications such as enterprise resource planning (ERP) like SAP, Oracle, and Infor; customer relationship management (CRM) like Salesforce, Oracle, and SAP; as well as human capital management (HCM) like SAP, ADP, Oracle, and Workday. These are an excellent fit for organizations that do not want to be bothered with managing the hardware necessary to support the application, not to mention the need to regularly update them. By accessing them in the cloud, they can be assured that they are always available and always up to date.

Jon Manis, CIO and Senior Vice President at Sutter Health in Sacramento California commented on his organization's cloud strategy by saying "We are using the cloud more and more, both for traditional workforce support applications like Microsoft Office and also for those collaboration and communication tools I mentioned. In many cases, they're already integrated into the available cloud solutions for workforce communication and support [4]."

Internal Cloud in Healthcare

For those larger healthcare organizations that have the technical capabilities, creating internal cloud and utility services can be a viable option. An internal cloud or utility service is an internal offering of a specific platform that can be used by multiple business units or application teams. If an application requires multiple platforms to function – such as a database which will be accessed via a web browser – then these could be hosted and distributed to users as an internal cloud solution. For example, many applications use Microsoft's SQL for their database and .NET for the web access. While this model does require a strong level of internal technical expertise and initial investment, there are significant savings and efficiencies to be found if the circumstances are right.

Common advantages to the internal cloud/utility service model include:

1. Faster
   - Time-to-market for internal business partners
   - Simplified procurement
   - Standardized system images
   - Instant capacity

2. Cheaper
   - Eliminates under-utilization and over-purchasing
   - Predictable cost based on resources allocated
   - Low cost of entry for new projects
   - Balanced budgeting over project life

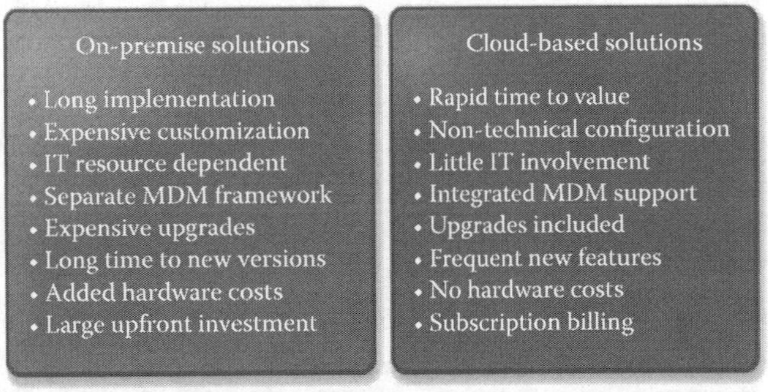

On-premise solutions	Cloud-based solutions
• Long implementation	• Rapid time to value
• Expensive customization	• Non-technical configuration
• IT resource dependent	• Little IT involvement
• Separate MDM framework	• Integrated MDM support
• Expensive upgrades	• Upgrades included
• Long time to new versions	• Frequent new features
• Added hardware costs	• No hardware costs
• Large upfront investment	• Subscription billing

Figure 3.3   Key differentiations of solution services.

    – No commitment to use excess capacity
    – Reduces costs of hardware, software, licensing, and power.

3. Better:
    – Higher availability
    – Stronger monitoring
    – Easier support from consistent deployment
    – Predictable, scheduled technical refresh
    – Built-in disaster recovery.

The following table outlines other factors which may influence an organization's willingness to implement an internal cloud solution (Figure 3.3):

Case Study

Penn Medicine is a $4.3 billion organization with more than 2,000 physicians providing services to the University of Pennsylvania Hospital, Penn Presbyterian Medical Center, Pennsylvania Hospital, Chester County Hospital, Lancaster General Health, and a health network that serves the city of Philadelphia, the surrounding five-county area, and parts of southern New Jersey.

Considered a leader in healthcare predictive analytics, the Penn Medicine data science team is dedicated to improving patient outcomes through analytics. Specifically, they want to harness the full power of clinical data to help clinicians identify patients at risk of critical illnesses that may have been missed by current diagnostic techniques. In the process, they are also developing solutions that will remove the barriers to developing analytic models and accelerate the deployment of analytic applications based on those models, all of which they intend to share with other health organizations via open source.

To accomplish this, Penn Medicine needed a platform for rapid development and deployment of predictive analytics applications that could be applied to detect patients at risk of critical illnesses. The platform they developed is called Penn Signals. Penn Signals is a collaborative data science platform developed by the Penn Medicine data science team that combines clinical data at scale with big data to allow researchers to explore solutions, allow developers to develop predictive applications, and provide a platform for deployment. The first applications of Penn Signals focused on sepsis and heart failure.

Key Challenges

- Harness clinical data to improve patient risk stratification.
- Deliver useful predictive alerts to clinicians.
- Accelerate development and delivery of predictive applications.

Solution

- Penn Signals is a collaborative data science platform that combines clinical data at scale with advanced analytics to develop and deploy predictive applications.
- Trusted Analytics Platform is an extensible open source platform designed to allow data scientists and application developers to deploy solutions without having to worry about infrastructure procurement or platform setup.

Benefits

- Identified patients at risk of critical illnesses that may have been missed by current diagnostic techniques.
- Reduced patient readmissions through early risk stratification and intervention.
- Improved patient care and well-being.
- Accelerated development of predictive applications.

According to a recent Gartner Group study of nearly 300 respondents, 65 percent cited their inability to identify the value of a big data system as the single greatest barrier that prevents them from adopting their own big data solutions. This implies a need for education and some guidance to help others take that first step, or at least prove the utility of such a deployment.

The healthcare industry can benefit greatly from the big data insights predictive analysis provides, as Penn Medicine's programs illustrate. Trusted Analytics Platform has the potential to make developing such cloud-based analytics easier for even small data science teams to implement successfully.

To this end, Penn Medicine is excited to share what they have accomplished in Penn Signals with other healthcare systems. The Penn Signals solution benefited greatly from the flexibility and scalability of this cloud solution. What Penn Medicine has seen, particularly in data science, is that cutting-edge technologies are often open source projects. Penn Medicine has built a foundation based on open source and now wants to contribute back to that community. For that reason, their long-term plan is to open source Penn Signals.

Conclusion

Clearly there are numerous ways to leverage cloud computing services in healthcare. Small to mid-size organizations have taken advantage of vendor hosted EHR solutions to relieve the need for internal infrastructure and technical expertise historically, and now larger health systems are positioned to do the same. For immediate value in cloud solutions, organizations are likely to continue taking advantage of SaaS solutions for back-office needs like ERP, CRM and HCM. Larger organizations with an interest and strong internal technical skills may see significant gains in operational efficiency through the implementation of their own internal cloud solutions in a high availability configuration. While there are many ways healthcare organizations can take advantage of "the Cloud," there should remain a healthy skepticism in the extent to which everything is moved. The Cloud is not the magic bullet that will eliminate local datacenters and the need for a local IT presence—at least not yet.

References

1. Brown, E. A. (2011, October). Final Version of NIST Cloud Computing Definition Published. https://www.nist.gov/news-events/news/2011/10/final-version-nist-cloud-computing-definition-published.
2. Eardley, R. (2016, March). Embracing the Cloud. Healthcare Informatics. https://www.healthcare-informatics.com/article/embracing-cloud.
3. Seshachala, S. (2015, March). Disadvantages of Cloud Computing. Cloud Academy. https://cloudacademy.com/blog/disadvantages-of-cloud-computing/.
4. Staff, H. (2017, January). Q&A: Jonathan Manis on IT Collaboration to Improve Patient Care. Health Tech Magazine. https://healthtechmagazine.net/article/2017/01/qa-jonathan-manis-it-collaboration-improve-patient-care.

Chapter 4

Manufacturing

Cameron Schmidt and Jake Ellis

Ford Motor Company

Contents

Introduction to Cloud Computing in Manufacturing

As covered in previous chapters, cloud computing provides companies with the capability to be flexible, scalable, and versatile enough to move at market speed. The manufacturing industry is no exception to these efficiencies, but there are unique variables to consider when examining the use of the Cloud in manufacturing. This chapter provides an understanding of the history of computing in manufacturing, different cloud business models, business efficiencies, and security considerations.

History of Computing in Manufacturing

The manufacturing industry has been defined by paradigm shifts that drive accuracy, speed, and efficiency. For example, the introduction of interchangeable parts during the Industrial Revolution led the charge during the late 1700s and changed the way innovators and businessmen of that era thought about mass production. Henry Ford revolutionized the industry in the 1900s with his introduction of the assembly line in the automobile manufacturing process. The assembly line had a substantial impact on the industry, and it is still used in auto plants today. These developments significantly affected the U.S. economy and helped pave the way for current manufacturing leaders in their search for new ways to achieve that same speed and accuracy that is sought after in every plant across the globe.

Today, in an era of technological trends like cloud computing, there is potential for exciting opportunities and unique challenges that could once again shift the paradigms of the manufacturing industry. In fact, there is already an industry term in manufacturing that is used to define this era of technological advancement: Industry 4.0. This methodology explains that the manufacturing industry is in the 4th stage of the industrial revolution. The first stage of the industrial revolution was characterized by the introduction of steam power, the second by the utilization of electricity in mass production, and the third by the introduction of computing and automation. The fourth stage of the industrial revolution, Industry 4.0, is characterized by the combination of cyber-physical systems, cloud computing and the Internet of Things to create "Smart Factories [1]." The chart below details out this progression of manufacturing revolutions and their respective degrees of complexity (Figure 4.1).

Computing in the manufacturing industry is generally not a new concept as computer integrated manufacturing has been around for over 30 years. However, the information and technological age of today demands speed, flexibility, and data processing. These demands have manufacturing companies looking to the Cloud to embrace their computing power needs and to stay relevant in a highly competitive environment. In surveys conducted by the Economist Intelligence Unit and sponsored by VMware, senior executives from the manufacturing industry familiar with cloud computing revealed that there is great opportunity for the Cloud to penetrate the manufacturing industry. The following graphical representations depict the importance of the Cloud in various sectors of the industry (Figure 4.2) [3].

Business Benefits

When talking about cloud adoption in manufacturing it is important to distinguish between the different ways in which the Cloud can be used in this industry

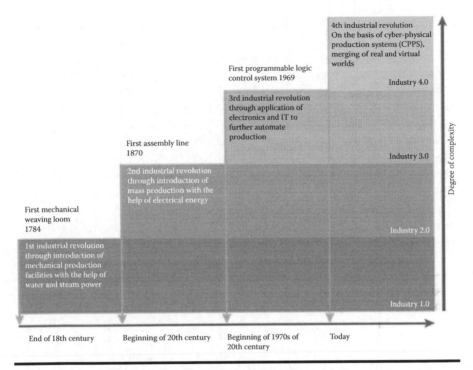

Figure 4.1   Definition of Industry 4.0 [2].

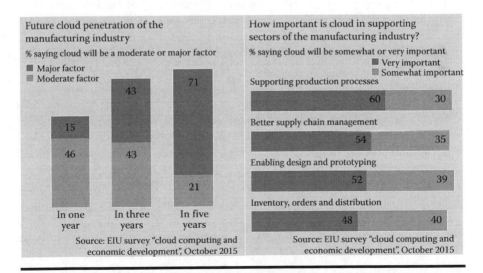

Figure 4.2   Number of breaches by victim industry within Cyber-espionage, numbers within parentheses are the industry NAICS codes.

as their adoption rates historically are not the same. The first is utilizing the Cloud on the business side of the enterprise. This utilization is much more common as all companies can benefit from the same features that cloud providers offer with commodity based services such as HR and Payroll. Another use in this sense is within the advanced data analytics of both business and plant operations. These analytics can be used to show productivity, quality, and safety of manufacturers' plants in real-time. In the latter, large-scale operations often require high compute power to process such a large amount of data gained from all the sensors, computers, and other devices that are gathering this data. Utilizing an Amazon Web Service, IBM, or Microsoft-type cloud provider offers companies enough workload to handle these advanced analytics. With the ability to process data faster than ever, employees are able to monitor plant operations on a proactive basis rather than a reactive one. Real-time inventory control, supply chain management, and automated processes are also on the rise in this industry. Additionally, the implementation of Platform as a Service (PaaS) is quite common as it allows the enterprise to move quickly and deploy services at market speed. These different models will be covered more in depth in the Case Study section where the various use cases are discussed.

Historically Slow Adoption

With all of the positives that cloud utilization promises, there are still companies in the manufacturing sector struggling with the adoption of this technology. Spinning up cloud instances obviously makes more sense in some areas than others. For instance, cloud utilization in the actual manufacturing process, in the form of Infrastructure as a Service (IaaS) for example, has been much slower to adopt for a couple of different reasons. First, there is a huge emphasis placed on the quality and efficiency of production line operations. Therefore, when companies entertain the idea of having their systems transferred to a cloud service provider, it comes with trusting that provider with any issues that may arise. Large-scale plants simply cannot afford to run into computing issues as any production downtimes can result in large losses. Unfortunately, unlike Customer Relationship Management platforms or other commodity based services that are common uses of the Cloud, plant and manufacturing operations are oftentimes not able to experience many downtimes with their infrastructure without cost. Another reason why the manufacturing industry has been slow to adopt cloud computing close to their plant operations is because of the idea that the standard manufacturing technology, in a lot of cases, is stagnant and in legacy form. In this case, companies may be running operating systems that are used to repeatedly completing the same tests and analytics so there is no need to upgrade these systems, nor would they even be interoperable with the Cloud without a complete overhaul. Moreover, upgrading legacy systems and integrating current processes to the Cloud can take a large number of skilled resources and may put time constraints on operations to complete. Lastly, the integration of IT into manufacturing is a learning process that takes time, resources, and patience. The connectivity of all of the various physical systems and applications on premise to the Cloud is a major challenge to overcome and poses major cyber security questions.

Security Considerations

The manufacturing industry is home to some of the most highly valued intellectual property, which means that these types of assets come with a large amount of threats and targets. In fact, according to the 2016 Verizon Data Breach Investigation Report, over half of all breaches in the Manufacturing industry were due to cyber espionage, which is defined in the report as "external threat actors infiltrating victim networks seeking sensitive internal data and trade secrets [4]." Figure 4.3 below details out the cyber espionage attacks by industry.

As one can imagine, ensuring proper security measures such as access control and network protection services are implemented should be among top imperatives of all companies—not only manufacturing, but all industries.

A large issue is that some companies simply are not aware of which vulnerabilities they are susceptible to and often times, the legacy applications and hardware with known exploitations and older protocols are much harder to protect than modern technologies. In some cases where manufacturing companies have not reached their security maturity level yet, they may seek out cloud services to

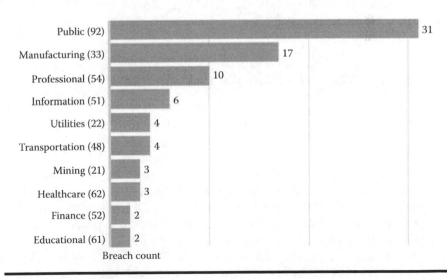

Figure 4.3   Detailed number of Cyber-espionage attacks by industry

provide security to their organization. When entertaining the thought of integrating cloud computing into their environments, trusting that critical assets will be sufficiently protected in the Cloud is a large fear to overcome. It is important that due diligence is taken when deciding on partnerships with cloud providers. For example, in a PWC Study, even though 61% of businesses surveyed from the manufacturing industry had some sort of cloud computing in their environment, only 53% of respondents stated they had a defined security strategy. Working with cloud business providers to ensure a company is fully protected in a way that makes sense for its business and most valuable assets is crucial [5]. Having a cybersecurity strategy defined and thoroughly communicated is just one step to take in order to ensure compliance and security across all areas of the business.

There are a couple of major security considerations that companies need to examine when making the move to the Cloud. The first of which is knowing what controls to place on high value assets such as designs, prototypes, and other IP. Knowing who has access to what data and systems becomes increasingly difficult to protect with the connectivity and remote availability of resources. Companies also need to consider which assets/services to keep on premise and which assets/services to move to the Cloud. Doing so will allow the company to categorize and value their assets, providing a better understanding of the threat landscape for those particular assets. On the other hand, if lower risk assets are moved to the Cloud, companies can trust the cloud service provider (CSP) to take care of these services, freeing up more company resources. The last consideration is how companies plan on protecting the integrity of their data and operations. With the potential to have an exponentially higher number of connected devices and other resources, there is a parallel increase in the need to make sure that the data stays secure and that critical operations do not come to a halt due to distributed denial of service attacks and other types of malicious activities.

Adoption Where It Makes Sense

While there are many challenges with cloud adoption in manufacturing, this should not deter companies from considering its use or offered solutions. Companies can still benefit from using the Cloud in some areas of their business as it is not an "all or nothing" model. For instance, virtualizing hardware in order to build redundancy in their operations may be very beneficial. Also, utilizing servers off site for the advanced analytics has its benefits for certain organizations. Both examples can be implemented in conjunction with any on premise data centers or systems that the company may already use and have no intent to move to the Cloud.

When making these types of decisions there are many factors to be considered, and it is important to conduct risk assessments of all assets and processes. This is to ensure that cloud services are only being utilized in areas that make sense to the business and its operations. Often times businesses benefit from implementing cloud services in small projects or taking advantage of the "low hanging fruit" in order to gain familiarity and confidence in the migration and connectivity of the Cloud with the core business or an organization. In the next section, a case study analysis is provided to highlight some of the potential Cloud adoption models in manufacturing.

Case Study

Throughout the previous chapters, the various models of cloud computing have been introduced and supported by evidence that has given answer to why it has been the buzz for several years in the computing industry. The manufacturing industry as a whole is not unlike other industries in adopting at least some part of each of the three major components of cloud computing. Each industry has determined its place on the Diffusion of Innovation Curve. Defining the role of Software as a Service (SaaS), Platform as a Service (PaaS), and Infrastructure as a Service (IaaS) is not industry specific. It would be easy to write a case study on a single manufacturing company and imply that it applies to every manufacturing company in the industry. Such thinking would be false and, frankly, dangerous. The goal of this section is to provide more than one perspective in order to allow readers to take the information and make rational decisions based on each set of unique circumstances. For that reason, the Case Study section will be written from two perspectives. The first perspective will be of a large established company with an already established infrastructure. This company will be referred to as Company X. The second will be a newer company looking to scale up over the next 10 years. This company will be referred to as Company Y.

As stated earlier in this chapter most manufacturing companies have strict guidelines around production quotas and allowed stoppage times. Basically, the old adage "time is money" holds true in the manufacturing industry as much as any other. Each hour of downtime could cost Company X millions of dollars. That being said, in a company like Company X you will most likely find both legacy hardware and software in a very segmented network environment. As long as these networks are secure, there is no business justification to take the manufacturing environment offline for an extended period of time to upgrade legacy equipment. What will eventually be found is that these environments will become increasingly virtualized and secured at the network level (there could be some additional security at both the Hypervisor and OS level, but that is not in the scope of this book). Does this come as a surprise?

Now that the actual manufacturing side of the manufacturing company has been discussed, how could Company X, a large manufacturing company, leverage the Cloud to its advantage? There are the three standard models, and in this case, there is a fourth to explore as well. Suppose Company X has an aging on-premise data center. Company X sends a request for proposal (RFP) to the major cloud providers (Amazon, Microsoft, Google, IBM) for a cloud solution. Surprisingly, IaaS is immediately dismissed as an option. More specifically, IaaS provides the hardware, storage, computing, etc. for a business. Because it is a service, the service provider is profiting in some way. What needs to be determined is if that profit is less expensive than having an on premises data center. Essentially, they are building massive server farms and renting space on them to many different companies. Is the problem clear yet? Here's an analogy to help build understanding. Say that Bob, a college student, needs a new laptop. He finds a deal for $1500 dollars, but also realizes he could rent the same laptop for $2000 dollars. His roommate is willing to share the cost with him, essentially a 50/50 split. In return for the $500 dollar savings, Bob's roommate would expect 50% of its use. However, Bob needs the laptop 90% of the time. In this model Bob would be expected to pay 90% of the $2, 000 dollars. The sharing model no longer makes sense. The same is true when discussing IaaS. In order to accommodate certain organizations' IaaS needs, the CSP would need to scale up so much that it would no longer be cost efficient, not to mention the speed loss moving from an intranet-based environment to an internet-based one.

So, if IaaS is out, PaaS and SaaS are the two remaining. A PaaS like Microsoft Azure provides a development stack that would certainly provide an advantage to a company like Company X. For instance, developing and deploying new applications can cut development time in half [6]. This is no small feat as large companies often have departments devoted entirely to creating, testing, and deploying new applications. To have the entire stack live in one place could revolutionize the application development business model. SaaS is probably the most widely adopted of the three models. Why? Well, first, thinking from the viewpoint of a systems administrator, it would be seen as a hassle every time a new version of software was released and needed to be integrated. New versions of software usually suggests, at best, a complicated upgrade path with the potential to lose all of the users' data in the process. With SaaS, all of the upgrades and customer data are handled on the backend while everything works seamlessly. Additionally, one advantage is that each instance of the software can be customized for the user of the business. For Company X, this is an amazing development for business purposes. Let's explore an example. The main vendor of Computer Aided Design (CAD) software is a company called Autodesk. Before Autodesk launched their SaaS all CAD drawings were hosted locally. What's worse is that Autodesk would update their software yearly and Autodesk seats were complicated and costly. Now, Autodesk has a cloud solution where CAD drawings can be stored safely in the Cloud [7]. Company X has a customized solution that caters to their needs and gives them exactly as many seats as they need. All of the updating of the software occurs on the test servers before it is moved into production, preventing any possible complications for Company X, avoiding the dreaded downtime.

The last aspect to explore with cloud computing and Company X is Big Data. Without making assumptions about what kind of company that Company X is, let's assume the Petabyte as a unit of storage will be a thing of the past. Would it make sense to leverage the computing power of the cloud to analyze this massive amount of data? Can Hadoop's HDFS be configured across a cloud environment? This thought grasps onto the nature of the Cloud vs. traditional data center argument. The answer calls back to the IaaS argument for a company this size. The simple answer is the more data a company has, the faster and cheaper it is going to be able to process at the traditional data center.

Now, apply the same aforementioned conditions to Company Y. Company Y is a smaller company that has unpredictable, but expected growth over the next 10 years. The same guidelines for downtime hold true, but what if the Cloud model could work differently for Company Y? Company Y currently has an old outdated OS server running all of its applications. Moreover, there is no segmentation between any of its services. An RFP was sent to the same CSP as discussed earlier.

Company Y has a lot of concerns. First, if they are on an OS that is no longer supported, it is a major security risk. The lack of separation is also a concern. Company Y is small enough that IaaS could be a reasonable solution. Company Y has two options. The first option would be to invest in all new hardware and software with the risk of needing at least one major tech refresh in the next 5–10 years. On the other hand, IaaS would be able to scale up and down and the software could be updated as needed.

PaaS may not play a large role at first, but could be integrated as the company grows. The development stack is a key feature that every company should integrate. Company Y could also move away from standalone copies of software. SaaS software, like Salesforce, has become the industry standard and provides customized solutions for companies of any size.

Conclusion

Cloud computing, like everything, is driven by the economics of the situation. With a better understanding of each scenario and business model, companies will have the best possible insight of both the product and the customer. As stated previously in the chapter, the role that the Cloud can play in a manufacturing company's computing environment can range from partial to total. In some cases, that role has yet to be fully defined, but the model is robust in what it has to offer and will continue to evolve.

References

1. Marr, B. (2016, June 20). What Everyone Must Know About Industry 4.0. Retrieved from https://www.forbes.com/sites/bernardmarr/2016/06/20/what-everyone-must-know-about-industry-4-0/#349f08d5795f.

2. Georgakopoulos, D., Jayaraman, P. P., Fazia, M., Villari, M., & Ranjan, R. (2016). *Internet of Things and Edge Cloud Computing Roadmap for Manufacturing. IEEE Cloud Computing*, 3(4), 66–73. doi:10.1109/mcc.2016.91.
3. VMWare (2016). *Ascending Cloud: The Adoption of Cloud Computing in Five Industries Executive Summary*. Retrieved from https://www.vmware.com/radius/wp-content/uploads/2015/08/EIU_VMware-Executive-Summary-FINAL-LINKS-2-26-16.pdf.
4. Verizon Enterprise (2016). *Verizon 2016 Data Breach Investigations Report* (Rep.). Retrieved from http://www.verizonenterprise.com/resources/reports/rp_DBIR_2016_Report_en_xg.pdf.
5. Symantec (2016). *Smarter Security For Manufacturing In The Industry 4.0 Era*. (2016). Retrieved from https://www.symantec.com/content/dam/symantec/docs/solution-briefs/industry-4.0-en.pdf.
6. Top 10 Advantages of Platform-as-a-Service. Retrieved from http://www.engineyard.com/whitepapers/top-10-advantages-of-platform-as-a-service.
7. Cloud Services (2017). Retrieved from https://www.autodesk.com/360-cloud.

Chapter 5

Cloud Marketing

Joe Ciuffo

Gensys

Contents

What is Marketing/Benefits?

Marketing represents an ever-growing field of professionals, and a substantial portion of many corporate budgets. Why is it so increasingly important? A company must promote itself to individuals identified as a good fit for the product. Thus, marketers position the message and branding of a company to closely align with those that would be interested and driven to do business with the company. Marketing professionals must relentlessly review data to confirm how well their message is received by their target group. Understanding the success of a marketing campaign allows a company to keep building upon a success, or pivot if the message is powerless. The field of marketing may illustrate the benefits of cloud computing more than any other area of business. Cloud computing has contributed to feats that simply

weren't possible for most businesses, from a marketing standpoint. Using cloud technologies, marketers can develop more effective campaigns to promote their products
to prospective buyers, and return an enormous amount of data to understand the
potency of their message amongst a target audience (Jeknic and Kraut, 2015).

At the very core, Marketing is meant to resonate amongst a defined target.
Imagine a person playing darts, where the objective is to hit the bullseye on the
dartboard. In marketing, the campaign is designed to have maximum potency with
those expected to be interested in the product. Much like darts, a company creates a campaign attempting to hit their bullseye. However, without actionable data
regarding the performance of a marketing campaign, the organization can't fully
understand if it was successful. Would someone really want to play competitive
darts with their eyes closed? Assuming the person is not capable of super-human
feats, they would ideally want to gauge their next throw based upon the result of
their first attempt. In marketing, a company collects data on the effectiveness of
their campaign to then judge how they will attempt the next. Failure to improve
upon marketing campaigns could result in wasted resources, and potential failure
as an organization (ExactTarget, 2014). This text will evaluate the current methods
Genesys has employed to market their products, and how the Cloud has affected
each item for the positive. The items examined are customer engagement, marketing automation, and marketing content creation.

Customer Engagement

Customer engagement is a connection, through various mediums of communication, between a company and a consumer. As organizations move away from traditional forms of media, such as television advertisements, marketers are looking for
new ways to connect with specific audiences. Customer engagement can occur in a
wide range of ways, from a booth at a trade show, to specific user targeted ads on a
social media page. It is becoming clearer that companies are looking to target their
marketing campaigns for higher effectiveness with a defined audience, rather than
blasting a message to unspecific mass audiences (Hollebeek, 2011). To better clarify
Genesys' customer engagement practices the use cases examined are trade shows,
lead generation, and digital marketing tools.

Trade Show

Trade shows are large physical events typically centered around a specific industry
or product. In the case of Genesys, the marketing team will attend trade shows
based around unified communications or contact center technology. The events
represent a great opportunity to connect with individuals who are open minded
to, or actively looking for, a new software provider. The Genesys team will usually

construct a large booth, typically 20 feet by 50 feet in size, highlighted by eye-catching branded content and computer displays to demonstrate the product. Physical events like trade shows generate a lot of foot traffic and conversations between the Genesys team and potential customers, so it is very important to track this information for immediate lead generation. In the past, most record keeping of conversations was done through business card collection or an excel spreadsheet (ExactTarget, 2014). The lead generation team would then do their research on the potential customer and follow up after the event.

With the advent of software as a service (SaaS) providers, the physical space has been revolutionized to take advantage of captured data. The Genesys demonstration booths are aided by cloud controlled wi-fi systems. Essentially these routers pull their saved configuration from a central host, negating extensive setup times and router configurations. The routers also understand if there are other connected repeaters that would extend the coverage of the wireless network. Together, the devices create a wireless mesh network, which allows the entire Wi-Fi coverage to operate under a singular connection name. A sales representative walking through-out the booth, providing a demonstration would not have to disconnect and reconnect to a new wireless network depending on their proximity to devices; rather he or she would seamlessly transition between each access point. The devices also provide detailed usage reports, giving further insight to those visiting the booth location. The reports show the average length of time users stayed by the booth, based upon connection to the network. This data can then be cross-referenced with the attendee list, which contains user specific information, to gauge how long potential customers were at the booth and frequency of visits. Setup teams are no longer fighting the clock to quickly configure the networks at tradeshows. The managed routers pull down the latest firmware automatically, assuring a fully optimized experience. Providing connectivity within a demonstration booth environment can now be as simple as plugging in the router and allowing the device to pull down all relevant configuration from a central location (McNamee, 2013).

Physical lead tracking has also received the SaaS treatment, using badge scanning and lead logging. When a user registers at the very beginning of a tradeshow, they are given a name badge to wear for the entire event. These badges show others their name and title, while also serving as a form of credentials to access tradeshow-specific events within the venue. Embedded in the badge is a near field communication chip which can be wirelessly read from scanning devices. As attendees walk up to a booth, their badge is scanned and logged to a central repository for that specific company; in this situation Genesys. Sales representatives can then access this repository, through a phone application, to store additional notes from conversations with each respective attendee. The notes are used to highlight that potential lead's needs and relevant items that would help within a future sales discussion (Interview Friio, 2017). Having a central repository to store lead information allows the teams to track the entire journey of client interactions. Instead of referencing a large excel spreadsheet that holds no readily relational data, a sales representative could see all the past interaction notes

Genesys has had with that individual. What if this potential customer moved to a new company, or become more receptive to new vendors? Stringing customer journey data together gives the company a clearer view as to where that person may be on their sales cycle. It also provides a greater depth of information so the sales team can pull from multiple conversations, instead of the last interaction. When an employee responds to an important business email, it is helpful to see the previous responses in that email thread. Without the previous responses, one would simply respond to the latest reply without any context. Consider this same situation when meeting attendees at a tradeshow; having context of previous meetings can greatly improve the current conversation (Kantrowitz, 2014).

Digital Marketing

Digital marketing represents a space growing at an exponential pace in applicability and competitiveness. Many of the tools that exists in the digital marketing space did not exist pre-cloud technology boom of the late 2000s. What makes digital marketing so powerful is the ability to combine analytics with effective targeting. The foundational benefits start with user journey, captured with marketing intelligence. As an example, imagine someone browsing a travel website and they've visited a section for Punta Cana twice before, during previous visits. On the backend of the travel website are trackers that have identified this user as a unique individual; collecting information such as time on website and areas and dates most frequently searched. The user's past browsing habits on the site will influence the content presented to them. On the user's third visit, all of the upcoming deals on the website might only show Punta Cana and advertise a special pricing that *just so happens* to be the same dates the user has been searching. The travel company might also integrate this data with social media platforms, and pay to advertise Punta Cana vacations to this specific user on Facebook or Instagram. To tie that all together, a user's browsing history for a potential vacation has drastically affected the content that a travel website displays on their main page and the advertising presented on social media platforms. The travel company didn't have to create generic ads, because the user's browsing history told them exactly what they needed to know. The ads are directed towards potential customers with extreme precision, which could lead to a large increase in the company's return on advertising investment. Cloud computing enables all of this data to be consumed and dynamically acted upon in almost real time; while also speaking natively with other third-party platforms, such as social media (Bonometti, 2012).

In Genesys, digital marketing all starts with robust analytics collected from a user's history on the company's website. If a prospective customer visits the company website and downloads a whitepaper, it will be tied to their history. If that customer received an email from Genesys and opened it to read the contents, or called into its customer service line for more information, it will be tied to their history. Much like a personal Facebook page where a user has a collection of their posts, Genesys creates a page for prospective customers and each post is a record of user interaction history. Accumulation of customer interaction data is important because it shows the big picture of their relationship with the company (Interview Friio, 2017). A sales team can see how invested a potential customer might be if they've been actively interacting with the company website and marketing items over a long period. This collection of data is usually defined as the customer journey, which represents a collection of touch points between the customer and the business. Traditionally, this data is *massaged* into various formats and lists to assist with other company initiatives. For example, if the Genesys team would like to hold a global webinar for their cloud communication software, how would they identify interested attendees? The data collected from previous touch points could serve as indicators that a company may be interested, based upon activity such as downloading of whitepapers.

The team could also log this data within a customer relationship management (CRM) that fully illustrates the lifecycle of customer interaction to end sale. A unique benefit of the cloud is having a single point of reference for data that can be accessed from anywhere. A CRM is a platform that contains all information about a customer in a single location. Items such as phone calls, emails, and various forms of marketing interaction could be captured there and displayed in chronological order. The marketing team can use this as a ledger of items sent to the customer, and the sales teams can utilize the page to see where the customer might be in the sales cycle, potentially indicating their readiness to buy. A CRM in the cloud, such as Salesforce, easily enables input from other pieces of software, regardless of location, to collect centrally. This information can be consumed by employees regardless of location, instead of traditionally having to be within company network to access the information. Having this information stored within the CRM's datacenter not only increases availability, but durability of data as well. If a customer was to house their own CRM, they would not only need to maintain expensive hardware, but also redundant pairs of servers as backup, in case of a failover situation. If a tornado were to hit a company's headquarters and destroy the primary and backup servers, everything would be lost. Data, in a cloud-based CRM, is redundant physically and geographically. If the same tornado destroyed a data center in the south, there would be a replicated version of that company's CRM in a different part of the country. Data availability and durability is not easily matched in an on-premises situation, without exorbitant costs. Therefore, organizations that are smaller in size (less than 1000 users) or those that are geographically diverse can greatly benefit from a cloud based CRM (Rouse, 2014).

Lead Generation

Once data has been captured and collected in a central repository, a company must make actionable insights on the information. In Genesys, the lead generation teams are responsible for taking the vast collection of data and using it to generate further response. Lead scoring, or determining a numerically weighted fit of a potential customer, is essential to targeting marketing content (Pardot, 2017). Sending weekly emails, and pursuing a customer that isn't highly scored as a fit could kill the opportunity and hurt the Genesys reputation. Therefore, the lead scores are essential to nurturing the lead and placing opportunities that are ready in the correct set of sales processes.

To create lead scores, the team uses various metrics from customer interactions. Much like a student taking a test where certain answers might be worth more on a 100-point scale, lead scoring may weight interactions such as email subscriptions heavier than downloading a whitepaper. Metrics captured from digital marketing analytics are essential to building lead generation scores. If a customer spends a long time on the company website, downloads a whitepaper, and subscribes to product information emails, there is a higher likelihood they are interested in a potential purchase. If the interested party then fits the description of a target market for the product, the lead would be sent to the sales team for further follow up and direction through the selling process. It is very important for the lead generation scores to be accurate, as the sales teams need genuine leads continuously funneled through the sales pipeline (Pardot, 2017). If these lead generation process isn't precise, sales teams could be wasting extensive resources for no realized gain.

These scores are built from user interactions throughout a variety of mediums; therefore, it is imperative the lead generation software can integrate with the various points of engagement. A cloud-based platform has the benefit of easier integration with third party products by use of an open API (application programming interface). An API is very similar to a menu at a restaurant. A potential diner would look at the menu, decide on an item along with any order modifications, and ask for it from the waiter. The API is a published document of all actionable items within the software, such as points of data or input, and allows for developers to order the actionable items to be used with other pieces of software. Over time, as the company uses more or different point of engagement, they will still be able to collect all that information in one central database and provide detailed reporting (Interview Friio, 2017). If the lead scoring wasn't all-encompassing for the entire spectrum of customer engagement within an organization, the end score would not be truly indicative of a potential selling opportunity.

Marketing Automation

Marketing data collection, and lead scoring has existed for quite some time; well before the implementation of cloud computing. However, the effect of cloud computing on these items is undeniable. The elevation of marketing tools due to cloud computing has been so successful that it birthed a completely new space: marketing automation. Marketing automation refers to tools that enact a set of work flows based upon defined criteria (Casey and Pilecki, 2017). To better define capabilities, imagine a bank website where users could begin loan applications right from the website. As the user is filling out the form, the website will automatically present a "speak with a live agent button," if the user enters a loan amount above $50,000, and begins alerting a customer service representative on the back end. The automation tools identified the customer amount was above the loan threshold, and then secured an agent on retainer to assist the customer in real time. Other organizations may take lead scoring into account, and build branches of tasks triggered upon the scoring category of a potential customer. The company may have automation set to email every lead that has created an account on the website once a month. If a user has downloaded information from the company site, it may trigger additional emails for new white papers that were recently published. Have you ever received a welcome newsletter directly after creating an account on a website? You have marketing automation to thank for the emails filling your inbox. Amazon traditionally uses these set of tools to follow up with customers after they have purchased a product to make sure their experience was satisfactory. Marketing automation tools are not simply limited to emails. In fact, many companies utilize different mediums of communication, such as an email 1 month and a text message the next, to avoid spamming a potential customer (Mcrae, 2012).

The benefits of automation tools increase over time, as companies analyze the performance of previous campaigns. The cycle will start over again: data is collected, potential customers are then re-scored, and automated campaigns are triggered, all considering learned behavior from previous actions. Did a user never open a sent email and unsubscribe from text messages? These items must be refactored, and the data re-analyzed to see which campaigns are generating actual revenue as opposed to frustrating would-be customers with spam. The technology gives marketers a chance to constantly learn, then refine their methods to better reach the targeted audience. Continuous improvement upon marketing automation is a key concept to nurturing potential leads. Overloading a lead with too many emails and too much information could cause frustration. Nevertheless, sending just the right amount or inviting them to informational webinars can foster trust and a long-lasting business relationship (Coveney, 2017).

Through the use of marketing automation tools, such as Marketo or Salesforce's Pardot, Genesys has transformed its lead generation. As a company with multiple products in its portfolio, serving very different types and sizes of customers, lead nurturing is done very differently depending on the category of potential customer. The company uses automation to reach out to existing and potential leads through a variety of email newsletters. Each newsletter is specific to a product. Customers smaller in size, with smaller IT departments, are targeted with informational content focused on speed of deployment, and comprehensive out of the box functionality. Larger corporations with extensive development bandwidth are targeted with a different set of products that highlights adaptability to that company's vision and broad customization capability for developers (Interview Friio, 2017).

Marketing Content Creation

An indirect effect of cloud computing on marketing has been content creation. In the past, teams working on marketing material would share Word documents with defined versions. If they were to collaborate on the same document, all revisions would go through a single user at a time and then be shared with the rest of the team. The potential for team members to be working on incorrect versions of marketing content and for confusion with collaboration from remote team members was high. Cloud collaboration tools like Google Drive and Microsoft Office 365 enable real-time coauthoring between all users sharing a document. In this situation, marketing content creators could be working on the same document at the same time, from any Internet-connected location (Padilla et al., 2015).

At Genesys, the marketing teams are constantly working on whitepapers, website changes, blog posts, and other content-based items that require team collaboration. As a company with a Chief Marketing Officer from the Netherlands and countless marketing teams in satellite offices around the world, real-time collaboration along with a centrally located master document is crucial. A blog post to advertise a global webinar may be written by authors located in North Carolina and Indiana at the same time, likely using video conferencing between offices to collaborate. Afterwards, that document is reviewed with their team lead, located in California, while the graphical content is inserted by designers from England. This type of cooperation would have taken days, and endless chains of emails, in the past. Now, it can happen in real time with less confusion along the way (Interview Friio, 2017).

Conclusion

The advent of cloud-based innovation is visible in every corner of the marketing industry. Whether it be a company's booth at a tradeshow or personalized content for web site visitors, cloud solutions have elevated the potency and availability of a marketer's tools. Cloud solutions have not only given way to the mass collection of data, but also the ability to draw deeper correlations or relationships between the information (Jeknic and Kraut, 2015). Marketers have applied this deeper understanding by developing curated plans of engagement with consumers based upon learned attributes from each specific person over time (ExactTarget, 2014). The marketing content then used for engagement is created by tools that are designed to be more highly available, and collaborative than ever before (Padilla et al., 2015). While this may appear complex, the end goal remains simple; hit the bullseye on the dartboard. Cloud Computing has played an essential role in the marketer's heightened ability to generate awareness and call consumers to action.

References

Bonometti, R. J. (2012). Technology considerations for competing in the big data—Social-mobile-cloud marketing space. *Competition Forum*, 10(2), 209–214.

Casey, S. and Pilecki, M. (2017). The top emerging technologies for B2B marketers. Forrester. April 6, 2017.

Coveney, J. (2017, March 11). What is marketing automation? 21 pros weigh in. Retrieved March 12, 2017, from http://revenginemarketing.com/blog/what-is-marketing-automation-top-answers-from-industry-thought-leaders/.

Hollebeek, L. (2011). Exploring customer brand engagement: Definition and themes. *Journal of Strategic Marketing*, 19(7), 555–573. doi:10.1080/0965254X.2011.599493.

Interview with Andrea Friio vice president of Gensys Technical Marketing [Telephone interview]. (2017, March 12).

Jeknic, J. and Kraut, B. (2015). Cloud services and marketing. MIPRO, 1492–1498. doi:10.11099/MIPRO.2015.7160508.

Kantrowitz, A. (2014, May 19). Pros and cons of the marketing cloud you should now. Retrieved March 7, 2017, from http://adage.com/article/digital/pros-cons-marketing-cloud/293258/.

McNamee, M. (2013, April 5). Cloud controlled wireless vs. cloud managed wifi. Retrieved from https://www.securedgenetworks.com/blog/Cloud-Controlled-Wireless-VS-Cloud-Managed-Wifi.

Mcrae & Co. (2012, May 7). What is marketing automation? Our top 10 FAQs. Retrieved March 5, 2017, from http://www.mcraeandcompany.co.uk/Blog/what-is-marketing-automation-top-10-faqs/.

Padilla, R., Milton, S., and Johnson, L. (2015). Components of service value in business-to-business cloud computing. *Journal of Cloud Computing*, 4(1), 15.

Pardot. (2017). *The Complete Guide to B2B Marketing*. San Francisco, CA: Salesforce.

Product keynote: ExactTarget marketing cloud. (2014). Fair Disclosure Wire. Retrieved March 5, 2017.

Rouse, M. (2014, November). Customer relationship management. Retrieved March 1, 2017, from http://searchcrm.techtarget.com/definition/CRM.

Chapter 6

Government Agencies
Making the Case for the Cloud in State Government

Jared Linder

State of Indiana Family and Social Services Administration

Contents

Introduction

Health and human services is not traditionally the swiftest-moving of industries. Unfortunately, state governments can be even slower. Within the state of Indiana, the Family and Social Services Administration (FSSA) represents the government-sector agency for health and human services where we are always working to increase the pace of our information technology maturity, including looking toward advancements like the Cloud for future IT development, system deployment, and support.

The public sector is no stranger to partnering with organizations and companies who specialize in various service offerings, including business process and workforce outsourcing, strategic planning coordination, IT staffing and outsourcing, and managed services. This partnering model is typically advantageous for all parties and holds true for several reasons: access to IT talent, training and development capabilities, and access to global best practices and knowledge bases, all while allowing all parties to focus on core competencies (Quelin, 2015).

Therefore, given the advancement in data center support and the push to host supporting IT functions in the Cloud, it absolutely makes sense for government health and human services organizations to work with partners to explore strategies around off-premises models, including cloud computing and how to best support large-scale government systems and applications through continued advancement in various service offerings, including software as a service, platform as a service, and infrastructure as a service.

This brief exposition of cloud computing as it relates to state government and the near-term future will serve as an exploration of ideas based upon current state findings within Indiana's specific technology environment. This chapter will explain Indiana's current landscape, explore a few possible candidate options for cloud readiness, define why a state would make those decisions, and discuss possible next steps.

Indiana's Current Landscape

In Indiana, the FSSA serves as the agency responsible for enrolling and managing the health care and human services benefit programs for our citizens for large governmental programs like the supplemental nutritional assistance program, temporary assistance for needy families (TANF), and Medicaid. As of 2017, we currently serve through those programs approximately 1.5 million Hoosiers at any given time, which represents about one out of every five citizens in Indiana (KFF, 2017). To more completely and more efficiently serve those citizens, we are always looking to understand and stay current with all technological enhancements critical to managing our IT and operations environment. It cannot be overstated that one of our primary goals as a health and human services organization is to deliver accurate, timely, consistent service delivery for our constituents (FSSA, n.d.). Therefore, our goal as an IT organization within the agency is to ensure that service delivery all happens as well, as efficiently and as manageable as possible.

As with any large organization in the early 21st century, we have a complex IT environment filled with aging legacy systems. We are currently in various phases in the system development life cycle of replacing many of those systems and have been exploring various models to develop and support those applications. These modernization activities are at the forefront of our policy and operations teams' priorities: we currently employ over 4,000 employees, including field workers who need access to our systems on a daily basis, so getting the IT right is crucial.

To further define the FSSA systems and application environment, we currently manage over $100 MM annually in IT and support contracts that support the policy divisions and the state and federal programs that fall under our purview. We also spend millions more a month in IT infrastructure costs at our Indiana state data center to support those efforts. We have historically been running a few large mainframe applications, several smaller applications that run on aging technology like Microsoft Visual Basic, and a series of various homegrown applications. In addition, we work together with our Indiana Office of Technology to run and support six state hospitals, including all the technology needed to fully operate remote, always-on healthcare facilities.

With the injection of enhanced federal funding resulting from federal initiatives like the Patient Protection and Affordable Care Act (PPACA) and Health Information Technology for Economic and Clinical Health (HITECH), Indiana has worked since 2010 to modernize its health and human services portfolio of applications and systems. We as a state are not unique in that endeavor, as the availability of funding has led most states down the same path of simultaneous legacy system replacement and technological and functional enhancement. It has also mobilized a workforce of private sector IT organizations and consulting firms who have specialized in the health and human service space while also continuing to evolve their industry best practices, including offering new solutions like platform builds, modular system architecture design, and alternative hosting and support models.

Much of this innovation has also come directly from guidelines laid out by our federal partners at the Centers for Medicare and Medicaid Services (CMS), a branch of the U.S. Department of Health and Human Services (HHS). CMS has worked for several years to provide varying levels of guidance to states regarding system design and architecture, data models and standards, interface creation guidelines, and modular procurement methodology (CMS, n.d.). Even the Unites States CIO's office has outlined their plan for IT modernization and improvement, including a cloud-first designation for new IT systems (ASA/OCIO, 2012).

This involvement at the federal level regarding technology and maturity enhancements has also then carried into funding availability and guidance regarding how states must plan future endeavors in an orchestrated, relatively common fashion. This includes the creation of, and adherence to, funding requests; conducting state self-assessments around Medicaid Information Technology Architecture focusing on business processes, data architecture, and technology architecture; and designing manageable project deployment plans, as well as developing roadmaps for future development as it relates to overall program success. And, although it could seem potentially restrictive to have regulations handed down to states regarding IT systems and funding, it has been beneficial in that we have mobilized nationwide around several shared concepts and a common nomenclature regarding how we define and work to implement successful IT projects at the state level. It has also created a known, knowledgeable workforce nationwide around all sides of the table, both public and private sector, as well as relationships with our federal partner organizations. It is with this army of industry players and these published guidelines that we then set out to create our future IT roadmaps and strategies.

Why the Cloud?

Indiana has been using different hosting models over the years, varying from on-premises infrastructure and support, to partner-hosted data centers, to light application support in what our users simply see as "browser-based." Mainly, we have been willing to explore a few different models, oftentimes in large-scale manners. The following section will describe our current attempts as well as outline recommendations and challenges we are experiencing in the current market.

In the largest example of FSSA moving infrastructure, applications, and hosting support out of our data center, we currently choose not to host our own Medicaid and healthcare claims processing systems. We currently do most of our fee-for-service claims transaction processing and HHS integration work with the support of our prime system vendor out of a private data center in the southeast United States. We are colocated here with other state HHS systems where we can leverage cost and resource synergies across states. With collocation, we can use our combined partner resources to ensure we can efficiently run large enterprise claims management systems for multiple states within the same data center. Indiana originally embarked upon this plan in late 2012, moving from an off-site, single instance of a private data center to this colocation model. The next step will conceivably be a larger leap toward no longer supporting infrastructure.

Now, it is naïve to think that no one runs a data center in a cloud-hosted situation, but the immediate benefit is that we will be moving away from running and managing site support and moving more toward outsourcing and trusting partners to help run our systems for us. We currently have been successful with application development and code promotion in multiple environments, and anticipate that our development teams will continue to successfully build and manage apps regardless of whether that application is hosted in the Cloud or a remote, privately-run data center. However, what we will probably see next is that state and partner organizations will then need to reeducate our workforce or find new employee candidates who have the available skills to help run modern systems through cloud-based techniques instead of needing on-premises support skills.

What we are now also seeing is a shift in some product offerings which is causing us to have to lean toward cloud solutions as the only future-proof offering. For example, in a few situations we are seeing vendors alter their product offerings in the name of obsolescence: on-premises models and licensure offerings are being eliminated in favor of either hybrid-usage or cloud-only support models for major systems offerings including Customer Relationship Management (CRM), email, and basic office and management software. While we are working to adapt to those models, we as a state can potentially be hamstrung by the inflexibility of solutions that force state clients to purchase licensure models that force them into a cloud-based hosting model. It would be preferable to work collaboratively to find models that are more flexible for state clients which vendor partners can support where the client-partner relationship and licensure/support model is mutually advantageous and not necessarily dictated solely by the technology roadmap of a product offering.

Alterations of licensure offerings of previously-purchased products cannot be the driver to move governmental solutions to the Cloud. The premise that merely moving from an on-premises to a cloud license equals moving systems to the Cloud is disingenuous and potentially damaging to the process of making the shift to cloud-based technology and infrastructure. If state clients are convinced to believe that making the strategic decision to move to the Cloud is as easy as purchasing new licensure, we will be doing ourselves a great disservice by not thoroughly planning and architecting our systems' needs in and for the Cloud. This cannot be a move made from procurement necessity, but must be made from the desire to completely reengineer and rearchitect the human service enterprise around principles that are grounded in future proofing, technological architecture design ideology, and overall desire to move IT maturity into the future.

What is of necessity, however, is security: this is one of our primary current concerns. States are working hard to keep up with the needed security activities while focusing on how to find trained resources to support that critical part of the enterprise. Currently, FSSA conducts several periodic audits of our security controls and protocols as part of our role as the state human services agency. Our federal partners, Food and Nutrition Services, a branch of the U.S. Department of Agriculture, conduct periodic, 3-year rotating system audits for our eligibility determination system which we use to distribute food stamps, Medicaid benefits, and TANF dollars. The current effort is intensive for all parties. This would be an excellent place for cloud-hosted environments to serve their fittest purpose and to excel as the technology of the future today—by allowing states and other clients to buy hosted environments that are essentially templates of combined security protocols and guidelines wrapped around industry best practices for server and infrastructure builds. Building and hosting environments around preestablished guidelines that also had this built-in auditability would be most welcome and most likely achieve cost savings by reducing the administrative and research burden needed to conduct those activities.

So, when we think about the benefits of cloud, we need to move beyond the storage discussion. Storage has become cheap enough that it is not really a primary driver of the reason to go cloud-based. Security, system and data center management, and new system development are the real reasons that states and other clients are seriously viewing the Cloud as a primary answer to large IT environments. Why this is important to Indiana specifically is that we run combined models throughout the state with different system deployments. Our state Office of Technology also manages our disaster recovery environment in a remote site on-campus at Indiana University in Bloomington. What this means is that we essentially replicate our production environments across the state, including incurring costs for installation, licensing, hardware, staffing, and maintenance. This also means we must schedule purchasing, installation, and set-up time for state staff as well as for hardware and software partners to help guide state staff on support activities, especially when dealing with specialized applications and appliances. Without saying, this of course increases state costs at every stage of the system planning, development, and support lifecycles. It would be ideal to shift the focus away from managing IT toward putting those dollars back into state programs or creating efficiencies where possible.

Next Steps

In addition to the possibilities for improvement that have been mentioned in the previous sections, what we are currently focused on is improving our overall footprint and increasing our technical capabilities. One example we are currently exploring focuses on models for running the IT environment for Indiana's state hospitals. We currently have six state behavioral health hospitals across the state that take care of some of our most vulnerable citizens. Some of these facilities are in rural or remote parts of the state. Currently we support those hospitals with in-field, on-premises hardware and software for many operational functions including data and record storage, network connectivity, and access to many local software programs. We do currently run an electronic medical records (EMR) system at a centralized location and pipe connectivity out to each of these six hospitals.

We host that EMR system at our centralized state data center, and much like all on-premises solutions it is subject to the rules and provisions placed upon it by the data center and its staff, including routine maintenance, hardware resets and maintenance, and application and workstation patch deployment. This centralized IT management of our EMR application at times causes issues with our decentralized hospitals who want to be in more control over their applications to be able to schedule outages and maintenance around critical hospital activities like new patient admissions and pharmaceutical distributions.

As we continue to modernize our enterprise, we are currently working to build a new state behavioral health hospital, and our approach will be to not just centralize our IT systems, but to replan and thoroughly consider the Cloud for our EMR system at a minimum, and our remaining IT needs where possible. We are leaning toward creating a model that absolutely leans toward a cloud-first approach, or at least a model that has us deploying locally the minimal amount of IT infrastructure necessary, knowing that the need to just deploy the IT needed to run the operations will still be substantial.

To explore models like the one previously described also takes more than technological planning: procurement and budgetary requirements must also be satisfied. States need to work with their procurement agencies to write request for proposals or other procurement documents where they offer respondents an ability to propose cloud or off-site hosting. If a state procurement process or guideline is prohibitive to creative IT solutions, the challenge lies with the partnering organizations and the state client to adapt to the current procurement models. Much like the licensure challenge mentioned in the last section, the purchasing model and the product offering must line up in order to successfully plan and purchase IT solutions for states. Nationwide, organizations like the Nationwide Organization of Procurement Officers work to continually improve the procurement process, including offering cooperative purchasing programs where states can spearhead projects and allow other states to partner on those solutions (NASPO, 2017).

In addition to procurement challenges, we are also seeing issues with our state budgeting process. Although one of the value propositions of cloud solutions is the reduction in initial purchase costs, often state procurement agencies have different guidelines and budgets based upon the difference between capital expenditures and operational costs. This is mainly due to tight operational budgets due to biennium budgetary guidelines, whereas large capital projects are not always subject to those guidelines due to the availability of other funding streams. Therefore, it is currently easier to implement a multi-million-dollar IT system including all the upfront hardware and software licensure costs than it is to engage a partner in a cloud-based solution that comes with lower up-front costs in favor of higher access fees or service rates.

Although it of course makes sense to try to minimize, control, or anticipate spend across the longer-term cost curve, this is a real impediment to altering the purchasing model. Also, this is a new problem that will most likely take exploration of how government entities and other organizations who create strict guidelines around funding allocations for distinctive capital and operational projects and expenditures must do business in the future. The market is changing and product offerings are becoming increasingly more cloud-based, or at least off-premises based, and purchasers of these products must adapt to meet this shift in the marketplace. IT partners must also remain cognizant of these challenges and work with states to produce solutions that work in both the near and long term.

Conclusion

Cloud computing is here, but there are evident challenges to the application of such technology within state government. What must happen is that we as an industry representing the government health and human services space need to focus on intentionally pursuing the alignment of technology availability and proliferation with and alongside of state and federal policy, compliance, budgeting, and procurement processes, as well as finding the political will to make broad changes to create positive outcomes for our programs.

What is critical, and that all parties also need to remember while pursuing these positive outcomes, is that in the health and human services space our goal is not to create world-class IT environments, but to deliver world-class services to our constituents through efficient and thoughtful usages of government funding and resources. Cloud-based solutions are very possibly one capable avenue to achieve those goals and those ends. What is needed next in addition to alignment of the above entities is a plan: we need to work together—state and federal government and technology partners and organizations—to create realistic approaches that modernize health and human services IT environments using logical and orchestrated game plans that capitalize on available technologies. It is also necessary for state clients or partner organizations who achieve success with projects develop case studies that enter the body of knowledge so that others can learn from and reference those activities when making IT decisions or selecting projects. If one of the main reasons to use the Cloud for future solutions is that we can leverage the expertise of others, then we need to continue to remember to do exactly that to ensure mutual success.

References

ASA/OCIO. (2012, March 28). Cloud Computing. Retrieved May 12, 2017, from https://www.hhs.gov/ocio/ea/cloudcomputing.html.

CMS. (n.d.). Medicaid Information Technology Architecture (MITA) 3.0. Retrieved May 14, 2017, from https://www.medicaid.gov/medicaid/data-and-systems/mita/mita-30/index.html.

KFF. (2017, May 18). Total Monthly Medicaid and CHIP Enrollment. Retrieved May 20, 2017, from http://www.kff.org/health-reform/state-indicator/total-monthly-medicaid-and-chip-enrollment/?currentTimeframe=0&selectedRows=%7B%22nested%22%3A%7B%22indiana%22%3A%7B%7D%7D%7D&sortModel=%7B%22colId%22%3A%22Location%22%2C%22sort%22%3A%22asc%22%7D.

Indiana FSSA. (n.d.). FSSA Mission and Vision. Retrieved May 13, 2017, from http://in.gov/fssa/4839.htm.

NASPO. (2017, January 12). Navigating the IT Procurement Landscape. Retrieved May 20, 2017, from http://naspo.org/Publications/ArtMID/8806/ArticleID/3409.

Quelin, B. (2015, October 20). Are Public-Private Partnerships the Best Way to Provide Government Services? Retrieved May 06, 2017, from http://insights.som.yale.edu/insights/are-public-private-partnerships-the-best-way-to-provide-government-services.

Chapter 7

The Internet of Things

Nick Chandler

ClearObject

Contents

The Internet of Things (IoT) has become one of the hottest technology trends of the early 21st century. A quick web search produces tens of millions of results for the phrase. It is a popular topic for both technical publications and business periodicals. But what is the "Internet of Things"? Consensus is difficult to find, and in fact, the Institute of Electrical and Electronics Engineers (IEEE) recognized the lack of a clear definition and compiled a paper, titled "Towards a Definition of the Internet of Things (IoT)," [1] to consolidate descriptions. But still, the definitions vary. For our purposes, we will use the following definition:

> The Internet of Things refers to the idea of putting intelligence (usually through small computing devices, known as embedded systems) into physical objects, so that relevant data can be collected from the objects and sent to other devices for processing and decision-making.

There are a multitude of technologies that enable IoT, from edge devices to cloud computing. The goal of this chapter is to provide a survey of some of these key enabling technologies. But before we begin the technical discussion, let us first take a moment to discuss the causes for excitement about IoT.

IoT as an Economic Disruptor

In late 2015, Gartner predicted that there would be 20.8 billion devices attached to the IoT by 2020 [2]. And, in early 2017, Boston Consulting Group reported that the IoT market in 2020 would be €250 billion (approximately $264.6 billion) [3].

But, what is driving such high expectations for IoT? Although IoT leverages numerous emerging technologies, it is far more than a buzzword. Unlike some advances in technology, it does not only enable traditional businesses to operate more efficiently—instead, IoT promises to change how traditional businesses go to market.

By adding intelligence to their goods, companies can proactively identify problems with their products, address them early, and improve the quality of experience for their customers. Consumers can take advantage of smart appliances to improve the comfort of their lives. Likewise, individuals and healthcare professionals can use embedded intelligence in medical equipment as well as personal health monitors to improve wellness. There are many use cases. The previously stated market penetration numbers are impressive, but McKinsey & Company believes the actual economic impact of IoT – in other words, the impact of the benefits driven by it – could reach between $4 trillion and $11 trillion by 2025 [4]. This is the kind of impact that makes IoT such a hot topic today.

To get the business advantages of the IoT, it is important to understand the technology behind it. Let us dive into some of the technologies supporting IoT.

Edge Technology: Embedded Systems and Connectivity

At the heart of IoT are network-connected devices that monitor and/or control the environment around them. These devices are the "things" in the IoT. Devices that monitor their surroundings are known as "sensors," while devices that control the environment around them are known as "actuators."

These devices can be thought of as embedded computer systems. The sensors and actuators are computer systems in that they require processing capabilities, memory, and storage to gather data and transmit it to other endpoints.

They are "embedded" in the sense that the computing device does not provide the key, defining service for the "thing." As an example from the consumer space, an activity tracker is not, by definition, attached to the Internet; you could simply use a pedometer to track your daily steps. However, by embedding intelligence into the device, your daily statistics can be uploaded to a cloud provider, allowing you to monitor your activity trends over time. As an example from the transportation industry, a diesel engine exists to move a vehicle from point A to point B. However, by embedding sensors into the engine, the performance and health of the engine may be recorded for analysis and proactive maintenance.

Embedded systems built for the IoT have some noteworthy challenges that traditional computers do not have. The devices may be battery powered, and, depending on where they are deployed, it may be difficult or impossible to replace the batteries. Additionally, these systems are generally small, which limits the processor, memory, and storage capacity for the devices. Even if the devices are not limited on processing power per se, no processing cycle should be wasted; greater efficiency reduces the amount of power that is required for the device. This necessitates using lightweight, specialized Operating Systems (OSs), such as pared down versions of Linux, or OS's like Contiki [5] or TinyOS [6]. Likewise, any software running on the system should be minimal and optimized as much as possible. In short, all of the intelligence in IoT systems must be optimized in such a way as to run with limited resources, using as little power as possible.

Network Access

Before IoT devices can communicate with the Internet, they must first have local network access. In general, access is wireless, as it is frequently unrealistic to run network cabling to IoT devices. Numerous access protocols are available, and several notable examples are described briefly in the next section.

The IEEE 802.11 [7] family of wireless protocols may be the first to come to mind when you think about wireless technology. After all, it is the most popular set of wireless protocols for standard laptops, smart phones, and tablets today. 802.11 offers high data rates and moderate coverage, which is great for standard computers. However, it requires significant power, making it a suboptimal choice for many IoT devices. For IoT, devices would need to either be hardwired for power or else be recharged frequently.

An alternative IEEE standard, 802.15.4 [8], defines low-rate Wireless Personal Area Networks (WPAN). It is the basis for numerous other WPAN standards, as 802.15.4 defines a physical and data link layer that upper-layer protocols can leverage. 802.15.4 operates over small distances (10 meters), with a data transfer rate of 250 kbps. For dense networks of sensors, this can be a good choice for network access technology.

One key note about 802.15.4 is that it does not provide a robust mapping to upper-layer protocols. For example, within an 802.15.4 network it is assumed that a single layer 3 protocol will be used, as there is nothing comparable to an Ethertype. It also dictates very small frame sizes. To run IPv6 over 802.15.4, the Internet Engineering Task Force (IETF) developed a series of standards, generically referred to as "IPv6 over Low-Power Wireless Personal Areas Networks" (6LoWPAN) [9]. 6LoWPAN provides header compression and other optimizations to enable IP connectivity to devices whose network access is based on 802.15.4. As such, it is a key technology for IoT in many cases.

For IoT applications where devices are highly mobile, cellular connectivity can be used. An example use case might be sensors attached to vehicles. Cellular coverage provides a vast network connectivity footprint; however, it requires a lot of power. In the case of sensors on a vehicle, it is assumed that the vehicle's battery will need to provide power to the sensor.

Application Layer Protocols

Now that we have discussed some of the lower-layer protocols available in the IoT space, let us turn our attention to the application layer. Protocols at this layer provide communication between embedded devices and the users, servers, or other things that need to interact with them.

As was the case with lower level protocols, application layer protocols must be lightweight to be most useful in IoT applications. To enable this, packet sizes should be kept as small as possible to reduce bandwidth and power requirements. Likewise, application protocols should not be any more "chatty" than required; there should not be excessive communication or polling between endpoints. Naturally, the less overhead required at the application layer the more efficient the lower layer protocols will be.

In addition to the previously stated goals, application layer communication should be able to compensate for untrustworthy network connectivity. In IoT deployments, it is very possible that bandwidth may be minimal, latency may be high, and basic connectivity may not even always be possible. This is especially true for devices that are deployed in particularly rugged or remote environments. Because networks may not be consistent, applications and application layer protocols should be resilient.

Application developers could certainly create their own application layer protocols for IoT, but there are several open standards that are in common use today. Examples include protocols such as Apache Kafka [10], the Extensible Messaging and Presence Protocol [11], and the Message Queue Telemetry Transport (MQTT) [12]. To illustrate how IoT application layer communication may be realized, we will take a closer look at MQTT.

MQTT

MQTT is a client/server-based messaging protocol, which allows clients to exchange information with one another through the server(s) without explicit knowledge of all the other clients with which they are communicating. It is an open source protocol, and the standard is maintained by the Organization for the Advancement of Structured Information Standards [13].

MQTT offers a Publish/Subscribe messaging model, which allows one-to-many communication between clients. Clients may be either Publishers, Subscribers, or both. Publishers generate messages containing data, and send these messages to brokers (e.g., MQTT servers) to distribute to interested Subscribers. Streams of related messages are identified by "topics." A topic is simply a label with which to identify related content. Subscribers inform MQTT servers when they want to receive messages for a given topic. Once a client has subscribed to a topic, any future messages that another client publishes for that topic will be forwarded to the subscriber via the broker. Figure 7.1 illustrates the high-level process used for communication in an MQTT environment.

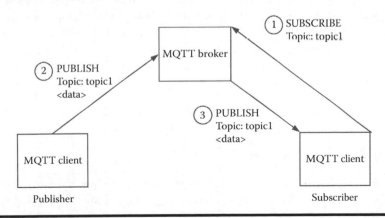

Figure 7.1   MQTT publish/subscribe operation.

In an IoT environment, sensors would fill the role of Publishers, as they need to send their data to other interested parties. The application servers that process this data would fill the role of Subscribers.

MQTT is well suited to IoT environments because it is lightweight. It includes only a 2-byte header on each packet. The less data that must be transmitted, the less power required to send that data. Additionally, MQTT's code base is small, which is a benefit to devices that are constrained on CPU, memory, and storage.

Standard MQTT is designed to run over a Transmission Control Protocol/Internet Protocol TCP/IP stack. It can run over either unencrypted or encrypted TCP. Alternatively, it may also run over the Websocket protocol (which, itself runs over TCP). For wireless sensor networks that do not support native IP, an alternate specification, MQTT for Sensor Networks [14] may be used to provide a gateway into a standard MQTT infrastructure. For example, this may be useful in 802.15.4 environments where 6LoWPAN is not used.

There are a handful of MQTT broker servers to choose from. Mosquitto [15], HiveMQ [16], and IBM MessageSight [17] can all operate either on-premises or may be deployed in the Cloud. Public cloud providers are also beginning to offer MQTT managed services as well. For example, AWS Device Gateway is part of the AWS IoT Platform [18], and Microsoft offers MQTT services through the Azure IoT Hub [19].

IoT Application Infrastructure and the Cloud

We have discussed the IoT Edge and how smart devices or sensors communicate. Now, let's turn our attention to the computing infrastructure for IoT–where cloud computing comes into play.

IoT is built using new application architectures, custom-designed and implemented for the organizations deploying IoT. Organizations can reuse some components, namely open-source frameworks; however, new code must be developed for each IoT implementation. This offers a great chance to build for the Cloud, as developers are not necessarily tied to legacy infrastructure to deploy these applications. The elasticity, unlimited scale, global reach, and reduced need to manage infrastructure to support these applications are primary reasons why cloud is a natural fit for IoT.

Microservices

Because applications are built new for IoT initiatives, the applications may be built to take advantage of cloud's characteristics. Legacy applications, designed prior to the growth of cloud computing, commonly put many components into a single, "monolithic" package. The entire software stack would be deployed on one, or a few, servers. Scaling the application required moving the entire application to a more powerful server—a process known as "scale-up." Problems with one software component could easily impact other components of the application; patching generally required upgrading the entire software package as opposed to just the component that had experienced issues. Figure 7.2 shows a conceptual diagram of a monolithic application, where components are tightly coupled and communicate with one another via system calls or else an API defined within the program itself.

On the other hand, cloud-native applications are commonly built in a "microservices" architecture. A microservice architecture breaks large applications up into component services that can run on independent systems. Each software component can be deployed separately, and it communicates with other components via the network. In fact, these services can communicate using the same messaging protocols as IoT devices use – that is to say, MQTT (or other similar protocols) can allow microservices to communicate with one another. By moving the interface between components from the local programming interface to the network, each component can be built using different programming languages or OSs, using whatever tools make the most sense for the job of that component. Figure 7.3 provides a conceptual outline of communication between microservices. Each service runs in isolation; for example, as its own container (see the subsequent section on containers for more information) utilizing the network for communication between components. Compare this to Figure 7.2.

When a component has a bug and needs to be upgraded, only that system needs to be touched. Additionally, components may be designed for scale-out performance gains rather than scale-up performance gains. This means that if a component needs some extra performance, administrators can simply bring new systems online that run more instances of that component. Or even better, the underlying

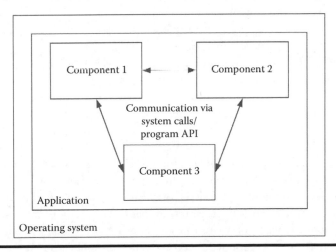

Figure 7.2   Conceptual diagram of a monolithic application.

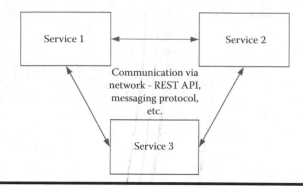

Figure 7.3 Conceptual diagram of communication between microservices.

cloud can watch for performance thresholds and automatically bring new instances online to add performance or take instances offline to reduce capacity during slow periods.

Two delivery mechanisms are generally a good fit in a microservices architecture: (1) containers or (2) Platform-as-a-Service (PaaS).

Containers

Containers offer a lightweight alternative to virtual machines. With virtual instances (such as AWS EC2 or Google Compute Engine machines) administrators typically deploy only a single application. In a microservice architecture, it would be even more likely that a single application would be loaded per virtual server, so that there would not be any more coupling between components than needed. However, this can be a lot of overhead, as each virtual machine has its own complete copy of an OS, taking up unnecessary storage, processing, and memory resources simply to maintain the OS.

Containers provide virtualization at the OS layer, however. Applications can run as completely isolated processes on the same OS, but each application believes that it has a server all to itself. This improves resource utilization, as numerous applications are now able to use a single underlying OS instance, saving on storage, compute, and memory. Another benefit is that containers can start and stop incredibly quickly—after all, they load and unload as fast as a process on a server can change state. Figure 7.4 provides a high-level comparison of virtualization and containerization. Note that for very high resource utilization, you may even deploy a container layer on top of an OS that is itself running on a virtual instance. This is a common container deployment pattern in public cloud environments.

Aside from higher resource utilization, another key benefit is that containers allow packing up all components necessary for an application into images and deploying them from container registries. By building images this way, containers

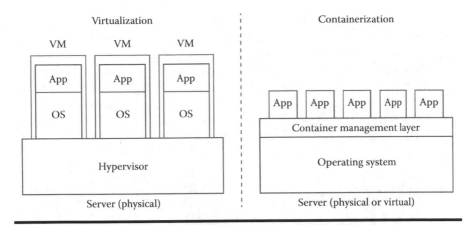

Figure 7.4 Comparison of virtualization and containerization.

allow application developers and operations team members to reduce "configuration drift" between different application instances within an environment.

There are currently two major container vendors: Docker [20] and CoreOS [21]. Many public cloud providers have container offerings, generally built on one of those two technologies, as well. For example, Amazon has AWS EC2 Container Service [22], Google offers Container Engine [23], and Microsoft offers the Azure Container Service [24].

PaaS

Containers provide many benefits compared to standard virtual server instances. However, there is still some degree of infrastructure to manage in a container environment – the underlying OS still needs to be patched and managed. Another common microservice deployment option is PaaS.

PaaS offerings may leverage containers on the backend, but deployment of applications can be more straightforward to software developers than a native container environment. When deploying an application to a PaaS, the PaaS provider can pull the application code directly into their platform, transparently load up the infrastructure necessary to run it, and then bring the application online. Cloud providers generally also offer auto-scaling, such that if a node that is running a PaaS application is too busy, it will automatically bring other instances online; likewise, it will take instances offline if less capacity is needed during slow times. The elimination of need for traditional operations processes in this model is sometimes known as "No Ops."

Whereas container platforms pull images from registries, PaaS can integrate directly with software version control systems and continuous integration/continuous deployment systems. This further reduces friction for software developers. The tradeoff is that there is less flexibility compared to containers, as PaaS systems support only certain programming languages and may not offer the full suite of features available to developers when code is packaged into a container.

Outside of public cloud providers, one popular PaaS vendor is Pivotal [25], which offers a paid version of the open source Cloud Foundry [26] platform. Among public cloud providers, the mega cloud providers all have products to offer: Amazon offers AWS Elastic Beanstalk [27], Google has Google Application Engine [28], and Microsoft offers Azure App Service [29].

Cloud Data Storage

Cloud storage offers a great way to keep data from sensors over time. Numerous storage options are available from all public cloud providers. Offerings range from object storage to block storage (typically for virtual instances) to various forms of managed database services.

For the purposes of collecting and acting on information from sensors, a database solution is required. However, unlike traditional relational databases, a better solution in many cases may be NoSQL databases. NoSQL databases differ from relational databases because they do not require the strict schemas associated with relational systems. This flexibility means that data can be written even if a record contains more or less data than other, similar records.

As an example use case for this, consider a newer model sensor that is able to send additional telemetry readings than an older model sensor. We want to collect all data from both models of sensors, and we may want this stored in the same database. However, we do not want to have to rebuild our database structure just to accommodate this. This is where the flexibility of NoSQL comes into play.

The major cloud providers offer managed (or "No Ops") NoSQL database services. Amazon offers DynamoDB [30] and Microsoft's service is DocumentDB [31]. Google has two NoSQL offerings currently: Cloud Datastore [32] and Cloud Bigtable [33].

Big Data and Analytics

As our numerous sensors send data to us, we have choices to make about what we do with potentially huge amounts of old data. Of course, we can use short-term data to make short-term decisions, but when data is no longer useful in the immediate term, do we delete it? There may be valuable long-term insights we can gain from our data if we keep it. However, if we do not delete it, we need to be able to scale our storage cost-effectively. Thankfully, cloud technology allows easy scaling, and public cloud providers offer different tiers of storage so that we can manage our costs.

Up to this point, we have discussed how sensors get data to the cloud to be processed by applications that can make decisions in real time. For example, if an environmental sensor suggests that temperatures are getting too high, application servers might notify a person to address the issue or else instruct actuators to address the issue. However, beyond short-term decision making, data from numerous sensors can be stored and aggregated to find trends and enable businesses to make longer-term decisions. This becomes even more powerful when data from sensors can be combined with data from other sources as a basis to perform analytics. The storage and evaluation of potentially huge datasets such as this is known as "Big Data."

Big Data refers to techniques required to process and analyze sets of data that are so large that traditional tools are insufficient. The datasets associated with Big Data are generally very large, but the phrase tends to also go hand-in-hand with analytics—we are not only concerned with how we store large datasets, but we also want to get insights from the data. The tools you might use to analyze data in a database of thousands of rows might differ if instead you had tens of millions of rows. Further still, the tools would differ if that data did not always fit into a standard relational database structure.

In the following sections, we provide an overview of one of the key Big Data frameworks available today: Apache Hadoop.

Apache Hadoop

Hadoop [34] is one of the most popular Big Data technologies available today. It is a framework for distributed storage and processing, targeted at processing and analyzing very large amounts of data. The initial inspiration for Hadoop came from two papers published by Google in the early 2000s: *The Google File System* (October 2003) [35] and *MapReduce: Simplified Data Processing on Large Clusters* (December 2004) [36]. Hadoop development was originally led by Yahoo, but it is now an open-source project, maintained by the Apache Software Foundation.

Unlike traditional scale-up storage and processing architectures, Hadoop is a scale-out architecture. Hadoop relies on the concept of clustered computing, both for storage and for processing. Traditionally, if more processing power or more storage were needed, an organization would need to replace their systems with larger, more expensive servers. Hadoop's scale-out architecture, however, allows organizations to simply add additional smaller, cheaper systems, known as "nodes." This allows organizations to scale their capabilities and costs linearly, while keeping the relative price of processing and storage the same. This elasticity lines up nicely with the core tenets of cloud computing, and we will discuss how cloud providers support Hadoop later.

Before we discuss specific offerings, however, let us go into a bit more detail on key components of the Hadoop ecosystem.

Hadoop Distributed File System

The Hadoop Distributed File System (HDFS) is the storage element of Apache Hadoop. As the name suggests, it is a distributed system, meaning that data is spread among multiple nodes in a Hadoop cluster. HDFS is intended for large datasets, so data is split into large blocks (tens or hundreds of megabytes), and each block is stored on at least three nodes. These replicas protect against the impact of node failures. Also, as the name suggests, HDFS is a filesystem, much like an OS's filesystem. This means that files may be accessed similarly to how you would access files in an OS.

HDFS operates in a master/slave configuration. A single controller node, called the "NameNode," is responsible for tracking which files are currently available on which storage nodes (or "DataNodes"). The NameNode simply keeps a record of which files are where; it does not store any data of its own. When external clients wish to access data that is stored in HDFS, they first communicate with the NameNode to identify where that data may be found. From there, the clients communicate directly with the DataNodes to retrieve or store data. This behavior prevents the NameNode from becoming a bottleneck in the HDFS architecture. If data had to traverse a single NameNode, then the performance of the entire system would depend on the capabilities of the NameNode. However, by making the NameNode responsible only for directing traffic, the Hadoop goal of linear scalability can be realized.

Although HDFS provides a scalable storage architecture, it is not intended to replace long-term persistent storage. It is designed to support high-performance analytics. Data must be pulled into an HDFS cluster before jobs begin, and there are several tools to allow this. One such tool is Apache Sqoop [37]. Sqoop is designed to transfer data between Hadoop clusters and other structured datastores, such as databases. We will discuss alternative data ingestion techniques in public cloud Hadoop offerings later.

Hadoop Distributed Processing: MapReduce, Spark, and Related Projects

Whereas HDFS provides the distributed storage capabilities of Hadoop, MapReduce provides distributed data processing. It consists of two primary steps: "map" and "reduce." Map processes involve some transformation or evaluation of input data. During the Map phase, worker nodes apply these processes to their own local data blocks, presented through HDFS. By working on local data, network bandwidth requirements are drastically reduced, as data does not need to be moved to an application server—instead, the server logic is moved to the storage.

The Reduce phase is used to run functions on the results from the Map phase. Depending on the algorithms used, there may be a Sort or Shuffle step in between

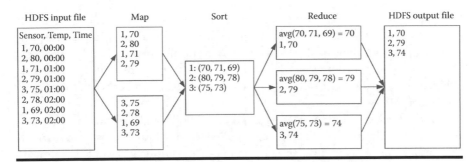

Figure 7.5 Sample MapReduce process.

Map and Reduce; by ordering the data coming out of Map, the Reduce phase can be performed more quickly.

Figure 7.5 illustrates an example MapReduce process. In this example, we are getting temperature readings from multiple sensors. We want to calculate the average temperature for each sensor. We have a file loaded into our HDFS filesystem with raw data from the sensors, including sensor name, temperature reading, and the time that the reading was taken. The first step is to split out the work between an appropriate number of workers; for our example, we assume two worker nodes are used. In our example, the only mapping required is to split out the necessary data fields, which is the sensor ID and the temperature; we do not care about time for the analysis we are doing right now. Once the data is mapped, MapReduce performs a sort operation, combining all of the data for each sensor as a list of values associated with the sensor ID. This data is fed into the Reduce step, and for our analysis we are simply calculating an average of all of the values associated with each sensor ID. Finally, we concatenate our results into an output file on our HDFS filesystem.

Getting processes dispatched to the proper nodes is a critical element of a Hadoop system. MapReduce provides a mechanism to achieve this natively. However, another popular technology has been developed to provide scheduling: Yet Another Resource Negotiator (YARN). One of the key benefits to YARN is that it allows multiple processing engines to be used in the same Hadoop cluster. This allows alternatives to MapReduce to be used, providing users the ability to leverage the right processing engine for the job.

In cases where a single MapReduce job does not yield the results that are needed, jobs can be chained together in numerous ways. The output of one job can be the input of another, or a series of MapReduce operations may need to happen on one dataset before bringing in another dataset at a later job. For each one of these MapReduce jobs, data is read/written to disk. Although storage is distributed, and processing is coresident with storage, disk I/O can still add considerable latency to jobs when complex processing is required. This has led to MapReduce being considered a better fit for batch processing rather than real-time processing. This is where Apache Spark comes in.

Spark [38] is an alternative to MapReduce, designed for handling large-scale data processing in-memory. Rather than writing all operations to disk throughout complex jobs, intermediate results are kept in memory, drastically improving execution times. In doing so, the project claims to run up to 100× faster than MapReduce. Spark jobs can be scheduled using YARN or other similar tools, such as Apache Mesos.

Some level of programming is required to build and execute Hadoop jobs, regardless of the processing engine. MapReduce, for example, is written in the Java programming language, and jobs can be easily written in Java. Spark provides libraries so that jobs can be written in popular programming languages, such as Java, Python, R, and others. It may be easier to interact with data using a traditional data management language such as SQL, especially if users come from a database background rather than a programming background. Spark provides Spark SQL, which provides an SQL interface into Spark. There are other similar tools in the Hadoop ecosystem to allow similar interaction with MapReduce. For example, two other popular projects, Apache Hive [39] and Apache Pig [40], provide higher-level interfaces for creating MapReduce jobs. Hive provides an SQL-like interface, and Pig provides a procedural interface for defining jobs.

Hadoop Providers

As described, Hadoop is an open-source framework, supported by many open-source projects. Like other open-source projects, several businesses have been built around Hadoop to provide product verification, support services, and professional services to organizations who wish to use Hadoop but who do not have the resources or knowledge to take this on themselves. Companies like Cloudera [41], Hortonworks [42], and IBM (through their BigInsights [43] portfolio) provide such products and services. These can be deployed on-premise or in the cloud, offering organizations the ability to tailor their solutions but at the cost of still having to operate the systems. An experienced Hadoop managed services organization can help businesses who elect to go this route, so that business users can focus on leveraging these Big Data systems, rather than operating them.

Alternatively, large cloud providers have begun to deploy analytics systems based on Hadoop. For example, Google Cloud Dataproc [44] is a Big Data solution, offering Hadoop, Spark, Pig, and Hive support. Dataproc allows users to build and deploy Hadoop clusters, scale them up or down, and turn them off as needed. Amazon has a similar offering, Elastic MapReduce (EMR) [45]. Again, EMR allows users to build Hadoop clusters as needed in the AWS cloud.

Earlier, we touched on the need to ingest data into Hadoop from other sources to perform analytics. We mentioned Apache Sqoop as one tool for this. A nice benefit of using native Hadoop services offered by cloud providers is that they commonly provide interfaces to simplify data ingestion from their long-term storage services into their Hadoop services. For example, Google Cloud Dataproc integrates natively with their Bigtable, Bigquery, and Cloud Storage offerings. Amazon EMR offers similar integration with S3 and DynamoDB. For IoT solutions, this could be a compelling integration. After all, if a business stores its IoT data in a cloud provider already, the ease of ingesting that data into a cloud-provided Hadoop instance makes sense.

Conclusion

In this chapter, we presented a brief overview of some of the technologies that are useful in today's IoT. The embedded systems at the edge of the IoT are sophisticated systems, but their size, power requirements, and potential mobility requirements yield some challenges that traditional computers do not have. Even the networking protocols used by these devices differ from traditional computers because of some of these challenges.

Cloud computing offers an excellent platform on which to build the applications to process data from these devices. As a business needs to process input from hundreds, thousands, or more devices, the ease of scaling cost-effectively has led many organizations to elect to build their IoT applications on the Cloud. Just as the processing capabilities need to scale, so too does storage capacity; again, the elastic nature of the cloud comes into play. For analytics, cloud-based Big Data solutions can be another nice tool to use.

The IoT promises to be a disruptor to existing markets while also creating new ones. Businesses can use intelligence from sensors to provide services to customers in real-time, and they can perform analytics on large datasets from sensors to shape corporate strategy and improve their products over the long term. The amount of disruption will be limited only by the innovative ideas that businesses come up with!

References

1. Amazon Web Services, Inc. (2018). Azure Cosmos DB – Globally Distributed Database Service | Microsoft Azure. Retrieved January 20, 2018, from https://azure.microsoft.com/enus/services/documentdb/.
2. Amazon Web Services, Inc. (2018). Amazon ECS - run containerized applications in production. Retrieved January 20, 2018, from https://aws.amazon.com/ecs/.
3. Amazon Web Services, Inc. (2018). Amazon EMR – Amazon Web Services. Retrieved January 20, 2018, from http://aws.amazon.com/emr.
4. Amazon Web Services, Inc. (2018). Amazon DynamoDB – NoSQL Cloud Database Service. Retrieved January 20, 2018, from https://aws.amazon.com/dynamodb/.
5. Amazon Web Services, Inc. (2018). AWS Elastic Beanstalk – Deploy Web Applications. Retrieved January 20, 2018, from https://aws.amazon.com/elasticbeanstalk/.

6. Amazon Web Services, Inc. (2018). AWS IoT Core Overview - Amazon Web Services. Retrieved January 20, 2018, from https://aws.amazon.com/iot-platform/.
7. Apache Hive. (2014). General. Retrieved January 20, 2018, from https://hive.apache.org/.
8. Apache Kafka. (2017). Retrieved January 20, 2018, from https://kafka.apache.org/.
9. Apache Software Foundation. (2018). Apache Spark. Retrieved January 20, 2018, from http://spark.apache.org/.
10. Apache Software Foundation. (2014, March). Sqoop -. Retrieved January 20, 2018, from http://sqoop.apache.org/.
11. Apache Software Foundation. (2014). Welcome to Apache™ Hadoop®! Retrieved January 20, 2018, from http://hadoop.apache.org/.
12. Apache Software Foundation. (2012). Welcome to Apache Pig! Retrieved January 20, 2018, from https://pig.apache.org/.
13. Cloud Foundry, Inc. (2018). Cloud Application Platform - Devops Platform. Retrieved January 20, 2018, from https://www.cloudfoundry.org/.
14. Cloudera. (2018). Home Page. Retrieved January 20, 2018, from https://www.cloudera.com/.
15. Contiki: The Open Source OS for the Internet of Things. (n.d.). Retrieved January 19, 2018, from http://www.contiki-os.org/.
16. CoreOS Inc. (n.d.). CoreOS. Retrieved January 20, 2018, from https://coreos.com/.
17. Dean, J., & Ghemawat, S. (2004, December). MapReduce: Simplified Data Processing on Large Clusters. Retrieved January 20, 2018, from https://research.google.com/archive/mapreduce.html.
18. Docker Inc. (2018). Docker. Retrieved January 20, 2018, from https://www.docker.com/.
19. Enterprise MQTT Broker. (2018). Retrieved January 20, 2018, from http://www.hivemq.com/.
20. Ghemawat, S., Gobioff, H., & Leung, S. (2003, October). The Google File System. Retrieved January 20, 2018, from https://research.google.com/archive/gfs.html.
21. Google Cloud Platform. (2018). App Engine - Build Scalable Web & Mobile Backends in Any Language | Google Cloud Platform. Retrieved January 20, 2018, from https://cloud.google.com/appengine/.
22. Google Cloud Platform. (2017). Bigtable - Scalable NoSQL Database Service | Google Cloud Platform. Retrieved January 20, 2018, from https://cloud.google.com/bigtable/.
23. Google Cloud Platform. (2018). Cloud Dataproc - Cloud-native Hadoop & Spark | Google Cloud Platform. Retrieved January 20, 2018, from https://cloud.google.com/dataproc/.
24. Google Cloud Platform. (2018). Datastore - NoSQL Schema Less Database | Google Cloud Platform. Retrieved January 20, 2018, from https://cloud.google.com/datastore/.
25. Google Cloud Platform. (2018). Kubernetes Engine. Retrieved January 20, 2018, from https://cloud.google.com/container-engine/.
26. Horton Works. (2017). Retrieved January 20, 2018, from https://hortonworks.com/.
27. Hunke, N. (2017, January 05). Winning in IoT: It's All About the Business Processes. Retrieved January 18, 2018, from https://www.bcgperspectives.com/content/articles/hardwaresoftware-energy-environment-winning-in-iot-all-about-winning-processes/.

28. IBM Corporation. (2016, January 01). Products. Retrieved January 20, 2018, from http://www.ibm.com/software/products/en/iot-messagesight.

29. IBM Analytics. (2016, June 01). Retrieved January 20, 2018, from https://www.ibm.com/analytics/us/en/technology/biginsights/.

30. IEEE Get Program. (2018). Retrieved January 20, 2018, from http://standards.ieee.org/about/get/802/802.11.html.

31. IEEE Get Program. (2018). Retrieved January 20, 2018, from https://standards.ieee.org/about/get/802/802.15.html.

32. Knolleary, A. (2014, November 7). Retrieved January 20, 2018, from http://docs.oasis-open.org/mqtt/mqtt/v3.1.1/os/mqtt-v3.1.1-os.pdf.

33. Kushalnagar, N., Montenegro, G., & Schumacher, C. (2007, August). IPv6 over Low-Power Wireless Personal Area Networks (6LoWPANs): Overview, Assumptions, Problem Statement, and Goals. Retrieved January 20, 2018, from https://tools.ietf.org/html/rfc4919.

34. Manyika, J., Chui, M., Bisson, P., Woetzel, J., Dobbs, R., Bughin, J., and Aharon, D. (2015, June). Unlocking the potential of the Internet of Things. Retrieved January 19, 2018, from http://www.mckinsey.com/business-functions/digital-mckinsey/our-insights/the-internet-of-things-the-value-of-digitizing-the-physical-world.

35. Microsoft. (2018). App Service. Retrieved January 20, 2018, from https://azure.microsoft.com/en-us/services/app-service/.

36. Microsoft. (2018). Azure Container Service (AKS). Retrieved January 20, 2018, from https://azure.microsoft.com/en-us/services/container-service/.

37. Microsoft. (2018). IoT Hub. Retrieved January 20, 2018, from https://azure.microsoft.com/en-us/services/iot-hub/.

38. Minerva, R., Biru, A., Rotondi, D., (2015, May 7). Towards a definition of the internet of things(IoT). IEEE. Retrieved from http://iot.ieee.org/images/files/pdf/IEEE_IoT_Towards_Definition_Internet_of_Things_Revision1_27MAY15.pdf.

39. Mosquitto: An open source MQTT v3.1/v3.1.1 broker. (2018). Retrieved January 20, 2018, from https://mosquitto.org/.

40. MQTT. (2014, November 7). Retrieved January 20, 2018, from http://mqtt.org/.

41. Pivotal Software, Inc. (2018). Home. Retrieved January 20, 2018, from https://pivotal.io/.

42. Stanford-Clark, A., Truong, H., (2013). MQTT for sensor networks (MQTT_SN): protocol specification. IBM Corporation. Retrieve January 20, 2018, from http://mqtt.org/new/wp-content/uploads/2009/06/MQTT-SN_spec_v1.2.pdf.

43. Tiny OS. (n.d.). Retrieved January 20, 2018, from http://www.tinyos.net/.

44. Van der Meulen, R. (2015, November 10). Gartner Says 6.4 Billion Connected. Retrieved January 18, 2018, from http://www.gartner.com/newsroom/id/3165317.

45. XMPP. (n.d.). Retrieved January 20, 2018, from https://xmpp.org/.

Chapter 8

Customer Services

Joe Ciuffo

Gensys

Contents

Customer service is a core competency for a successful organization. Successful execution of customer server not only helps retain current clientele, but promotes best practices of the company's product. Genesys provides customer service in the form of support for existing customers using its suite of contact center software. The support personnel are responsible for identifying bugs within the software, correcting misconfigurations of the system, and distributing information knowledge-base articles, which are responsible for providing education content. Support personnel, otherwise known as technical support engineers, triage a numerous and diverse amount of customer inquiries that originate from various mediums. The use of cloud computing in the customer service field provides a greater quality of service through better availability, delivery, and quality of information.

To fully understand how Genesys has benefited from cloud computing, it is important to first examine the concepts and scope of work that exist in the daily operations for a customer service department. The company provides highly technical customer service though their Customer Care Technical Analysts for a suite of customer engagement and unified communications software platforms. Customer engagement software is a set of technologies designed to easily connect a customer service representative to an end-user through a medium of communication. Typical mediums of communication could be text messaging, phone call, website chat client, or email. Unified communication is the integration of real-time communication services such as video, voice, instant messaging and more, all tied to a single user, with presence information indicating if the user is available (Pleasant, 2008). From the perspective of the Customer Care Technical Analyst and the customer, it is vital that lines of communication and information given remain available and durable. A customer in need must be able to reach a technical analyst at any time. If there is an outage for one form of communication, there must be a backup solution in place to provide support to the customer. The information received by the technical analyst must exist in spite of any outage. Technical analysts require the provided customer information to correctly diagnose a problem, and document the history of past inquiries or issues. Much like a patient's medical history is utilized by a doctor, technical analysts require customer service history as it may contain relevant information correlated to current and future issues (Windley, 2002). From the perspective of a Customer Care Technical Analyst, there are many tools utilized when helping the customer. These tools are essential to providing the highest level of service, and have been heavily impacted by the "cloud-ification" of software. The areas examined within Genesys customer service and their impact from cloud computing are

- Customer mediums of communication
- Internal mediums of communication
- Knowledge-base management system
- Customer incident ticketing system
- Internal infrastructure management system
- Data driven metrics

Mediums of Communication

Customer Care Technical Analysts utilize various forms of communication to engage with the customer, depending on inquiry's level of severity and timeliness of resolution. Many customer service departments, including at Genesys, use a contact center solution for their organization. A contact center solution is a means of routing all incoming communications or interactions through an organization (Fallon 2014). The interactions are sent to an agent or person who would be most helpful to the specific needs of each unique situation. The mediums of communications that will be examined are phone call, email, instant messaging, and video.

Phone Call

Traditionally, most forms of customer inquiries, especially those of highest severity, enter as a phone call. From the customer end, a phone call is a relatively simple procedure that requires calling a designated number for service with the expectation of reaching a live Technical Analyst. On the customer care side, there is a set of procedures that takes an incoming call and eventually routes that phone call to the most relevant, readily available agent at that time. A phone call routed to a Technical Analyst generally goes through three segments; the Interactive Voice Response (IVR) call flow, the assigned queue or desired workgroup, and available agent selection process.

The IVR is a system that allows the caller to interact with a set of prompts via number input from a phone or voice recognition. The responses provided by the caller will then change the trajectory or navigation of the call path; the path of a call is defined as a call flow. The IVR is designed to allow caller navigation through a set of menus, just as you would call your cellular phone service provider and press 1 or state "Customer Service" to speak with a live agent regarding your phone bill. In the technical customer service environment, the IVR is used to narrow the scope of the caller's specific issue. After navigating through a brief set of IVR menus, the system will know the product and product-specific area associated with the inquiry. From this point, the call is then transitioned to a unique call queue for this item (Roos, 2017).

Call queues are waiting rooms for incoming phone calls within a customer service organization. However, it is important to note that there are many queues within a company. Each queue would represent a workgroup, or team, that is specialized in a set of items. Within this technical customer service organization there would be a queue that deals with questions regarding data, another that specializes with phone call recordings, and others such as user-interface design. The purpose of dividing teams into specialties is so technical questions receive answers from subject matter experts. Many of the incoming callers have a technical background and a deep understanding of the product. Therefore, it is essential for the teams to have a deep, vertical understanding of their specialty rather than shallow, horizontal knowledge of the entire product suite (Meyers, 2016).

Email

Emails are as common to a customer service department as calls, albeit with a lower priority and assumed response time. Most organizations will funnel all emails through a single account, such as customersupport@company.com. This process is to take away confusion from the side of the customer and provide a point of contact that is easy to access. On the customer service side, software is used to *scrape* key identifiers from the email so that it is routed to the correct team. The software enables the customer service process to be unobtrusive for the customer, simply requiring an email to the customer service team directly. To clarify further, Genesys' customer care team uses email filters on the main service email to identify certain words, such as database or broken phone, then route the email to the appropriate team resources to perform further analysis of the problem. Email rules within the company's routing system define which keywords correspond to a certain team (Roos, 2017).

Instant Messaging

In the past, traditional customer service has been driven through phone calls and emails. However, instant messaging between a customer and technical analyst has increasingly become a preferred method of communication. The rise of web chats can be attributed to many customers being familiar and comfortable with chat applications through use of social media and smartphones. Prompting the web chat between a customer and a technical analyst can be done in a variety of ways – such as customer initiated or proactive web chat prompts. Customer web chats also serve as an alternative form of communication if phone lines were down. Having a backup communication system for customers is essential to customer satisfaction, especially in emergency situations.

A customer initiated chat would begin with the end-user pressing a "speak with an agent" button on a website or within an application. After the user has initiated the chat, the interaction is then ACD routed to an available agent where the scope of the inquiry can be further narrowed or transferred to the most capable team (Brown, 2016).

A proactive chat can present a chat window to the customer in a variety of ways, based upon an organization's defined criteria. As an example, if a customer was to request more information about Genesys' software and had an estimated seat count—or number of individual licenses purchased for users (above 500 in this case)—we would prompt the user with a chat box on the bottom right of their screen. A potential customer with such a large seat count is a great opportunity and source of revenue; therefore, it is important to have a technical analyst on standby via chat to make the experience more personal. The analyst could be on standby to address any immediate technical questions that might dissuade the potential customer from pursuing the software (Interview Friio, 2017).

Video

As cellular and home Internet speeds have increased, along with an increase in monthly data limits, video communication has become a common communication platform. Customer service departments such as Amazon Kindle support and Quicken Loans were swift in realizing the value of this medium. Both companies highlighted this feature as a key differentiator in their product support offering, and noted faster issue resolution times as well as higher customer satisfaction scores. The ability to see the customer, face-to-face, can lessen the amount of anger directed towards a support representative (Paresh, 2014).

At Genesys, we use video to share a user's computer screen during a support inquiry. Due to the highly technical nature of the unified communications industry, it can be difficult to talk through troubleshooting steps, while others may find documentation confusing. A screen share presents the opportunity for the technical analyst to quickly see the problem and show remediation steps in real time on the user's machine, instead of referencing further technical documentation. Video can cut days of confusion out of a customer service request because the issue is presented live, mitigating any confusion potentially brought on from written problem descriptions.

Agent Selection Process or Skills Based Routing

A customer service department can receive thousands of calls, emails, and web chats in one single day. How are these routed to employees efficiently? Automated call distribution (ACD) is the process of routing interactions from the very beginning of customer interaction to the company employee who picks up the phone or answers the email. An interaction is the term used to define the multitude of communication mediums that enter a customer service department; these are not limited to calls, emails, and web chats. At its very foundation, ACD examines basic employee metrics to route a call, such as how long the employee been available to take an interaction, time since their last interaction, if the employee is currently utilized on an existing interaction, and if the user set their software status to available for incoming interactions. These variables and more are taken into an algorithm which then decides the most applicable technical analyst for the incoming interaction. This is done within milliseconds, and usually requires a high amount of computational power depending on the variables in the call routing path (Geraghty, 2013).

This type of routing can be taken even further depending on the intricacies of a company's customer service department. Call routing, based upon predefined employee skillsets, is one of the most essential competencies within Genesys' customer service department. Imagine calling a computer software company for a problem that is specific to a Microsoft Windows Laptop, but the call is routed to a representative who only has knowledge of the Apple iPhone version of the software. The agent would be extremely uncomfortable providing support, and the customer might exhibit immediate frustration in lack of progress on the issue. It is extremely important to route incoming calls to the appropriate queue, such as a customer service team and a technical analyst with the applicable skillset. Genesys uses its own software to provide skills-based interaction routing, or the assignment of incoming interactions, to an agent who can best solve the inquiry of the customer. The routing software utilizes a set of processes that evaluate where an agent is most skilled, based upon previously defined criteria, and if that agent is currently available to pick up the phone at that very moment. The implementation of routing software ensures timely assignment of incoming interactions to the most appropriately skilled technical analyst, in the fastest time possible based upon needed criteria (Brown, 2016).

Internal Communication Systems

Technical Analyst fielding customer service inquiries are quickly realizing the importance of internal communications systems as a means of collaboration and internal education. Internal messaging tools, such as Slack or Microsoft Skype, facilitate quick one to one or group chats. These tools also allow for video conferencing, and easy upload of images. At Genesys, the customer service department uses a *follow the sun* practice, which means support is available 24 hours a day and geographically diverse. Technical Analysts working in Australia need a simple way to communicate with a technical team lead in Indianapolis. Communication must be simple and robust, otherwise an internal breakdown would immediately affect the support given to a customer.

Knowledge-Base Management System

A knowledge-base (KB) system is used to store documents that are frequently referenced items used for configuration, maintenance, or general troubleshooting of a product. Companies traditionally have two variants of a KB system, one that is customer facing and one that is internal for Technical Analysts. It is imperative that a KB system remain available and durable for both variants. A customer's administrator of the product often relies on the knowledgebase articles for daily tasks and use of this system reduces overall customer service inquiry volume, enabling technical analyst to not become overrun by rudimentary or redundant requests. The technical analysts rely on the internal KB articles to gain familiarity in areas they lack experience, which promotes self-service and preservation of useful team information. The knowledge base cuts down on customers having to wait on the Technical Analysts, and the analysts having to wait on further knowledge before they can assist with the issue (Frost, 2017).

Thus, it is vital that this information is available to both parties and is durable, and that it is not possible to be permanently deleted due to hardware failure.

Customer Incident Management System

Inquiries submitted to a customer service department are tracked through a customer incident management system, or ticketing portal. These systems, such as ZenDesk or SalesForce Service Cloud, serve as a central repository for customer incidents. To further illustrate, if a Genesys customer noticed an odd bug within the software, such as users automatically logged out of the product after 24 hours, they might email a question to customer service asking if this is desired functionality. The ticketing portal would automatically generate an email receipt response to the customer, acknowledging the inquiry and providing a ticket reference number. The ticket number is a unique identifier generated for each inquiry that comes into the system. The customer can easily reference this number if they call customer service, or check the status of their issue via Genesys' support portal website. From the Technical Analyst perspective, the ticket number can be used to conveniently track all correspondence on the incident and see an entire conversation history. Having a single place of storage for all forms of communication on the ticket permits other Technical Analysts to help in case of an agent's absence or need for further assistance (Kansky, 2010).

Internal Infrastructure Management System

Managing a software as a service (SaaS) platform requires precise organization of resources to maintain uptime for consumers of the product. With a slew of development teams constantly modifying code and implementing the changes into a production environment, disaster is constantly right around the corner. Many software organizations utilize the Information Technology Infrastructure Library, framework as a broad set of best practices for implementing changes, IT processes, and customer satisfaction in a production software environment (Mochal, 2006). Much like a ticketing system, an internal infrastructure management system is a repository for all information regarding hardware information and change control. By use of a single repository, other teams in the company could avoid catastrophe, such as accidentally turning off machines when another team might be using it for testing. Additionally, if a customer is experiencing a problem with the software, internal analysts can quickly identify what may have caused service disruption by referencing the ledger of changes within the infrastructure management system. Due to the serious importance of change control within a SaaS organization, it is vital the infrastructure management system be easy to access from any location and consistently available to all users.

Data Driven Metrics

As a SaaS provider, data is everything. Contracts with customers are built upon service uptime service level agreements that return heavy discounts on monthly charges if the product is not working within the guaranteed amount of time. Teams of technical analysts are judged upon their ability to answer incoming calls within a given time threshold, so that the end customer isn't consistently waiting on hold. Average response times for follow ups with the customer are held to set standard of time based upon the business impact of the inquiry (Windley, 2002). For example, issues that are business impacting would contractually require a response time of one hour. While the scenarios can go on, the main take away is that data drives business monitoring and continual improvement. Customer service management relies on data collected to ensure the teams are fielding and responding to inquiries in the appropriate amount of time. If teams are overwhelmed with a volume of inquiries then management would have actionable data to increase staffing and increase the number of technical analysts on a given team. In the case of service uptime agreements, the lack of accurate uptime data could result in lost revenue if a customer contests the veracity of stated system availability. On a more positive note, collection of data can result in positive improvement by identifying knowledge gaps. Are there certain service tickets that are taking longer to resolve? Are certain Genesys products causing much of the incoming service tickets? Analysis of the data can quickly highlight these items, and build business processes to *fix the leak* (Genesys, 2017).

Cloud Solution Benefits

The "cloud-ification" of communication technologies has become enormous, causing many technical departments to wonder if it is time to move away from traditional on-premises systems. While the hype of the technology could be considered overzealous in praise, there are clear and very serious benefits to cloud-based communication platforms. At Genesys, many customer service teams utilize the organization's cloud-based communications system, Purecloud. While the organization still focuses heavily on non-cloud solutions as well, there are distinct benefits to a cloud solution within a customer service department.

At the very core of a cloud solution is the utilization of scale to solve problems. Traditionally, many phone systems and contact centers relied on a central server to perform much of the processing using an on-premises platform. While the solution has been to have a back-up central server to switch over to in case of failure, there are immediate red flags in this scenario (Brown, 2016). Imagine having one person, plus a backup, in your organization that is responsible for everything important. If they were to call in sick, there would only be one other person capable of fulfilling their duties. This puts an organization in emergency mode the moment the first person is unavailable, as they are now down to a single resource. Switching the focus back to a central server, these on-premises servers must be capable of operating at maximum load or work capacity. Envision building a seven-lane highway, and deciding on seven lanes because the roads are busy enough a few times a year. Wouldn't it seem to be a waste of money if 80% of the time a two-lane highway would suffice? In an on-premises based architecture, the organization must purchase servers that can handle peak capacity even if it is rarely realized in daily use. This requires a much more expensive solution based on theoretical usage, and if it isn't enough when that time comes, the organization is in panic mode. Cloud based solutions solve this problem through scale using micro services, and flexibility. Microservices take portions of the central server, such as chat or voice, and allow them to operate independently (Brown, 2016).

Returning to the one person responsible for everything situation, what would happen if that company divided the important person's responsibilities to independent teams of people? In a contact center platform one microservice could simply handle voicemail, one could be for web chat, while another is responsible for routing all incoming calls to the right people. In this situation, if there was a problem with just the web chat microservice, it would have no effect on call routing or general telephony. Essentially, these servers take on a specific task and operate independently, while communicating with each other to work as a team. System survivability is also increased because the microservices can be geographically redundant. Instead of having a primary and backup server in the organization's headquarters, micro services can utilize data centers that are diversified throughout a country, or even globally. If there was a natural disaster that directly affected an organization's contact center in Virginia, the system would immediately reroute all traffic to systems in Denver data center (Brown, 2016).

Cloud computing also enables scale as a solution to cost and flexibility. Organizations do not have to retain servers that would be considered overkill out of fear they need to meet peak usage for the organization. Cloud computing resources can utilize elasticity to grow, or shrink depending on current usage. For example, if an organization was having a special holiday sale and incurred more calls than ever before, the microservices that deal with calls could increase their amount of resources to help handle the current volume. Immediately after the spike in calls, the micro services could then scale back down to normal usage. In this scenario, the organization would only increase costs for the peak time usage, rather than the entire life of those servers.

The benefit of scale through microservices and elasticity is again apparent during upgrade cycles. In a premises environment, performing upgrades on servers can take an extremely large amount of human resources and time. The upgrades should be scheduled months ahead to not impact peak business processes or negatively affect customer service employees during business hours. In a cloud platform, developers will create new instances, or sets of servers, to deploy the most recent version of the product. Envision instead of upgrading your laptop to the newest version of Microsoft Windows, someone simply handed you the exact same laptop with the newest version already installed and configured. This type of deployment permits businesses to experience no downtime between upgrades. Additionally, if there was a problem with the newest version of the product after upgrade, the previous version is still stable and easily reverted to (Li, 2016). Resolving bug fixes in this manner enables quicker resolution times and tremendously lower business impact from software-related downtime. The result is saving business man-hours that could be better spent on optimizing business processes and increased confidence in the stability of the platform.

Cloud computing's impact is not just felt within the contact center industry, but in collaborative business tools as well. Knowledge-base and infrastructure management systems must have the highest amount of availability and durability. It is imperative that customers have an outlet to reach support, where documentation of past incidents and current technical analyst recommendations can be consumed. This information must be persistent, and the customer service teams would be weakened if they lost these items. Even if the system was to go down temporarily, and availability was limited, it is more important that the information is still there. Data durability and availability is a clear proficiency of cloud based systems through sheer amount of redundant data storage, and geographical diversity of the backup systems.

All this scale increases the capability to capture an immense amount of raw data. For many organizations, large databases were simply too expensive to implement and maintain. However, as hardware maintenance and costs are expenses managed by the cloud provider, more organizations can take advantage of big data. Innovations such as non-relational databases enable organizations to take advantage of raw processing power through cloud resources and build flexible data models. More specifically, data can be captured and filtered down later to identify relevant business use cases, instead of having to scope the needed information at the very creation of the database structure. This gives businesses a chance to develop greater processes, recalculate past metrics at any point, and have further insight into company execution (Harrison, 2010; Homan, 2014).

The implications of cloud platforms are also felt on the front-end, or user interface, providing end-users applications that are operating system agnostic and easy to access. As most of the computing is done within the cloud data centers, end-users can access cloud applications via their web browser of choice. This alleviates the need for software to be installed on workstations and IT teams juggling various versions of the software depending on the user's operating system. Users can access the company platforms from their phone, laptop, desktop, or any device that is convenient in that current situation. Remote employees, or those that spend time out of the central office, have an easier method of accessing corporate applications. Every user is on the latest version, so employees receive the best of the product without needing to constantly update. These benefits extend to the internal IT teams as well, as the engineers encounter fewer issues regarding company applications and can quickly test for organizational-wide issues within the central cloud platform (Brown, 2016).

In conclusion, cloud-based technologies, even in the simplest use cases, enable users to do more. Like mortar that fills the space between bricks, cloud computing fits where needed, enhancing existing business processes and collaboration through ease of system access and device agnostic applications. Cloud platforms are built with inherent features that lead to drastically higher system uptime and durability of data. Technology is only as useful as the people who consume it. Cloud computing is supporting useful applications to be in the hands of those who are best equipped to innovate the customer service landscape.

References

Brown, D. (2016). Purecloud competitive advantages. Interactive Intelligence. Daly City, CA.

Fallon, N. (2014, August 6). The new customer service is here, there & everywhere. Retrieved March 9, 2017, from http://www.businessnewsdaily.com/6927-omnichannel-customer-service.html.

Frost, A. (2017). What are knowledge management systems? Retrieved March 1, 2017, from http://www.knowledge-management-tools.net/knowledge-management-systems.html.

Genesys. (2017). Workforce optimization overview. Retrieved February 19, 2017, from http://www.genesys.com/solutions/employee-engagement/workforce-optimization.

Geraghty, S. (2013, April 13). What is acd? Retrieved February 28, 2017, from https://www.talkdesk.com/blog/what-is-an-acd/.

Harrison, G. (2010, August 26). 10 things you should know about NoSQL databases. Retrieved March 1, 2017, from http://www.techrepublic.com/blog/10-things/10-things-you-should-know-about-nosql-databases/.

Homan, J. (2014, April 6). Relational vs. non-relational databases: Which one is right for you? Retrieved February 15, 2017, from https://www.pluralsight.com/blog/software-development/relational-non-relational-databases.

Interview with Andrea Friio vice president of Gensys Technical Marketing [Telephone interview]. (2017, March 12).

Kansky, M. (2010, October 5). Understanding how ticket management systems work. Retrieved February 28, 2017, from http://blog.livehelpnow.net/understanding-how-ticket-management-systems-work/.

Li, R. (2016, August 4). Microservices essentials for executives: The key to high velocity software development. Retrieved March 1, 2017, from https://www.datawire.io/microservices-essentials-executives-key-high-velocity-software-development/.

Meyers, L. (2016, May 9). Universal queues are more than technology. Retrieved March 15, 2017, from https://www.callcentrehelper.com/universal-queues-are-more-than-technology-86512.htm.

Mochal, T. (2006, November 10). 10 things you should know about ITIL. Retrieved February 15, 2017, from http://www.techrepublic.com/article/10-things-you-should-know-about-itil/.

Paresh, D. (2014, August 11). More companies adding video to personalize online customer service. Retrieved March 1, 2017, from http://www.latimes.com/business/la-fi-video-customer-service-20140812-story.html.

Pleasant, B. (2008, July). What UC is and isn't. Retrieved from http://searchunifiedcommunications.techtarget.com/feature/What-UC-is-and-isnt.

Roos, D. (2017). How interactive voice response works. Retrieved from http://electronics.howstuffworks.com/interactive-voice-response.htm.

Windley, P. (2002). Delivering high availability services using a multi-tiered support model. Retrieved from http://www.windley.com/docs/Tiered%20Support.pdf.

Chapter 9

A Movement Toward SaaS and the Cloud

The Evolution of IT Services in Higher Education

Kirk Young, Ruth Schwer, Rob Hartman,
Chris Ardeel, Tom Janke, Zach Skidmore,
and Peter Williams

Butler University

Contents

Introduction

As the United States approaches the year 2020, higher education faces a unique set of challenges. In the aftermath of the 2008–2009 recession and ongoing international economic strife, the financial cost of pursuing higher education caused many students and parents to question the value of the college experience. Increasing enrollments at for-profit institutions caught the attention of nonprofit school administrators and illustrated just how much demand might be going unmet. At the same time, the high executive compensation and questionable employment outcomes (Kirkham, 2012) of for-profit school graduates caused a backlash of increasing regulatory scrutiny that impacted both sectors. Combined with declining funding from federal and state budgets, nonprofit schools struggle to fund routine operating expenses, satisfy regulatory reporting, and meet students' increasing expectations for their college experience (Center for Analysis of Postsecondary Education and Employment, 2012). Beyond dipping into the endowment or raising tuition, what can higher education do to remain relevant and sustainable?

The exponential development of technology over the last decade (Greenwald, 2011) can play a disruptive and innovative role in enhancing or even changing the student experience. Whereas information technology departments hitherto played a support and service-focused role, these business units have now begun to seize opportunities to provide additional value to their organizations through a model focused on partnership.

In general, the role of technology can be approached from two different perspectives in a university setting. Technology's place in assisting with, shaping, and even at some level driving academic pedagogy clearly plays a very large part in an organization's instructional strategy and philosophy. It can also be provided from an environmental standpoint; faculty may not want to change their teaching style based solely on their use of email, but they do want reliable email service. From these two vantage points, many institutions create teams or departments focused on technology from the academic perspective or the support and environmental perspective; at Butler University, the Center for Academic Technology champions the former while Information Technology champions the latter. Working together, these departments work to fulfill the needs of all of campus. True partnership with the rest of campus, however, provides the opportunity to change this dynamic in powerful ways.

In the case of Butler Information Technology and the support and environment side of technology, adjusting team structure represented a key component of the move toward the posture of partnership. In order to change the perception and focus of an IT team, they needed to change their focus from deep support of every system to free up resources for optimizing remaining solutions. This initial shift in reducing second and third tier support from on premise solutions to an increased preference for cloud services did not impact the first tier of support; however, it offered a new complexion for the time management of the resources on the teams in the background of IT. The next shift involved further reduction of infrastructure toward cloud-hosted services, clearing existing solutions and actively reducing the technological footprint on campus in ways that changed the application inventory beyond just a higher utilization of cloud products at the time of purchase. Coupled with this shift is an intentional expansion of skillsets and roles within the team to provide vendor management, relationship management, project management, business analysis, etc. to contribute value to clients in a completely different and much more holistic way than ever before.

By reorganizing and refocusing IT and its services to approach the institution's portfolio of projects and initiatives in an intentional way, IT strategy can more closely align with overall university strategy. The cloud plays a pivotal role in enabling such a strategic shift; by equipping the organization to operate in an increasingly agile nature using Software-as-a-Service (SaaS) across a variety of functional roles, the institution can devote more resources to differentiating and revenue-generating initiatives, while also facilitating better connections with the community and prospective students utilizing the power and potential of all of the data being collected. Colleges and universities must embrace the digital push in order to address the challenges currently facing higher education, and each driver of change holds its own relevance to the cloud.

Driver: Offering More Services at a Lower Cost

As with most organizations, colleges and universities constantly seek new ways to reduce costs while maintaining the same services. The rising scrutiny on the costs and benefits of higher education will only heighten this strategic movement. Given technology's ability to drastically change the way we work and live, the cloud offers an attractive vision for reducing costs while continuing to provide dependable services. The opportunity exists, but not as cleanly as many institutions hope.

In the past, Butler University's IT department included support as a key component of every team. While development and analysis of varying levels took place in the areas of Client Services, Administrative Computing, and Network and Infrastructure, the top priority of every team was customer support and service. As a result, for many years post-ticket surveys consistently demonstrated glowing feedback for the support experience provided by the department; however, comments made it clear that service was lacking when it came to deeper connections with the campus community (i.e., collaboration, cooperation, and innovation). Fortunately, a strategy for addressing these needs aligned well with an increased utilization of cloud services.

When support-oriented organizations make a change toward a partnership model and greater focus on cloud based offerings, it can scare both the resources involved with the shift as well as the customer base. Will the quality of support suffer? Will headcounts be reduced to take advantage of outsourced functions and reduce costs? Change management plays a critical role, and a core component of that requires understanding the true implications and considerations of moving to the cloud. Vendors will not hesitate to tout the potential cost and time savings available should their services be procured; in fact, many will make it a key selling point in their proposal. Their pitch will resemble something like this:

■ Time Savings
  - Decreased time spent on supporting the customer
  - Decreased time spent updating servers

■ Cost Savings
  - Decreased cost of maintaining server on site
  - Decreased cost of human resources supporting product and customers

Unfortunately, the benefits of cloud services often do not translate this directly and clearly. When considering customer support, simplifying the experience for the end user still trumps all else; at Butler, first tier support still takes initial calls and creates cases to track issues, escalating to second tier or directly to the vendor as appropriate. Second and third tier support no longer spend time updating the server or software, but instead begin to manage the "instances" of cloud products, keeping track of its integrations with the on-premise environment and other systems, as well as the overall data flow so that service is maintained uninterrupted.

Email serves as an excellent example of the complicated nature of justifying cloud services. For higher education, email represents a litmus test for the cloud. It is a commodity service offered to workplaces by established and dependable providers, the most well-known being Google and Microsoft. Transitioning to cloud-based email service carries lower risk and a perceived higher reward. As Butler moved to Microsoft's Exchange Online from on-premise service, first tier support experienced no change in the general amount of time allocated to the service, while second and third tier support notably recognized a shift in time spent from updating Exchange servers to managing the cloud instance of Exchange, as well as regularly updating integrations with our authentication and account provisioning tools. An additional wrinkle presented itself in terms of backup services; a legacy policy needed to be reassessed after the migration due to changes in how it would have to be carried out. This resulted in additional time and cost. Strictly in consideration of email itself, at the end of the project the transition to the cloud resulted in negligible savings in terms of a time and cost perspective.

If cloud services do not always represent substantial cost and time savings from the standpoint of the individual product or service itself, then where do any benefits manifest? The answer depends on the answer to another question: what is the organizational strategy for the time savings gained by moving more and more services to the cloud? Many might worry that any time savings achieved represents an opportunity to reduce workforce costs by either outsourcing remaining work or outright cutting total headcount. This can have an adverse effect on the end user support experience, team morale, etc. which may eventually counteract and supersede any financial benefits of the original decision and move. Another option involves refocusing the existing resources' efforts.

As a result of claiming what time savings are realized by moving to the Cloud and utilizing SaaS, organizations have the opportunity to expand skillsets and improve the technical and consulting capacities of their team members. When not involved in support and operational work, focusing this newly acquired time and energy toward more intentional relationship management, project management, and change management can have positive ripple effects across an entire institution. If better planning sets teams up for better results, then consulting with clients to meet their needs provides the chance to more efficiently and effectively work with them and arrive at successful and sustainable solutions. Coupled with better planning and execution, the increased focus on process improvement and business analysis work done in collaboration with clients can also lead to increased time savings. Though it may not be a direct result of the transition to or increased utilization of cloud services, there exists great possibility for corresponding changes in resource allocation and time spent.

At Butler University, IT created its Partnership team to specifically dedicate resources toward these more consulting-based roles in interacting with clients, tying the development and support teams of the department closely together to meet constituent needs. Not only do the practices of process improvement; business analysis; and relationship, project, and change management benefit the IT department by streamlining the preparation and implementation of solutions, it also benefits the client areas by continuously partnering with them to streamline *their* business processes, thereby providing the client areas opportunities for buying back time for their own resources to focus on other needs.

Taking advantage of the promise of the Cloud in order to provide more service at a lower cost seems straightforward and simple enough, but clearly the considerations can be more nuanced and complex than anticipated. Calculating a return on investment strictly from the costs associated with an individual service may not come close to justifying a move or purchase; by developing a business case examining a solution from a holistic perspective and projecting the big picture benefits, higher education institutions can begin making the move away from the strictly support posture toward a partnership and cloud services model. In the case of Butler University IT, while support remains a core component of the department's mission, its complexion has changed. The additional focus on partnership and consulting services now complements and strengthens the department's support team, increasing the strategic and holistic interaction with clients and making work across the entire university more effective and efficient. For decentralized business units at larger higher education institutions, the same strategies and tactics can be adopted at the divisional, departmental, or team level; the change to the Cloud can be driven from the ground up.

Driver: Access Anytime, Anywhere, Perpetual Access

Just as disruptive and innovative as technology may be in enhancing and changing the student experience in higher education, so too are the students themselves. Every year, a new class arrives with greater expectations of their institution and its technological capabilities; their digital citizenship begins from a more advanced place than some of the faculty, staff, administrators, and even some of the other students! By and large, K-12 institutions have made great strides innovating with and adopting cloud-based academic technology (EdSurge, 2017). They have set a high bar for higher education institutions. While the rapid development of technology and its fast-paced adoption by students can present additional challenges and pressures on higher education, these factors can also be viewed as positive enablers of change. Rather than updating a service to cutting-edge and forcing end users to adopt the change, colleges and universities have the unique opportunity to capitalize on their core constituents' enthusiasm for technology and use that momentum to guide possibly more resistant members of faculty, staff, and administrators through their own change cycle.

96% of undergraduate students have smartphones (Brooks, 2016), so an established audience is waiting for institutions to increase their mobile presence and engagement. The trend amongst cloud services to include optimized mobile access of some kind further solidifies this directional shift. Butler University kept this in mind when considering a challenge nearly all higher education institutions have faced or are currently facing: if students want to engage with their university on their mobile device, what should that app look like? What are the ultimate goals of the mobile app? How will it interact with and support existing systems, processes, and services? The result was the Butler App developed in a unique partnership with ClearScholar.

ClearScholar, a startup technology company local to Butler's own Indianapolis, began developing their student engagement mobile app in 2016 with Butler University as a founding investor and subject matter expert. A pilot group was quickly formed with a small group of students for the first semester of use, and the app was fully released to all Butler students in 2017. Since that time, 70% of target students have actively utilized the app (Clearscholar, 2017). Current functionality covers basic needs, with future developments and releases intended to more fully incorporate the app into business processes and student communication throughout campus. In the future, Butler and ClearScholar envision the mobile app as serving as the primary gateway for students to engage with Butler, enhance their student experience, and strengthen their already considerable bond with their university.

Our increasingly accessible world reinforces the need for a core mobile portal to campus services. Online file storage has enabled and enhanced productivity and collaboration across campus as students make use of services such as Google Drive for Education, OneDrive, DropBox, Box, and others. Having a mobile app,

Learning Management System (LMS), and other systems easily integrating with these various options is not only a convenience for students, it is a necessity. As mobile technology intersects with pedagogy and the classroom setting, this seamless access becomes necessary for faculty as well. Instructors are increasingly working with the Center for Academic Technology to brainstorm ideas for appropriately incorporating all of the digital tools at their disposal into their teaching, whether it involves receiving assignments electronically via the LMS or using Panopto, Poll Anywhere, or other services for in-class polling to adjust their lesson plan in real time to meet the needs of their students. The Center for Academic Technology champions the effective use of educational technology through such collaboration with the Butler community to foster 21st-century skills and to nurture innovation. Building on the theme of change management mentioned earlier, in essence the Center for Academic Technology aims to move beyond simply being a service point into the role of accomplice with faculty in optimizing the way technology supports learning. Cloud-based tools and any-time access, now ubiquitous in the workplace, are an essential extension of the ever-evolving learning environment, and academic technology centers play a crucial role in coupling use of these new tools to sound pedagogical practice. Academic technology centers are well positioned as primary conduits between the academic community and the IT organization.

Mobile access and engagement will only continue to gain significance in higher education as the industry approaches the next decade. Having an environment with enough flexibility and adaptability to incorporate myriad disparate services into a single mobile portal begins with a strategic shift toward cloud services. By providing easy access to as many tools as possible, colleges and universities will better enable their students and faculty to enhance the learning experience, assist students with their development into world class citizens, and provide greater service.

Driver: Quickening Pace of Technology Development/Change Need for Agility. Inseparability of LMS Tools

As mentioned previously, the higher education industry must embrace and actively develop flexibility and adaptability to meet the needs of a digitally fluent student body, rapidly changing technology, and the effects of the intersection of both of these factors in the classroom setting. In the past, higher education institutions have been slow to change, partially due to the occupation of a strange place in the technology sector; there exists the need for standardization and management throughout the higher education organization in order to maintain a certain level of service quality, whereas there is also a competing need for open access and compatibility in order to encourage the nexus of diverse ideas and experiences amongst all campus constituents, including at the level of technology. For example, the ability for Blackberry devices to connect to Butler's network was supported arguably

2–3 years past the point where it was worth the effort to ensure compatibility; most telling about this fact may be whether incoming students today even recognize the brand.

Given the competing needs of higher education information technology departments, the tendency of cloud services to include an optimized mobile experience provides an attractive option for increasing the compatibility of an organization's environment. Students consider technology to be a significant contributor to their success (Brooks, 2016), making it all that more important to provide an environment in which they can easily work and learn. 81% of institutions will invest more resources in the cloud in 2017 (Schaffhauser, 2016), and 79% say they are already using cloud services in some capacity (Vion, 2016). By strategically shifting more towards the utilization of SaaS and cloud computing, academic institutions can position themselves to better serve their constituents and the student experience. Faculty and students are aware of the new ideas and tools all around them, bringing them in to try out constantly; they only lack access. This makes a flexible learning environment critical to the experimentation and exploration necessary in the classroom.

Driver: Clear Differentiation/Value in an Industry under Scrutiny

In addition to rapidly evolving technology, with incoming students who are more digitally savvy than ever and the rising scrutiny on cost versus value provided by institutions of higher education, the pressure to keep costs stable while finding ways to provide improved service results in the need for additional resources and therefore additional revenue. From where can these new and untapped funding sources possibly originate? Innovation has become an imperative within higher education as institutions struggle to recognize new ways to operate. Internal consulting programs and process improvement offer one avenue for streamlining workflows and freeing up time for resources to take on more strategic challenges. Exploring partnerships to open up new revenue streams and opportunities for brand recognition and reinforcement are another method of pursuing additional funding for programs and resources.

Where does the Cloud factor into the potential for revenue generation? By creating a flexible environment with easy connection and integration points, colleges and universities can place their programs in a position to take advantage of opportunities for new revenue and community engagement. At Butler University, a niche program in one of the most respected colleges recently developed an online certificate program in a matter of weeks by using cloud services and quickly connecting as needed to the overall environment, allowing a partnership with community businesses to move from ideation to execution without missing a beat.

Examples such as this are possible throughout every college and academic program. Partnerships with community organizations not only enrich the student experience, they also carry the potential for brand recognition and additional revenue streams. Colleges and universities do well to find the thriving sectors in their areas and form relationships with businesses in those industries that align with their programs. These symbiotic arrangements offer ample opportunity for investment and revenue sharing, much like Butler's partnership with ClearScholar. Guaranteed internships can also benefit both the students of the institution as well as the business in need of additional resources, and with the right match of brands this type of agreement can increase the positive reputation of both organizations. Beyond just providing revenue opportunities, these additional immersive learning experiences for students help justify the costs of attending a college or university, especially with respect to their more robust and established programs.

Conclusion

With technology developing at such a rapid pace, what might be the future of the Cloud and SaaS in the higher education industry? If every app and every system exist in the cloud, what becomes of an institution's central infrastructure? The architecture of a technology environment with the cloud in mind does not stop at the applications and systems in use, it even extends to the core infrastructure. Butler University recently moved on premise infrastructure to a new solution which resembles Butler's own mini-cloud. This was a first step toward an eventual shift to cloud infrastructure hosting services, such as those provided by Amazon or Microsoft, which would represent a dramatic shift in technological capabilities and resource allocation toward more strategic and value-added areas on campus. Differentiation comes as a result of giant leaps, and Butler has begun its running start.

Where does the student experience fit into the Cloud of the future? Looking forward, the Cloud will continue to make it easier for learning analytics to be quickly harvested and purposed toward improving student experience and learning outcomes. Having an environment with seamless and very expansive data flow opens up entirely new possibilities for serving students and enhancing the learning experience. Data can be leveraged at the micro and macro levels, keeping well established general business processes running smoothly while also opening the door to more tailored interaction with constituents to truly meet them where they are. Using this customer relationship management approach, higher education could radically transform the educational experience while staying true to the central purpose of the college and university setting. The Cloud represents possibility, and the shift has just begun.

References

Brooks, D. C. (2016). *ECAR Study of Undergraduate Students and Information Technology, 2016*. Louisville, CO: Educause Center For Analysis and Research.

Center for Analysis of Postsecondary Education and Employment. (2012, February 21). For-Profit College Students Less Likely to Be Employed After Graduation and Have Lower Earnings, New Study Finds. Retrieved from CAPSEE: https://capseecenter. org/for-profit-college-students-less-likely-to-be-employed-after-graduation-and-have-lower-earnings-new-study-finds/

ClearScholar. (2017, March 6). Butler University Sees Success Leveraging ClearScholar Student Engagement Platform. Retrieved from ClearScholar: https://clearscholar.com/ butler-university-sees-success-leveraging-clearscholar-student-engagement-platform/

EdSurge Research. (2017). The Most Important EdTech Trends of 2016. Retrieved from EdSurge Research: https://www.edsurge.com/research/special-reports/state-of-edtech-2016/k12_edtech_trends

Greenwald, W. (2011, January 4). Top 10 Most Influential Tech Advances of the Decade. Retrieved from PCMag: https://www.pcmag.com/article2/0,2817,2374825,00.asp

Kirkham, C. (2012, January 30). For-Profit College Executives Make Much More Than Their Higher Education Counterparts [INFOGRAPHIC]. Retrieved from Huff Post: https://www.huffingtonpost.com/2012/01/30/for-profit-college-compensation_n_1229284.html

Schaffhauser, D. (2016, September 22). Higher Ed Cloud Adoption on the Rise. Retrieved from Campus Technology: https://campustechnology.com/articles/2016/09/22/ higher-ed-cloud-adoption-on-the-rise.aspx

Vion. (2016). Trends in Cloud Computing. *eCampus News*.

Chapter 10

Implementation and Benefits of Cloud Services in Higher Education

Dan Jones
Ball State University

Contents

Introduction

As the use of cloud computing continues to grow in business, 50% of the top 1,000 global companies store their customer's data in the Cloud (Bhatiasevi & Naglis, 2016). It appears that higher education institutions are falling in line and following the example of the business world. Before examining how cloud computing is being implemented in higher education, as well as the advantages and disadvantages for students, it is important to establish a definition of cloud computing and the services that are offered through the Cloud. For the purposes of this chapter, the definition provided by The National Institute of Standards and Technology (NIST) will be used. NIST defines cloud computing as "a model for enabling convenient, on-demand network access to a shared pool of configurable computing resources (e.g., networks, servers, storage, applications, and services) that can be rapidly provisioned and released with minimal management effort or service provider interaction" (National Institute of Standars of Technlology, 2010). Within that definition lay many different uses of cloud computing. A common way for businesses and higher education to be successful in their implementation is for administrators to be knowledgeable about "networking, virtualization, routing, data movement, data use, process management, and security to be helpful to an organization using cloud computing" (Morrill, 2011). The other commonality that exists between business and higher education is that a transition to cloud computing services is often done to reduce costs on hardware and information technology (IT) staff. Cloud computing can help to accomplish these savings because it moves hardware and some IT responsibilities into the hands of a cloud computing services provider. This is similar to the concept of how utilities, such as water and electricity, are provided to buildings and homes. The basic cost savings come through the cloud computing services provider leveraging their centralized management approach across multiple customers helping to keep the economies of scale down and offering their services at a lower cost than higher education institutions running the same system within their own network (Jaeger, Lin, & Grimes, 2008). Like the utilities model, the cloud services providers assume the large financial burden of system management and data protection (Jaeger et al., 2008) which allows their customers to better utilize the services to suit their needs. For example, a higher education institution might use a cloud file management system such as box. com or dropbox.com to allow their faculty to store files for their courses. The institution can then customize the service by buying a set amount of storage for the entire institution, for each department, or for each individual. The capacity of the cloud services provider assists in keeping costs low by allowing the institution to create a flexible model and offload the responsibility of the servers and data centers to the cloud services provider.

This chapter will focus on the following items: (1) cloud services used in higher education; (2) considerations for higher education when moving to cloud technology; and (3) negative and positive impact on students in higher education.

Cloud Services Used in Higher Education

The most common methods in which cloud services are provided are through three approaches (Wheeler & Waggener, 2009):

- Infrastructure as a Service (IaaS)
- Platform as a Service (PaaS)
- Software as a Service (SaaS)

IaaS is the cloud equivalent to being able to control the backend of a network. A few common services offered through IaaS are virtual computers, servers, and storage (Sultan, 2010). IaaS provides infrastructure resources that allow the institution to move from having the expense of maintaining in-house equipment to outsourcing it and having effective, efficient scalability in services to meet increasing or decreasing demands by students and faculty. While most students and faculty will not knowingly access the IaaS services of a cloud platform, it is normally accessed by institution administrators through a dashboard which they will interact with indirectly. For example, if a student or faculty member grants permission for the helpdesk to take remote control of their computer in order to diagnose a problem, the IaaS component is allowing this connection. This approach is beneficial to the student or faculty user because they do not have to be concerned about buying, installing, or upgrading any software to allow the helpdesk to remote into their computer (Aharony, 2015). A major function of higher education that begins to differentiate the needs from business is the need for capacity and privacy to store research data. IaaS also serves as the conduit for students and faculty to the servers and storage provided by the selected cloud service to securely store and share research data (Mathew, 2012).

PaaS builds on the services offered by IaaS and is based off the traditional model of computing where each user installs software or applications on the hard drive of their personal computer. PaaS allows a higher education institution to offload the expenses of maintaining and updating all the software on the computers they own and makes it easy to push software to students for installation on their own computers. With PaaS these updates and maintenance issues are now controlled remotely by individuals within the institution that have been granted the appropriate security privileges (Sultan, 2010). The largest benefit for higher education is that it can offer powerful operating systems and application tools to students and faculty from a central location. In turn, this helps to ensure the latest versions are being used, and updates can be pushed out to users. Both features help to secure access to the system and the data stored at the IaaS level. (Aharony, 2015). Another benefit of PaaS for higher education is it allows students and faculty to experiment with building software and applications. This could be extremely useful in a computer science course. PaaS gives students and faculty the ability to "build their own application without the cost and complexity of buying and managing the underlying hardware and software layers" (Mathew, 2012). The final piece is then to run software and applications in the cloud environment, which leads to the SaaS component.

One common theme for higher education institutions that makes SaaS popular is the implementation of a Learning Management System (LMS), such as

Blackboard, Canvas, or Desire to Learn. An LMS permits students to submit academic artifacts (i.e., papers and portfolios) and take quizzes (Aharony, 2015). The LMS allows faculty to grade the artifacts, provide feedback, and submit final grades to the Registrar's office. SaaS provides means for the LMS and other applications (i.e., WebEx for conferences and Box.com for file storage) to be delivered through an Internet connection making the applications accessible twenty-four hours a day, seven days a week (Sultan, 2010). Students and faculty will also use SaaS to access their personal data stored in a Customer Relationship Management (CRM) application. Students might use the CRM to register for classes and check their balance on their lunch card. Faculty might use the CRM to view their paychecks or vacation balance. The student and faculty will interact with the application in the SaaS environment through an interface designed by the cloud service provider, often referred to as a dashboard, and the ability to easily use this interface is critical to the implementation of the application (Masud, Huang, & Yong, 2012). The ease of use connects with the concept of self-efficacy, which will be discussed in more detail later in the chapter. With the amount of personal data being stored, it is important for the higher education institution to evaluate the cloud service provider and make certain they have a robust security system. The security components and functionality of SaaS can be monitored and controlled by IT administrators, and this is paramount to a successful implementation of SaaS (Masud et al., 2012). For example, an LMS running as SaaS can be updated without needing to be taken offline. If an LMS is not running SaaS and updates are needed, the entire system will need to be taken offline for the updates to be performed. As a result, no students or faculty can access the LMS while it is down. Upgrades are normally done during a time when there is minimum usage (i.e., Saturday morning between 2 a.m. and 4 a.m.). However, it is still two hours where everyone is locked out from the system, and the next time the program is launched the update will be available. With SaaS these updates can be completed without interrupting the user experience. Once individuals log in, they will see the changes. When accessing a critical enterprise system piece such as the LMS, the less downtime the better.

Before moving onto the benefits of cloud services in higher education, a summary of the three services is provided below (Colman, n.d.):

- IaaS is a system that is built to an institution's specifications and includes virtualization, servers, storage, and networking that are managed by the cloud service provider.
- PaaS is used to deploy software and updates to users and builds off of IaaS to manage and install operating systems.
- SaaS is used to deliver software and applications that have been licensed by the institution and builds off of IaaS and PaaS to deliver the services to the end user.

The remainder of this chapter will focus on the SaaS system since IT has the greater direct impact on students and faculty. Also, the benefits and risks of implementing cloud services will be examined.

Benefits of Cloud Services for Higher Education

The major benefit of cloud services is the financial savings gained by offloading the need to purchase and maintain computer equipment, especially servers, which can lead to other savings through having a smaller IT staff or, at a minimum, allowing IT staff to concentrate on other technology concerns. As part of the Enterprise Resource Planning (ERP) process, a university can recognize the following benefits from cloud services (Goel, Kiran, & Garg, 2011):

- Reduced Cost: The purchase of additional hardware and software updates is now the responsibility of the cloud service provider.
- Unfettered Access: Students and faculty members can access the system, such as the LMS, through any wired or wireless devices.
- Uptime: Almost zero downtime can be expected.
- Manpower: Limited manpower is required to run and implement cloud technology.
- Future Needs: If the university increases in students or faculty, it is easier to scale up because the investment in hardware is absorbed by the cloud service provider, and the uptick in cost to the institution for additional services is minimized.
- Customization: The institution can select the services they want to implement based on specific requirements and budgetary allocations.
- Emergency and Disasters: Distribution of the data across the cloud service providers data centers can help to recover from an emergency or disaster at the institution.

Beyond saving money, another value for higher education institutions is that cloud services can help them to keep pace with changing technology, and this can be used as a marketing tool to attract students (Sultan, 2010). An institution can research the typical ways their students use cloud technology and leverage this information to make sure current and future students are aware that the institution is keeping pace with technology. Typical services that higher education takes advantage of with cloud services are (Masud et al., 2012):

- Personal Workspace in Classrooms: Used to provide an area for students to test development of an application in a workspace that is isolated in a virtual environment so the student cannot harm the computer they are working on.

■ Personal Learning Environments: Used by students as an alternative to institutionally controlled Virtual Learning Environments. The students are allowed to spin up their own instance of a virtual server and customize it to suit their needs for various classes or research.

■ File Management Convenience: No need to back up everything to a thumb drive and transfer it from one device to another or to transfer items to a new computer.

■ Mobility: Students and faculty can access files and information from any device (i.e., laptop, tablet, or smartphone).

Overall, the cloud environment should be less work than an all-physical IT environment, especially with institutions that have more than one physical location (Alam, 2013). New instances of virtual machines or access to software applications can be deployed or granted to any campus location. No longer does an individual from IT need to travel to a location to setup a server; it can all be done remotely, and this leads to additional cost savings.

Additional benefits come through the institution minimizing the servers that they own and having upgrades and migration of data being handled by the cloud service provider. This can help save time and money in migrating data from physical server to physical server. In addition, maintenance of key programs should be more efficient and create less calls to the helpdesk. In the case when the LMS is distributed over the cloud provider's infrastructure in the SaaS model, if one application server is lost, they will have redundancy at other locations and the people using the LMS will likely not notice any downtime. This leads to campuses having redundancy and resilience everywhere.

When implementing cloud services, a major benefit is going to come from availability and scalability (Ercan, 2010). If a university has a course that needs more hard drive space for a research project, they can simply request that space from IT staff or their provider and pay for the additional space. It is no longer required for the university to setup and maintain another server to fulfill this request for additional space.

In addition to the savings on hardware and IT staff, an unexpected area of savings could occur for students and allow the university more flexibility to hire faculty (Alamri & Qureshi, 2015). Because cloud technology provides for better options for high quality video and audio delivery, students can attend lecture through virtual classrooms. This helps the university to offer courses to any student globally. If students can come from anywhere, the institution can now hire faculty from anywhere, either full-time or adjuncts. This could help the institution boost the depth of faculty expertise which was not feasible in the past due to travel constraints. Even if the students and faculty are in the same city, cloud technology, such as WebEx, would allow students to continue to meet with faculty in case of a snowstorm or another emergency which closed campus. Cloud services can also be leveraged to bring in outside lecturers to the classroom.

Risks of Cloud Services for Higher Education

While cloud computing offers numerous benefits for universities, it also has some potential limitations or constraints. Even though research suggests that cloud computing will "facilitate more learning experiences for students by increasing access to information and enabling collaboration, correlation, and data sharing," (Odeh, Warwick, & Garcia-Perez, 2015) an institution must examine the risks, particularly with legal and policy constraints and take care to plan their implementation.

Potential risks for an institution are (Odeh et al., 2015) and (Katz, Goldstein, & Yanosky, 2009):

- Deterioration of customer care and service quality: When an institution gives up control of services to an outside provider, there is always a risk they will not perform the function as well as was done in-house.
- Departmental downsizing: One avenue where cloud services can help to save money is in reducing IT staff, but letting people go or outsourcing services can have a negative impact on the culture of the institution.
- Uncertainty about new technology: Whenever people switch to something new, there is almost always concern of how well it will, or won't, work.
- Lack of supporting resources: Switching is one thing, but getting students and faculty up to speed on how to use and implement the new cloud services is another. Training is important and will potentially cut into the savings offered by switching to cloud services.
- Poor or nonexistent service level agreements: If an institution is going to place their services in the hands of cloud service vendors, (i.e., the LMS), they must be sure to have agreements on services in place.
- IT not ready for the switch: IT staff may not be highly skilled in managing risk and service performance with third party vendors.
- Lack of trust and confidence: Once students and faculty find out their data is being placed in the hands of others, they will naturally be concerned, and steps must be taken to show how their data is secured.

These risks are not insurmountable and can be overcome with time and experience in a relationship with a cloud provider. Since cloud services in higher education are likely to be implemented in a similar fashion at other institutions, the challenges faced by a single institution are likely to be similar to another, and the normal culture of higher education is to share information for the greater good. This can help the institutions to support each other. Of course, an individual institution's problems can be magnified by the enrollment of students and the number of faculty, but a similar support system of sharing information is not likely to exist in the business world. This gives higher education an advantage during implementation as well as determining services moving forward.

Adoption of cloud technology can also face pressure from inside the institution, especially if changes in technology have not gone well in the past. An EDUCAUSE Center for Analysis Research survey found that institutional culture was the largest barrier to adopting cloud technologies; the second barrier cited was concerns about IT security; and the third barrier being regulatory compliance (i.e., concerns about meeting Family Educational Rights and Privacy Act) (Katz et al., 2009). These findings of cloud adoption are backed up by another survey conducted by the IDC Enterprise Panel (Tout, Sverdlik, & Lawyer, 2009) where they listed the following risks in cloud adoption:

1. Security: There are several concerns surrounding the implementation of security in cloud computing, especially in a university setting.
2. Performance and Availability: Concerns include how to guarantee performance from an outside vendor. This is especially true in higher education since student submission of work is typically tied to strict timelines.
3. Integration with In-House Programs: University IT administrators typically use their own house applications with a portion that is customized to their own IT lab structure. A paramount concern is the transitioning of applications to the cloud environment and how much of the customizability will be lost in that process.
4. Cost is another factor that may be introduced by additional vendor relationship management or additional measures that are unique to cloud computing.

From the results of these two surveys, it is apparent that security of information is a primary concern among students and faculty within the institutions that are, or might, adopt cloud technologies. Concerns include where the data will be placed, who will have access to the data, and if the data will be stored in different countries with potentially different data privacy laws. This concern is amplified in higher education because of the research information data that is part of academic studies which needs to be kept secure. Research data can range from basic information such as grade level and age to higher-level data such as issues of national security or hospital patients' medical information (Tout et al., 2009).

Even if the students and faculty aren't worried about security the IT staff will be concerned for them and the institution. The largest concern with IT managers is surrendering control and providing access to their data to outside cloud services who have the ability to change the underlying technology without customers' consent (Sultan, 2010). But the concern that everyone shares is the security of the data, particularly their own data. Cloud platform vendors will argue that their software, if run properly, isolates all user data and separates information from each person (Alam, 2013). But no matter how much security is put in place, there is still always the concern of human error when setting policies on the servers or when migrating to a different server.

One path to overcoming the security concerns is for the institution to share with its students and faculty how the cloud service providers are protecting and maintaining the integrity of their data. The normal methods of data protection are (Mathew, 2012):

1. Mask or de-identify of the data: If the data is hacked into, none of the information (i.e., grades) will be able to be tied to a student.
2. Firewalls: Help to prevent people from breaking into the cloud service providers servers and data center.
3. Encryption and decryption: Data can be encrypted, and if it is stolen, it will not be able to be read by anyone outside the institution.
4. Authorization identity management: Requiring a second login; for example, the Duo system that requires confirmation for logging into a system from a smartphone.

Along with the substantial benefits of cloud computing come potential pitfalls that can impede usefulness and cause substantial frustration. One concern is the prospect of uncontrollable downtime, which will vary by provider, and can occur as server maintenance is performed or as unforeseen outages occur (Behrend, Wiebe, London, & Johnson, 2011). Because software is accessed remotely through SaaS and applications may become unavailable, there may be a perceived or actual lack of control from students and faculty which will make them wonder when the applications will be available for use (Behrend, Wiebe, London, & Johnson, 2011). Despite these issues, it is clear that the cost savings and maturity of cloud technologies in providing a secure environment outweigh the risks, and the preference is to move from "on-premises IT and toward the auditable and highly professional practices of cloud service providers as this market matures" (Katz et al., 2009).

Considerations When Moving to Cloud Computing

The common reason for a higher education institution to switch to cloud services is "economic, relating to the reduction in funding and the need to increase competitiveness through better student and staff experiences" (Masud et al., 2012). Before adopting cloud technology, it is important for the institution to make sure they are not using cloud services purely for financial gain. The cloud services need to be in alignment with the strategic plans of the institution. This will help to make certain that there are systems in place to make and manage the change. A plan to transition to cloud services was developed by Tuncay Ercan and outlined the following needs (Ercan, 2010):

- Assess current costs and develop benchmarks for application support, provisioning, and ongoing resource consumption.

■ Identify opportunities to reduce costs and speed up service delivery via use of automation for integrated application and infrastructure provisioning.
■ Implement systems to monitor and integrate application performance and real-time capacity planning analytics with automated provisioning solutions.
■ Integrate security strategies and priorities across the application development, release, and operations life cycle. IDC recommends that organizations begin the journey toward integrated cloud management by targeting early pilot projects at developer teams and application environments that can deliver quick payback to validate the business agility benefits and operational efficiency improvements.

A cost that is often not calculated in switching to cloud technologies, and an area that is likely to offset the savings, especially the initial savings, is the "training and support for key stakeholders such as instructors, administrators, or IT professionals" (Behrend et al., 2011). If the support staff (i.e., helpdesk and faculty) do not have the knowledge to support or use the cloud services effectively, then the students will not likely utilize the technology on their own, especially since students are normally only motivated to use technology that is directly tied to a grade in the course. Faculty buy-in through training and support is critical, and it holds the key to successful implementation of cloud technologies in the university (Behrend et al., 2011). For the IT staff, the institution needs to provide training and possibly implement a revised process of career development so the IT staff are better prepared to aid in the transition because "setting clear direction through training programs to encourage the development of solutions with cloud components will help" (Wheeler & Waggener, 2009). Even with the introduction of great technology, if the technology has low usage or implementation throughout the institution, it will lead to "financial losses and bad organizational culture" (Wu, Lan, & Lee, 2011).

Along with training students, faculty, and IT staff, it is necessary to be aware of the following challenges that will be faced by the IT staff (Goel et al., 2011):

■ Elasticity Complexity: Because cloud technology has scalability, the demands and needs for the services can switch from day to day, and it requires a highly skilled IT staff to work with the provider to develop and maintain such applications.
■ Technological Bottlenecks: The switch from in-house technology to cloud services will likely require learning how to manage the new data structure, file systems, and storage technology. This will take time and can even force the institution to completely redo how they handle and manipulate data, especially research data.
■ Serializability and Consistency: Because cloud services are available 24×7, and from different parts of the world, the IT staff will need to work with the cloud service vendors to make sure software applications updates and migrations will occur at an opportune time.

■ Monitoring, Analysis, and Building Trust: Due to the scale and importance of the applications running and the data being stored, constant monitoring of the cloud servers is required. Regular reporting after proper analysis will help to build the trust of the users in cloud systems.

Impact on the Students

A big factor in implementing cloud services is the end user (i.e., student) and if they will actually be able to use the services with confidence. If the students do not have the self-efficacy or belief that they possess the resources and skills needed to perform and succeed in a specific task (Bandura, 1977), the cloud service will fail no matter how great the features. Although most students probably have the technical ability to use the cloud services, a major component of self-efficacy is tied to the motivation and effort required to complete the task and maintain persistence when facing obstacles. If the institution does not support the students and the faculty with training on the services being offered, the technology will likely fail (Aharony, 2015). The flip side of this is if the student sees the value and convenience that the technology brings to help them complete their assignments, this will push forward the use of the cloud services. Students will be more "likely to find cloud computing easy to use, as well as being useful, if they believe that they are confident and have the capability of using it" (Bhatiasevi & Naglis, 2016).

Helping Students Convert to the Cloud

A unique challenge for higher education institutions when using cloud computing services is the broad range of technical skills of their faculty and students, which can number into the thousands. If faculty and staff are struggling to utilize cloud services, they can often reach out within their institution and get help from colleagues or take advantage of scheduled training programs. But for students, particularly online students who are often isolated and working on their own, help is not always as available at all or in a timely manner. While faculty have incentive to work through their problems because it is part of their job, a student's reaction might be to drop out or move to a different school.

A question that arises when working with student's self-efficacy is if the students are more concerned about their ability to use the technology or the usefulness of the technology. Based on previous research, it has been found that the ease-of-use perception was a much stronger predictor of adoption than the usefulness perception (Behrend et al., 2011). This research indicates that while students may acknowledge the utility of a tool, they still might lack the motivation to use it because of their need to "balance multiple roles, they lack advanced technology skills, or they may not wish to invest the time needed to learn a new tool even if it is a useful one."

"Even if the results are a benefit in the long term, they will abandon it if it requires too much effort to learn how to use the tool" (Behrend et al., 2011). With this in mind, the institution must come up with a plan and method to provide assistance to students in a timely manner to encourage the adoption of the cloud services.

While training in cloud computing services has the potential for improving the efficiency, cost, and convenience for higher education, it has some perceived limitations by students. The limitations are (Mathew, 2012):

1. Risk related to data protection and security and its integrity, and students might not want to use certain services because of this concern.
2. Lack of organizational support or training can also cause a student to lose interest in using the cloud services.
3. Lack of Internet access and slow speeds can impact a student's ability to effectively use the cloud services.

Even with the potential drawbacks, cloud services provide higher education institutions a clear path to achieve the 4A principle of Anyone, Anytime, Anyplace, & Anything (Chandra & Borah, 2012) for their students. With this philosophy in place, online students may have the most to gain from cloud computing initiatives (Behrend et al., 2011). Online students or students from remote locations no longer have to commute distances, and cloud services can help to meet these "students' needs by providing a common interface to a class or a school and by providing rich content that allows the students to engage in learning regardless of location" (Behrend et al., 2011). For on-campus students, cloud services can also provide value. For example, the ability for an on-campus student to complete a technology assignment outside the classroom using a virtual computer or a simulation may mean the difference between staying enrolled and dropping out (Sander, 2008). While cloud services have their drawbacks and concerns, the world of possibilities it opens to support students in different ways cannot be ignored, and higher education needs to continue to push toward greater adoption of cloud services.

Conclusion

While both business and higher education face limited budgets, higher education is also charged with trying to keep tuition down. Therefore, they are restricted by having to keep the money flowing in from tuition at an acceptable rate while simultaneously figuring out how to deal with shrinking budgets. As a result, they are getting squeezed from both ends. One area where institutions have been trying to save money is by offloading their IT infrastructure into the cloud computing realm and switching their mindset to seeing computer hardware as a service provided by vendors instead of inventory they have to purchase, maintain, and hire staff to support (Mircea & Andreescu, 2010).

The impact of cloud computing can be a great benefit for higher education institutions in terms of cost savings and the ability to provide useful services to students. Major benefits include (Mathew, 2012):

1. Accessing files and data from wherever there is an Internet connection
2. Creating a backup of your data through the use of syncing tools
3. Sharing content more easily by giving someone access to data based on their email; for a university this makes it easier to share information with others outside the universities system
4. 24×7 access to infrastructure and content – a prime example is students having access to the materials for a course through their LMS
5. A lessening of computer equipment being used which has a positive impact on the environment
6. Increased exposure of new IT technologies to students that will help them to gain real world experiences for future careers

These benefits from implementing cloud services are based on a service-oriented architecture (Alam, 2013) that works well in the tight budget times with its pay-as-you-go and pay-for-what-you-need cost structure. According to a survey conducted by Ed Tech Magazine (Daly, 2013), higher education institutions gave the following reasons for switching to cloud technology:

1. Increased efficiency (55%)
2. Improved employee mobility (49%)
3. Increased ability to innovate (32%)
4. Freed current IT staff for other projects (31%)
5. Reduced IT operating costs (25%)
6. Enabled the college to offer new products/services (24%)

An interesting side effect to switching to the cloud computing model is it also creates a sense of openness and sharing, which is often a benefit to higher education institution because it aligns with the ideal of these education systems being founded as a means for individuals to share research (Katz, Goldstein, & Yanosky, 2009) (https://link.springer.com/chapter/10.1007/978-3-642-15877-3_15).

References

Aharony, N. (2015). An exploratory study on factors affecting the adoption of cloud computing by informational professionals. *The Electronic Library, 33*(2), 308–323.

Alam, M. T. (2013, July 22). Cloud computing in education. *IEEE Potentials*, pp. 20–21.

Alamri, B. H., & Qureshi, M. J. (2015). Usability of cloud computing to improve higher education. *International Journal of Information Technology and Computer Science, 9*, 59–65.

Bandura, A. (1977). Self-efficiacy: Toward a unifying theory of behavioral change. *Psychological Review, 84*, 191–215.

Behrend, T. S., Wiebe, E. N., London, J. E., & Johnson, E. C. (2011). Cloud computing adoption and usage in community colleges. *Behaviour & Information Technology, 30*(2), 231–240.

Bhatiasevi, V., & Naglis, M. (2016). Investigating the structural relationship for the determinants of cloud computing adoption in education. *Education Information Technology, 21*, 1197–1223.

Chandra, D. G., & Borah, M. D. (2012, February 22). Cost benefit analysis of cloud computing in education. Retrieved from IEEE Xplore Digital Library, http://ieeexplore.ieee.org/document/6179142/.

Colman, E. (n.d.). What's the difference between SaaS, Paas, and Iaas? Retrieved from Computenext, https://www.computenext.com/blog/when-to-use-saas-paas-and-iaas/.

Daly, J. (2013, February 25). The state of cloud computing in higher education. Retrieved from EdTech, https://edtechmagazine.com/higher/article/2013/02/state-cloud-computing-higher-education.

Ercan, T. (2010). Effective use of cloud computing in educational institutions. *Procedia Social and Behavioral Sciences, 2*(2), 38–942.

Goel, S., Kiran, R., & Garg, D. (2011). Impact of cloud computing on ERP implementations in higher education. *International Journal of Advanced Computer Science and Applications, 2*(6), 142–145.

Jaeger, P. T., Lin, J., & Grimes, J. M. (2008). Cloud computing and information policy: Computing in a policy cloud? *Journal of Information Technology & Politics, 5*(3), 269–283.

Katz, R., Goldstein, P., & Yanosky, R. (2009, January 22). Cloud computing in higher education. Retrieved from EDUCAUSE, https://net.educause.edu/section_params/conf/CCW10/highered.pdf.

Masud, A. H., Huang, X., & Yong, J. (2012). Cloud computing for higher education: A roadmap. *IEEE 16th International Conference on Computer Supported Cooperative Work in Design*, China, May 23–25, pp. 552–557.

Mathew, S. (2012). Implementation of cloud computing in education—A revolution. *International Journal of Computer Theory and Engineering, 4*(3), 473–475.

Mircea, M., & Andreescu, A. I. (2011). Using cloud computing in higher education: A strategy to improve agility in the current financial crisis. Retrieved from Communications of the IBIMA, http://www.ibimapublishing.com/journals/CIBIMA/cibima.html.

Morrill, D. (2011, September 12). Cloud computing in education. Retrieved from Cloud Ave, https://www.cloudave.com/14857/cloud-computing-in-education/.

National Institute of Standards of Technlology. (2010, November 15). NIST cloud computing program. Retrieved from National Institute of Standards of Technlology, https://www.nist.gov/programs-projects/nist-cloud-computing-program-nccp.

Odeh, M., Warwick, K., & Garcia-Perez, A. (2015). The impacts of cloud computing adoption at higher education institutions: A SWOT analysis. *International Journal of Computer Applications, 127*(4), 15–21.

Sander, L. (2008). Rising cost of gasoline pinches students at rural community colleges. *Chronicle of Higher Education, 54*(41), 17–21.

Sultan, N. (2010). Cloud computing for education: A new dawn? *International Journal of Information Management, 30*, 109–116.

Tout, S., Sverdlik, W., & Lawyer, G. (2009, January). Cloud computing and its security in higher education. Retrieved from ResearchGate, https://www.researchgate.net/publication/255618308_Cloud_Computing_and_its_Security_in_Higher_Education.

Wheeler, B., & Waggener, S. (2009). Above-campus services: Shaping the promise of cloud computing for higher education. *Educause Review, 44*(6), 1–16.

Wu, W. -W., Lan, L. W., & Lee, Y. -T. (2011). Factors hindering acceptance of using cloud services in university: A case study. *The Electronic Library, 31*(1), 84–98.

Chapter 11

Cloud Use in Consulting Services

Austin McClelland
Accenture Federal Services

Tucker Hale
Accenture LLP

Contents

Introduction

Cloud computing can set a valuable short term and long-term relationship for consulting firms and their clients. As many companies migrate over to cloud environments, we see the need for experienced professionals to help strategize, plan, and assist in the migration or implementation of a cloud environment. This presents a unique opportunity for clients to utilize consulting firms, as these firms can bring in experienced and specialized teams for each phase of the implementation. Following an implementation, consulting firms can help clients by offering solutions to manage the environment and minimize down time, assist in scalability, and ensure that data is secure.

The Trusted Relationship

The fast-paced industry of consulting is predicated on cost-effective, quick-to-market, industry-leading solutions with the client's best interest in mind every step of the way. The client-consultant relationship is vital in driving corporations to new heights by identifying inefficiencies and establishing strategic processes improvements. Here, at the intersection of leading technology and cutting-edge solutions, cloud computing is shaping the way consultants deploy and the standards in which C-suite executives enhance their workforce.

According to the International Data Corporation (IDC), the cloud industry is estimated to grow to more than $140 billion in revenue by 2019. Of that $140 billion, a large portion of the market share is comprised of consulting solutions built on Platform-as-a-Service and Software as a Service providers including Microsoft, ServiceNow, Salesforce, and Amazon Web Services (AWS) (IDC, 2016). With an industry rapidly on the rise, the continuous building of client-consultant relationships is essential to develop sustainable solutions while increasing opportunities for future proposals in order to grasp a larger piece of the multi-billion dollar-pie known as "the cloud."

Roadmapping

The key to a successful cloud environment is proper planning. This is where having experienced professionals involved can have the biggest impact on a project's success and create long term savings for clients. Before any cloud instances are spun up, roadmapping allows the clients to map out the current environment or requirements. Cloud offers a high level of scalability at lower costs, but it's still important to be sure the instances you deploy will cover the bandwidth you need without spinning up too many servers and adding unneeded costs. Even though cloud is "usage-based," having dormant servers and instances that are not utilized efficiently adds unnecessary costs.

During roadmapping, priorities are established. Migrating systems can take manpower and overlapping server costs. Companies often find it useful to migrate different parts of their environment to the cloud in stages to minimize the costs. This staggered approach also puts less risk on a client. If any issues were to arise during the migration it would be important to minimize the data that is affected. If an issue arises during a migration of an entire environment, all the client's data can be at risk.

Another important decision that often is overlooked is what cloud provider should be used. While most 3rd party products can be integrated into a range of cloud solutions, some cannot. It's important to look at business critical applications to make sure that they are compatible with the cloud solution you are looking at.

Consultant/Client relationships should be looked at as a partnership. As a consulting firm becomes more familiar with an environment they are able to make better recommendations. Having a good working relationship means clients get better tailored solutions and are made aware of technology changes that might affect them or improve how they do business.

Performance Benefits

Delivery to customers and clients is at the forefront of all business transactions. The best way to meet service standards and client expectations is through efficient business processes along with the support of innovative technology. Whether your business is operating locally or deploying overseas, cloud solutions offer a wide range of benefits enabling businesses to outperform their competitors.

Cloud brings many tangible benefits to an organization outside of scalability, such as usability, mobility, and accessibility. Each of these domains will look different based your organization, and consultants can use the roadmapping and requirements gathering to be sure that the cloud solution brings additional business value outside of data storage. Although all technological solutions present different challenges, cloud provides performance benefits to a workforce that cannot be ignored.

Usability measures the effectiveness, efficiency, and satisfaction of a product. Generally speaking, cloud applications are designed to mimic current systems in order to meet these standards along with streamlining the ease of use for customers. For consulting groups looking to implement new systems, cloud is at the forefront of request for proposal responses due to its flexibility. Enterprises have to adapt to changing business conditions, and cloud solutions offer the flexibility and speed to deliver as a critical component and selling feature in order to meet these changing environments. Other features that make cloud solutions enticing to prospective clients are the ability to offload system maintenance requirements. On premise solutions are expensive and often require around the clock surveillance and oversight. Additionally, any maintenance to equipment falls at the liability of the firm. Cloud computing allows for consulting agencies to save money for their clients by outsourcing and offloading these costs to a third-party service provider. In relation to this, an additional usability performance benefit includes the increased storage that correlates to cloud computing. Today, cloud providers such as AWS, Microsoft, ServiceNow, and others offer considerable amounts of infrastructure to clients for storage and data traffic. With workload volume spikes imminent in today's unpredictable landscape, the cloud offers the ability to scale dynamically, effectively, and efficiently.

Usability is the idea that the environment is going to be available to employees 99.999% of the time, and that it will help them perform their jobs more efficiently. Cloud allows data to be stored virtually, so it's not in a single location. In traditional IT infrastructure, the data is stored on a physical machine that may be manually configured, have high costs to provision, and be susceptible to problems such as power outages. With a cloud environment this data is stored in multiple locations so that it is always recoverable. Consultants can make the process easier when deciding how the data is stored and for creating disaster recovery plans in case something in the environment stops working, or a breach of the environment were to occur.

In addition to data being stored in multiple locations, users of a cloud environment can access their data from multiple locations. Rather than needing to be connected to a local network, users can access and collaborate on documents from anywhere. Consultants can help ensure that the proper checks are in place so that documents can be collaborated on by the right people no matter where they are physically located. Solution providers like Google and Microsoft have various applications and platforms that allow multiple users to make edits and changes to a document simultaneously. This can speed up project delivery and bring a higher level of efficiency to a team's deliverables. With that said, goals need to be met, which is where consultants can be useful in making informed decisions on which platform is best for your environment. There are different considerations that need to be weighed for your platform, such as the security of the product, how it integrates into the products you already have, and how much it will cost to implement.

Other performance benefits to offering cloud solutions fall under the adoption of a mobile workforce. The scale at which businesses conduct operations is expanding across new international boarders every day. An increased market size stresses the demand for expanded access to centrally located data. Non-cloud solutions minimize a workforce's ability to access internal networks across the globe. This feature of enhanced mobility is a key component for clients to transition to cloud computing. Cloud solutions like Google Drive, Dropbox, and SharePoint allow for international teams to store, share, and access documentation from any connected device. Consulting companies leverage these same principals as their transient workforce serves various clients across multiple intersections of the world.

These mobile benefits also shed light on related performance advantages, including accessibility. As corporations aim toward the standards of increased mobility, cloud offers consultants and their clients' accessibility into document sharing for increased collaboration. Having the ability to enable multiple users to work on documentation shared on the Cloud allows for real-time edits, increased collaboration, and reduced wait times. Cloud solutions have already been adopted by many consulting firms and their clients around the world, while the aforementioned performance benefits only add to its credibility and users' competitive advantage.

Accessibility across applications makes users life easier and more efficient. Enterprise Sign-On is the idea that users only need to login with their credentials and password once, rather than for each application they are using. Users don't need to enter credentials for email, then again for documents they are accessing. This not only makes life easier for employees, but can also improve a company's security posture. Rather than having multiple passwords to remember, and potentially write down, the users have the one password to keep track of. When implemented correctly security increases, but when done incorrectly it can pose an additional risk. If a hacker were to figure out a user's password they now can access all the files and applications that the user has access to. This is where consultants can help ensure that accessibility is optimal, without sacrificing your company's security. They may look for highly confidential file groups or people with administrative rights so that additional login steps and identity verification are added, and hackers aren't able to breach the organization.

Security Considerations

All data is not the same. Consultants can help clients decide the type of protection they need, and how to divide data into separate cloud instances to make sure their data is secure. Each company's data and environment are unique, so each security solution should be unique as well.

Traditionally, many companies had "hybrid" solutions where some data was hosted in the cloud, while other data used traditional IT infrastructure. The reason for this was due to governance, or who controls the data. Once data was in the cloud there was a gap between who owned the data and the security of it. Today, a new type of "hybrid" solution exists to minimize this by hosting data in public and private clouds. Public clouds are those solutions we come across most frequently in our daily life, like Google Drive or Dropbox. Then private clouds are those that are used only by a specific organization. Many cloud providers are able to provide both types of cloud. AWS, for example, is the largest cloud provider and has public and private cloud available.

In addition to what type of cloud, it's important to consider where the data for the cloud is being hosted. This is especially important for companies with a global presence. Different countries have different laws and regulations for how data is handled and stored. Germany has some of the strictest data privacy laws, and is often cited as a prime example in discussions for where users and their data will be located. Some cloud solutions, such as Microsoft's Azure, have an entirely separate solution for these territories complete with local data centers, residency, and different administrative credentials so that users are sure they don't accidently become non-compliant with German laws. These rules can be complicated, and vary heavily by region, so experienced consultants can help their clients navigate these rules and regulations so they can be sure they are working within the law.

Financial Benefits

The bottom line is the most important discussion for any business transaction, most notably in response to a business proposal. With consulting agencies routinely searching for products that meet client requirements and expectations, cloud solutions are at the forefront of cost saving implementations. Factors including speed to market, agile development, and scalability have provided consulting firms the ability to shorten timelines, ultimately cutting cost, to their respective clients. But implementation and deployment efficiency are not the only cost savers for cloud solutions; hardware and storage costs are where clients make up the majority of overhead savings through cloud solutions. AWS offers the ability to auto-calculate your potential cost savings through their case study tool. In the following diagram, companies switching business operations from a traditional data server to AWS save an average monthly cost of more than $35,000. The majority of those cost reductions come in the form of reducing a company's spend in server hardware and data center overhead.

Amazon Web Services Calculator

https://aws.amazon.com/tco-calculator/

By moving from on premise to the Cloud, businesses can not only operate more efficiently, collaboratively, and globally, but they can reduce a significant portion of overhead costs by shifting key responsibilities and maintenance to a third party. These significant cost savers, along with the aforementioned performance and security benefits have altered the way consulting firms operate internally in addition to the proposals they offer respective clients.

References

4 Problems with Traditional Methods of Data Storage. (2016, July 18).Retrieved June 02, 2017, from https://www.zadarastorage.com/blog/industry-insights/4-problems-traditional-methods-data-storage/.

AWS Total Cost of Ownership Calculator. (n.d.). Retrieved June 02, 2017, from https://aws.amazon.com/tco-calculator/.

Bertholon, B., Varrette, S., & Bouvry, P. (2011). Certicloud: A Novel TPM-Based Approach to Ensure Cloud IaaS Security. *2011 IEEE 4th International Conference on Cloud Computing*. IEEE.

Eijkenboom, P. (2017, June 02). Creating a Governance Framework for Cloud Security. Retrieved June 02, 2017, from https://www.cso.com.au/article/408853/creating_governance_framework_cloud_security/.

International Data Corporation. (2016, January 21). Worldwide Public Cloud Services Spending Forecast to Double by 2019, According to IDC [Press release]. Retrieved from https://www.idc.com/getdoc.jsp?containerId=prUS40960516.

Joe Panettieri. (2017, February 09). Cloud Market Share 2017: Amazon AWS, Microsoft Azure, IBM, Google. Retrieved June 02, 2017, from https://www.channele2e.com/2017/02/09/cloud-market-share-2017-amazon-microsoft-ibm-google/.

Microsoft Azure Germany. (n.d.). Retrieved June 02, 2017, from https://azure.microsoft.com/en-us/overview/clouds/germany/.

What is Cloud Security?—Amazon Web Services (AWS). (n.d.). Retrieved June 02, 2017, from https://aws.amazon.com/security/introduction-to-cloud-security/.

Chapter 12

Publishing
The Case for the Cloud in Publishing

Eric Germann

Contents

As an Information Technology decision maker, it's difficult to avoid the hype surrounding "moving to the cloud." This chapter will provide a brief recap of how cloud technologies have evolved and why they may make sense in some or all aspects of a business model.

A Brief History of Virtualization

The enabling force for cloud technologies is virtualization, initially patented by VMware in 1998 (Devine et. al, 2002) Prior to VMWare, virtualization existed on mainframe class machines, but its introduction brought it to standard server class machines. The first open-source virtualization platform, Xen, was introduced in 2003 (Knuth, 2007). Since that time, other platforms have been introduced, such as KVM.

Virtualization allows multiple "virtual" machines to run on one physical machine under the supervision of a hypervisor. A virtual machine is a completely self-contained installation of an operating system (the "guest OS") with resources such as the number of Central Processing Units (CPUs), memory and disk allocated to it by the hypervisor. The hypervisor marshals the guest onto the processor when it is time to run, emulates memory and network interfaces and provides a network connection function to connect the guest OS to resources outside the physical server. It also provides disk services to the guest OS, either through physical disks or via connections to storage systems such as Network File System storage or Storage Area Network (SAN) devices.

Virtualization has had a dramatic impact on corporate data center architectures in the past decade. Gone are the days or multiple models of tower servers lined up or rack mounted servers dedicated to a specific function. With virtualization, IT professionals have gained flexibility in deploying guest OSs. When a new "server" (a guest OS implementation) is needed for a specific purpose, it can be installed and spun up with relative ease, once all the virtualization components are in place.

However, on-site virtualization does have its limits. First, there is an initial planning stage. How many virtual machines (VM's) are going to run on the server? What are the storage requirements for those VM's? Do the intended applications require redundancy? Does that redundancy need to be manual or automatic? To what degree is redundancy required (hypervisor host, network, storage, etc.)?

After estimating all the requirements, specifications for quotes are then drawn up for purchasing. A typical redundant implementation with SAN storage, blade servers and software costs factored in can easily exceed $100K, a formidable capital hurdle for smaller businesses or startups. This also only accounts for redundancy in the server infrastructure, not Internet connectivity.

Another factor many don't consider when moving to virtualization in smaller businesses is the server environment. The server equipment requires considerable cooling. Uninterruptible Power supplies (UPSs) are required for sustaining uptime during brief power failures. If sustained runtime is needed, either significant UPS investments are required or a generator is needed. Operationally, offsite storage of backups become critical as many data assets are concentrated on a dense infrastructure.

Evolution to the Cloud

To overcome some of the limits of on-site data centers, organizations began collocating their virtualized data centers to service provider data centers ("colo facility"). By leasing a cage at a colo facility, the site operational burden for cooling, power backup and Internet connectivity was transferred to the colo provider. IT professionals then had to develop new processes to manage what, in effect, were remote data centers. This required either proximity to the data center for staff access or utilization of data center staff to provide a "remote hands" function under the guidance of the organization. In this model, increased bandwidth may be required between the site and the colo facility.

From a budgetary perspective, this required both an initial capital outlay for the virtualization equipment and monthly operating expenses for the lease on the colo facility. There also may be variable costs associated with use of colo staff for operational processes.

For organizations that did not wish to or did not have the resources for the initial capital outlay, data center providers started providing the virtualization hardware themselves. For a monthly fee, the service provider would handle all the capital outlay, hardware upgrades, software upgrades, storage, backup, connectivity, cooling and power requirements. This was the genesis of "the cloud."

Launch of the Public Cloud

Arguably, the beginning of public cloud services began on March 14, 2006 (Hamilton, 2016) with the launch of Amazon Web Services (AWS) Simple Storage Service (S3). Technically, the original service on AWS to launch was their Simple Queue Service in November 2004, but S3 was the primary event that drove people to consider what has become known as Infrastructure-as-a-Service. Since that time, AWS has evolved to over 70 services available globally. Other significant cloud providers at the time of this writing are Microsoft Azure, Google Cloud Platform and IBM Cloud. In early 2017, it was estimated that AWS had 40% of the market share, Microsoft/Google/IBM had 25% of the market and the remainder composed of niche players (Panettieri, 2017). The key innovation AWS delivered to the marketplace and that the others have emulated is a "pay-as-you-go" model. There are no capital outlays upfront and billing is based on utilization over time.

We'll now focus on the value proposition to businesses and startups of using public cloud services.

The Cloud Model

All the major cloud providers offer substantial benefits to organizations, both established and startups. Primary benefits are:

- À la carte services – Virtual machines can be started and stopped as needed. When changed, the pricing changes. Storage can be allocated on an as needed basis and paid for based on usage. Internet bandwidth is based on consumption, not fixed costs for lines to a facility.
- Elasticity – The sizing of the machines can be adjusted as needed as requirements change. Storage can be adjusted up or down as needed. Some providers offer multiple types of storage for different storage requirements. No longer does the business face the prospect of having to upgrade a shelf or disk unit in a SAN or server. Internet bandwidth in and out of the data center is virtually unlimited on the major cloud offerings. This burst capability is very appealing for unpredictable traffic patterns.
- Redundancy – The cloud providers provide redundancy within a regional offering and sometimes across regions. Multiple data centers in a region allow an architect to build redundant architectures leveraging the à la carte nature and elasticity of the underlying services.
- Geographic Diversity – Many of the cloud providers provide geographic diversity on an à la carte basis. For example, at the time of this writing AWS has 16 regions spread around the world. For organizations that wish to operate globally, this offers the ability to host content close to the consumer/user. As data privacy law evolves in various countries, this also allows the organization to maintain storage compliance for the area they are operating in.
- Cost Containment/Allocation – As resources are allocated in the Cloud, they can be segmented in such a way that the costs can be directly allocated to various lines of business. This offers a new level of transparency where lines of business within an organization have greater visibility into the cost of their offerings.
- Avoided Capital Costs – Since the model is consumption based and driven by need, there is no initial allocation of capital required. Also, because an asset is not being acquired, there is no depreciation on the assets associated with the service rollout. All costs become either an Operating Expense or a Cost of Goods Sold, depending on the business model of the organization.
- Avoided Operational Costs – Organizations can focus or refocus their efforts and human capital costs on developing the applications vs. operation of data center facilities. Developers have much more granular control of the infrastructure and costs associated with it.
- Ability to Innovate or "Fail Fast" – One of the key hindrances to many organizations is inability to innovate because of resource constraints in their existing IT infrastructure. Cloud providers offer the ability to test innovative

ideas with a relatively low-cost footprint and "Fail Fast" in proof of concept. Developers can literally provision a global test environment in minutes, test their application and turn it off or terminate it and only pay for the runtime and resources used. This encourages innovation within the organization and the ability for management to quickly evaluate whether to move to the next stage with a proposed project.

Getting to the Cloud

Organizations that have legacy server operations (i.e., are not a pure cloud play/ startup) generally follow a three-phase process in migrating to the cloud. These phases are:

1. Lift and Shift
2. Partial Optimization for the selected cloud provider
3. Fully Optimized for the selected cloud provider

Phase 1 – Lift and Shift

In this phase, the organization is not concerned with optimizing for the cloud provider chosen. In essence, they're treating the cloud provider as a traditional colo data center and simply building servers that mimic their on premise footprint. Production applications are installed on the built servers and data is then migrated in some fashion from the on-premise servers to the cloud servers.

This is usually the least cost-effective phase in the transition, as generally the staff is new to the selected cloud platform. This can lead to oversizing of servers and disks, but also provides the least risk for the organization. Other than being remote to the organization, the deployed applications "look" and are managed at the server level identically to their on-premise counterparts. This phase typically requires significant bandwidth, both to migrate and to operate the applications. Migrations of the data usually requires some blackout period in which the on-premise applications are unavailable so the data can be synchronized to the cloud servers.

Phase 1 is also the lowest risk phase. Since the cloud provider is treated as simply a colo facility, the organization is not inherently dependent on any one particular feature of that provider. If sufficient testing is done ahead of time, the project can be abandoned at any point up to migration if expected performance is not achieved.

While Phase 1 is lowest risk, when selecting a cloud provider it is important to plan for the end goal. Is your plan to stop at Phase 1 or follow through to Phase 3? If the former, a cloud provider can be selected based simply on cost. If the latter, much more careful selection needs to be done as the ability to migrate between cloud providers becomes much more difficult in Phases 2 and 3.

Phase 2 – Partial Optimization

After the frenzy of the initial migration, many organizations begin partial optimizations based around the cloud provider they have selected. In this phase, analytics may be used to optimize costs for storage and virtual machine sizing. It is very common in Phase 1 to oversize the selected servers in terms of memory and/or CPU. In this phase, when the applications have been running for a period of time, detailed data is available which allows more precise sizing decisions to be made. This can lead to significant cost savings if the servers were overprovisioned. Conversely, if the Phase 1 deployment was very conservative in sizing, bottlenecks may be exposed which can be remediated through proper sizing.

This phase is a good point to start rethinking some business processes. For example, an organization may have backed up their database by simply dumping it to disk on attached block storage. Once inside a cloud provider, it may be beneficial to consider moving those backups to object storage such as AWS S3 or Google Cloud Platform (GCP) Cloud Storage. For disaster recovery, this can even be done to another region, across the country or globe (subject to data privacy laws). Many of the providers offer tiered storage levels with different access times and associated costs. For example, database backups could be moved to AWS S3 on a daily basis with weekly, monthly and yearly backups automatically moved to AWS Glacier, a storage service similar to S3, but with longer access times for object retrieval and associated lower costs.

At this point, many organizations start moving to a DevOps mode of operation vs. a Systems Engineer mode. Automation can slowly be introduced and more insight can be gained from the analytics associated with the cloud platform. This provides keen insight for developers within the organization to move to Phase 3.

Phase 3 – Full Optimization

At this point, the organization is fully committed to their selected cloud provider. The transition from Phase 2 to Phase 3 typically involves a complete refactoring of the code involved. Developers will typically leverage all the services they can from the selected provider to provide the best end-user experience.

This mode is typically the leanest mode of operation. Costs are minimized by leveraging the complete suite of services within the provider, primarily elasticity. Infrastructure will auto-scale up and down based on load.

There are several drawbacks to Phase 3 however. They include:

■ Significant development costs to refactor code to leverage all services that are applicable.
■ Cloud provider lock-in.

At this point, it is very difficult to extract the organization from a particular cloud provider without performing another refactoring. While most of the services provided by the cloud provider are available through some open source or commercial product, moving out of the provider requires porting the application to the replacement services. If the goal of the organization is Phase 3, a careful analysis of cloud provider services is required up front in conjunction with the development assets available. If those development assets do not have the requisite skills, time and training need to be added to the budget for developing those skillsets.

Future Directions

While cloud providers have revolutionized development and deployment of applications, they continue to innovate. The current trend is to move towards containerization, which is an example of "application virtualization." (Docker, 2017) is one of the most popular container platforms and most of the cloud providers support Docker for application deployment.

In application virtualization, the entire operating system is not virtualized. Only the application, supporting libraries and data are virtualized and are run in a standardized environment. That environment provides scheduling, network and other resources.

The primary advantage of containerization is an entire operating system installation and associated licensing costs are avoided. The image that is deployed is fully self-contained ensuring that any dependencies used during development are carried forward to deployment. Multiple copies can be deployed across multiple hosts for increased redundancy. Since the entire operating system is not included in the container, the runtime footprint is significantly less. This allows for much higher densities of containers on a given host and better utilization of those hosts, leading to reduced costs. Finally, the application can be built and tested locally and then deployed in the local datacenter or deployed to a cloud provider without recompilation or bundling.

Multi-cloud strategies are also being considered for adoption. In this scenario, an organization builds in multiple cloud providers for either redundancy or feature purposes. This allows the organization to leverage the features unique to each cloud provider. If the unique offerings of a provider are avoided, this can avoid vendor lock in. If the unique offerings are leveraged, very powerful, if not complex, architectures can be built.

Cloud providers continue to look for opportunities to innovate. As new technologies are introduced cloud providers provide an excellent platform in which to try new services with low overhead and cost.

References

Devine, S. W., Bugnion, E., & Rosenblum, M. (2002). U.S. Patent No. 6,397,242. Washington, DC: U.S. Patent and Trademark Office.

Docker Inc.; Docker (2017).

Hamilton, J. (2016, March). A decade of innovation. Retrieved from Perspectives: http://perspectives.mvdirona.com/2016/03/a-decade-of-innovation/.

Knuth, G. (2007, August 16). A brief history of Xen and XenSource. Retrieved January 18, 2018, from http://www.brianmadden.com/opinion/A-brief-history-of-Xen-and-XenSource.

Panettieri Feb 9, 2017, J. (2017, February 09). Cloud Market Share 2017: Amazon AWS, Microsoft Azure, IBM, Google. Retrieved from https://www.channele2e.com/channel-partners/csps/cloud-market-share-2017-amazon-microsoft-ibm-google

Chapter 13

Telecommunications
A Race for Survival: Cloud in the Mobile Carrier Industry

Cheer Dheeradhada
Telecom Peers, Inc.

Contents

There is a formidable cloud looming over the U.S. mobile carrier industry. This dark ominous cloud of uncertainties is fueled mainly by a perpetual cyclone of competitive price war, hovering mists of unsustainable legacy infrastructure, and thunderous future demand trends unsupportable by today's technologies and standards. The existing telecommunications networks are bursting at the seams with exponential growth of digital data largely because the piping and moving, as well as handling of voices, videos, texts, and images have become commoditized with ever-increasing downward cost pressure. All signs points to a congested, uncertain time ahead—a crowded, cloudy future world for the wireless telecommunications industry.

The good news is that another rescuing cloud is forming, providing a potential way out for the telecommunications industry. However, not all U. S. mobile carriers are ready to accept this path. Selected few have enough resources and strategic urgency to embrace this new set of "cloud" and complementary technologies custom-built for the carrier industry. Others have to take a wait-and-see approach hoping to ride out the desolate storm of telecommunications battlefields ahead.

Alice and Bob: The Future of Smart Devices and Environment

It's 6:00 a.m. Bob's cloud-based intelligent personal assistant (IPA) named Alice sends a "Wake Bob" command to his bed. Bob's side of the bed starts to vibrate gently while his "smart" ergonomic pillow plays a soft orchestral Vivaldi Morning song. Accustomed to the routine, Bob wakes up, gets out of bed, and begins his day.

Just like any other day, Alice lights up each part of the house used by Bob in anticipation of his morning movements. She knows when and how to adjust the room ambient temperature, to adjust settings on his workout equipment, and to start the coffee machine in the kitchen.

Preprogrammed with Bob's healthcare provider virtual service, Alice constantly monitors his pulse, temperature, blood pressure, and respiratory rate via signals from his "smart" shirt. As always, she has already sent a command to adjust the dosage for his blood pressure medication dispenser based on Bob's historical and current medical readings. Alice has access to the cloud medical system of Bob's primary physician to exchange relevant medical information. This includes providing real-time health information, communicating concerns, receiving advice, and making medical appointments.

Alice is a secure cloud-based IPA accustomed to multitasking and analyzing massive amount of real-time information. She constantly monitors and reacts appropriately to detectors and sensors programmed by cloud service professionals and customized by Bob. With a virtual medical subscription service, Alice keeps track of calorie consumption, exercise routine, and medical status. For the virtual home automation service, Alice monitors security, energy usage, and Internet-enabled appliances. At work, she constantly assists Bob by tracking, analyzing, and prioritizing incoming communications, news of interest, personnel resource utilization, and strategic analytic data.

After sending a command to start Bob's self-driving car, Alice opens the car door to let Bob in and securely sync up with his car. She then connects to the car speakers reminding him of all his appointments for the day. Bob discusses the agenda and talking points of each meeting with her. He then dictates the answers to all the off-hours emails and messages received.

Arriving early, Alice asks if Bob would like her to take the car to the nearest gas station. The car is now less than a quarter tank full. "The one on Central and Washington?" Bob asks. "Yes, I'll take the car to Uncle Sam's," Alice replies with confidence even though there is another gas station right across from Uncle Sam's. Bob has mentioned to her before that he prefers Uncle Sam's gas to those of others. "We should be able to avoid the traffic and be back before the parking lot gets too full," Alice offers her analysis. "Thank you, Alice. I'll talk to you again when I get to my office," Bob ends the conversation with her knowing that by the time he gets to his office on the 77th floor, Alice would have already taken his car to the gas station, started the coffee machine in his office, and prepared the conference room for his first meeting.

The Alice technological ecosystem may seem farfetched but will one day become an everyday reality driven by continuing advancement in the Internet of Things (IoT) and its supporting and complementing technologies: radio frequency identification, embedded sensors, global positioning system based service, wireless, cloud computing, virtualization, big data, cyber physical systems, and machine learning. Component parts of this future are happening now: personal digital assistants (Sarikaya, 2017), smart home automation (Yadav, Borate, Devar, Gaikwad, & Gavali, 2017), IoT smart healthcare system (Vuha, Rajani, & Vineeth, 2017), cloud enterprise resource planning (Thangavel & Sudhaman, 2017), and ambient intelligence (Risteska, Trivodaliev, & Davcev, 2017).

The IoT: Connecting Anything, Anywhere, Anytime

The IoT is a foundational paradigm shift with potential to revolutionize health care, manufacturing, agriculture, transportation, military, education, government, and consumer products/services (Geng, 2017; Nguyen & Simkin, 2017; Saha, Mandal, & Sinha, 2017; Yeo, Chian, & Ng, 2014). The International Telecommunication Union (ITU) Telecommunication Standardization Sector (ITU-T), the standardization arm of the ITU, has defined IoT as "a global infrastructure for the information society, enabling advanced services by interconnecting (physical and virtual) things based on existing and evolving interoperable information and communication technologies" (p. 1). IoT provides the means to sense, monitor, manage, and control smart interconnected devices (Amadeo et al., 2016; Gubbi, Buyya, Marusic, & Palaniswami, 2013; Zhu, Wang, Chen, Liu, & Qin, 2010). In our futuristic example, IoT allows Alice to communicate, exchange, and control other devices from a coffee maker to self-driving car, to an enterprise resource system.

Cloud Computing

One factor underpinning the rapid development and adoption of IoT is cloud computing which has significantly driven down the operational and maintenance cost to transport, process, and store information (Brumec & Vrček, 2013). The National Institute of Standards and Technology defines cloud computing as "a model for enabling ubiquitous, convenient, on-demand network access to a shared pool of configurable computing resources (e.g., networks, servers, storage, applications, and services) that can be rapidly provisioned and released with minimal management effort or service provider interaction" (Mell & Grance, 2011, p. 2).

Cloud computing allows various users access to shared scalable networked computing resources. These resources include software applications, networking infrastructure, available computing capability, and data storage. The key complementary technology to cloud computing is virtualization. Virtualization is defined as a "framework or methodology of dividing the resources of a computer into multiple execution environments, by applying one or more concepts or technologies such as hardware and software partitioning, time-sharing, partial or complete machine simulation, emulation, quality of service, and many others" (Zamani, Akhtar, & Ahmad, 2011, p. 305). Users in separate geographical environments can share both physical and logical network resources in an aggregate on-demand manner. Virtualization is realized by virtual machine (VM), a networked collections of computing capabilities that emulate behavioral functions of a system. VMs are created, managed, and controlled by a hypervisor or virtual machine monitor. The ultimate goal of cloud computing and virtualization is to optimize and economize resource usage. This is analogous to building a public swimming pool serving many families instead of building a private swimming pool occasionally used by a single family. Both Forrester and IDC research firms predicted a rapid growth in cloud developments and deployments (Mohan, Yezhkova, Scaramella, & DuBois, 2016; Ried, Kisker, Matzke, Bartels, & Lisserman, 2011).

The U.S. Mobile Carrier Industry and the Race for Survival

Competition, regulations, and escalating customer demands often hastened the demands for cost-effective technological evolution (Awadalla, 2017; Pfeffermann, 2017; Shakya, Tehranipoor, Bhunia, & Forte, 2017; Zehavi & Breznitz, 2017). Strategy Analytics reported that the U.S. wireless market will reach 128% market penetration by the year 2020 (De Grimaldo, 2015). With a fiercely competitive and saturated market, the future success of the industry rests on customized targeted contents, bundled value-added services, and ubiquitous IoT support.

By the year 2020, 50 billion devices will be connected (Murray, 2016). With this IoT trend, the U.S. mobile carrier industry has to strategically position itself to effectively and efficiently market and support the ever increasing and accelerating demands for bandwidth, expansion of connected devices, intensive computing consumptions, and automated service lifecycle (Cisco Systems, 2015, 2016). In the mobile world, AT&T noted a 100,000% increase in traffic from 2007 to 2014 (AT&T, 2014). 4G traffic (which will represent 79% of all traffic by 2021) equates to 4 folds increase in processed data compared to 3G (Cisco Systems, 2017).

The legacy telecommunications infrastructure model where hardware network components and software functionalities are deeply interwoven requiring piecemeal developments, maintenance, and lifecycle management is no longer sustainable. These interwoven highly specialized networked systems translate to limitations and delay in time to market for new products and services as well as high operating costs. The survival of the U.S. mobile carrier industry now rests on the success and integration of three key technological concepts: Network Functions Virtualization (NFV), Software Defined Networking (SDN), and big data. Some carriers took a wait and see approach while others dived right into be innovators and early adopters hoping that their investment would put them ahead of the pack to support future mobile technology trends.

Network Functions Virtualization (NFV)

NFV enables telecommunications service providers to virtualize network functions through commercial off-the-shelf hardware. Virtualization technology is used in NFV to separate functionalities from physical location (Chiosi et al., 2012), which in turn provides a more agile, adaptive, and cost-effective network infrastructure compared to a traditional vendor centric hardware-software network model (Han, Gopalakrishnan, Ji, & Lee, 2015). Instead of using specialized hardware and software combinations, network operators can separate out the functions of the hardware and virtualize the functions across groups of off-the-shelf high availability servers in the Cloud. These software replicas of hardware-based network elements are called virtualized network function (VNF). NFV not only equates to lower development and maintenance cost (capital and operating expenditure), but also provides the means to decrease time to market for new products and services (Zhang & Banerjee, 2017).

Software Defined Networking

Offering complementary capabilities to NFV, the SDN is used to dynamically provision, manage, and control network functions and services by separating the control plane from the data plane. The control plan refers to the protocols, policies, functions, and capabilities that determines how to route network data. The data plane (also known as the forwarding plane) refers to the hardware and basic capabilities used to modify, remove, and forward data based on the instructions from the control plane. The control plane plans and instructs the data plane. The data plane executes the planned routes in order to get data to the destination. The separation of the hardware and basic functionalities from their programmable controls encourages rapid development and centralized management.

Big Data

Two NASA researchers Michael Cox and David Ellsworth coined the term "Big Data" to represent challenging datasets that were too large to process effectively due to computing resource limitations (1997, p. 236). By 2011, the term big data evolved and matured to refer to "a new generation of technologies and architectures, designed to economically extract value from very large volumes of a wide variety of data, by enabling high-velocity capture, discovery, and/or analysis" (Gantz & Reinsel, 2011, p. 6). For the carrier industry, big data complements NVF and SDN to provide for real-time, autonomic, and adaptable network management (Omnes, Bouillon, Fromentoux, & Le Grand, 2015; Yang Y., Cheng, Yang C., Chen, & Jian, 2015).

Lessons from History: Symbian and Android

Symbian is a smartphone operating system built to provide personal digital assistant functionalities while optimizing hardware resource consumption and power requirements.

Ahead of its time, Symbian was developed by Nokia, Ericsson, Motorola, and Psio through a formation of Symbian, Ltd. in 1998 (West & Mace, 2010). Via a licensing model, Symbian was meant to create a mobile operating system that set standard for the rest of the industry. By mid-2007, Nokia had 50% market share with Symbian operating on 65% of all smartphones. To combat the rising tide of Apple iOS and Android, in 2008 Nokia took control of Symbian and released its source codes to the open source community with the goal of propelling the platform forward (Best, 2013). However, Symbian steadily lost its market share due to its legacy codes, proprietary history, and lack of adequate third-party application support systems (Blankenhorn, 2010; Best, 2013). Nokia abandoned Symbian in 2011 for Windows Phone. By the end of 2016, Apple iOS and Google Android totally dominated the smartphone industry with a combined market share of 99.6% (Goasduff & Forni, 2017a). Symbian has now faded into obscurity with less than 1% market share (netmarketshare, 2017).

Compared to Symbian, Android has the necessary foundational architecture, complementary support systems, and widespread adoption suited for the mobile Internet era. Google open sourced Android operating system and launched the Open Handset Alliance with 34 other established founding members in 2007. When Android entered the commercial market in 2008 with 5% market share, Symbian was the dominant player in the smartphone OS ecosystem with 52% market share (Meulen & Petty, 2008). However, Android's global market share steadily climbed to reach 82% in 2016 (Goasduff & Forni, 2017b). The rise of Android has been fueled by its cloud computing capabilities and rapidly evolved ecosystem of complementary hardware, software, and community support (Kenney & Pon, 2011).

The Tale of Two Strategies: AT&T vs. Verizon

In the United States, AT&T and Verizon have been the most vocal proponents and early adopters of NFV and SDN (Meyer, 2016a) in order to reap first mover advantages (FMAs). For telecommunications service providers, FMAs refer to differentiated benefits resulting from innovation, pioneering technology, or market entrance (Bijwaard, Janssen, & Maasland, 2008; Jakopin & Klein, 2012; Muck, 2012).

AT&T's vision is to transform 75% of its network functions to the AT&T Integrated Cloud (AIC) network by the year 2020 (Donavan, 2015). To manage SDN, AT&T's Enhanced Control, Orchestration, Management and Policy (ECOMP) platform is used as an automated command center to create, monitor, analyze, and run all the VNFs inside the AIC network (AT&T, Inc., 2016). To AT&T, ECOMP is the operating system for SDN around which vendors can build applications (Rice, 2017).

After more than 2 years of development, testing, and deployment, AT&T announced the release of ECOMP to the Linux Foundation (Rice, 2017). This open innovation strategy is meant to propel the ECOMP platform to the next level by leveraging talents outside of AT&T. With ongoing engagement in ECOMP open source development, AT&T hopes that ECOMP will become the go-to operating system of the virtualized telecommunications network. To meet its aggressive 75% virtualized goal by 2020, AT&T is willing to collaborate with external talents, including those of competitors, to enhance and enrich its own knowledge while influencing the standards crucial to its operations. Earlier this year, the Linux Foundation announced the merger of the ECOMP project and its existing Open Orchestrator Project to create a new Open Network Automation Platform Project (Burns, 2017).

Verizon, on the other hand, is focusing its effort on its Enterprise Solution and support for future 5G Network (Meyer, 2016b). In collaboration with Cisco, Ericsson, HPE, Intel, Nokia, Red Hat, and Samsung, Verizon developed an NFV-SDN foundation architecture document (Verizon, 2016). Ericsson was selected in early 2017 to provide cloud-based NFV-SDN solutions for its flagship virtualized global Managed Network Services offerings (Ericsson, 2017). By partnering with telecommunications vendors, Verizon can ensure a gradual, measured path to technological maturity and foster widespread adoptions of complementary and supporting products.

In the world of telecommunication infrastructure, history has shown that standards driven by industries consortium are more crucial to widespread adoption than market force (Funk, 2002). In the mid-1990s, both Verizon and Sprint selected Code-division multiple access (CDMA) as its radio communication technologies to adopt in order to migrate away from their legacy analog technology. Pioneered by Qualcomm, CDMA (at the time of adoption by Verizon and Sprint) was a newer and faster technology offering more capacity and better quality compared to the Global System for Mobile Communications, commonly known as GSM (Baier, 1994; Chopra, Rohani, & Reed, 1995; Tscha, Choi, & Lee, 1993). Within a few years, however, GSM caught up. Backed by the industry consortium and propelled further by the European Commission legal mandate, GSM adoption steadily climbed to 83.5% of global mobile subscribers by 2009 (Frost & Sullivan, 2009). Verizon's current plan is to discontinue its 2G CDMA network by 2019 (Dano, 2016) and to gradually grow into an NFV-SDN architecture (Matsumoto, 2016).

T-Mobile, Sprint, US Cellular, and DISH Network

In 2015, the Federal Communications Commission completed the auction of Advanced Wireless Service 3 (AWS-3) bands consisting of 1695–1710 MHz, 1755–1780 MHz, and 2155–2180 MHz. The bid amount and the bidding firms involved provide some clues about the strategic direction of the firms and their financial ability to carry out their strategic vision. To fulfill the promise of future 5th-generation networks, mobile operators have to consider potential mobile technologies that shape the standards as well as spectrum utilization and usage.

Not surprisingly, AT&T and Verizon (the top two U.S. mobile carriers) outbid the rest with the total combined amount of more than 28 billion dollars. Sprint did not participate in the AWS-3 auction. Sprint is currently majority-owned by Softbank Group Corp., a Japanese multinational telecommunications firm. Sprint joined the Central Office Re-architected as a Datacenter in April 2017 to keep a watchful eye on the advancement and standardization of NFV-SDN to transform telecommunications central offices into datacenters. The cash-strapped Sprint is now rumored to be in talks to merge with T-Mobile, the third largest US wireless telecommunications operators (Baker, 2017). T-Mobile did participate in the AWS-3 auction and spent $8 billion to acquire about half of the low-band spectrum sold. The AWS-3 acquisition put T-Mobile in the position to provide nationwide coverage. However, T-Mobile contended that its modern core architecture equates to less urgency to embrace SDN and NFV (Marek, 2017). The merger between

T-Mobile and Sprint would help boost dwindling operating margins caused by the race to the bottom price war among mobile carriers.

US Cellular, the fifth largest U.S. mobile carrier, has had a growth issue mainly due to limited spectrum availability and market positioning (Kagan, 2016). To pave the way for competing with other mobile carriers, US Cellular conducted 5G with Ericsson and Nokia (Marek, 2016) and acquired low band licenses to grow their network and capacity (Jones, 2017). For Nokia as well as Ericsson, NFV and SDN are key technologies that make network slicing, a foundational 5G concept, possible. Network slicing is a method of logically separating network resources and functions and mapping them to required services to optimize utilization. By acquiring additional spectral licenses and working with key SDN/NFV vendors to conduct 5G trials, US Cellular is positioning itself to serve varying dynamic broadband demands of the future.

The surprise player was DISH Network, who aggressively acquired $10 billion worth of spectrum. DISH Network had already tried to acquire Sprint back in 2013 but lost to Softbank. T-Mobile, Sprint, and DISH Network are now strategically positioning themselves for merger and/or acquisitions while waiting for the dust of uncertainties to clear in order to reap the most benefits. This includes gauging the new Trump administration's position on a more consolidated telecommunications industry with fewer players and/or more tie-in relationships.

Survival of the Fittest: Stronger, Smarter, Slimmer, Simpler, Swagger Services

For the U.S. mobile carrier industry, the race toward an efficient, optimized, fast, adaptable, scalable, dynamic, resilient, on-demand, and service-oriented network infrastructure has begun. What is at stake is not just a technological evolution, but also the very survival of the industry. Fierce price competition as well as historical regulatory pressure have also contributed to the strategic shift in the U.S. mobile carrier industry's service offerings. These strategies include competitive bundled services that tie together voice, data, and video infrastructure as well as content services in a ubiquitous wireless access environment (Curwen & Whalley, 2017).

AT&T and Verizon are taking two different paths to evolve their network. Instead of waiting for the agreement and slow measured process of the industrial consortium standardization, AT&T is betting on the open-source model to propel the NFV-SDN architecture to the next level. Verizon, on the other hand, takes a more practical approach to work with established vendors to ensure future compliance and vendor adoptions. The rest of the mobile carriers are not as anchored or dragged by legacy processes and systems which means that they can wait longer to see how SDN and NFV shape up in terms of maturity and scalability. Unfortunately, there is no magic formula for an optimal time to adopt a constitutive, pioneering technology needed to survive the exigent IoT era ahead.

To succeed, each U.S. mobile carrier has to carefully adapt to the rapid pace of technological change and skillfully foster cooperative mutually beneficial ecosystems of customers, vendors, developers, and regulatory entities, as well as quickly transform itself into a non-commoditized service-based virtualized network company.

References

Amadeo, M., Campolo, C., Quevedo, J., Corujo, D., Molinaro, A., Iera, A., … Vasilakos, A. V. (2016). Information-centric Networking for the Internet of Things: Challenges and Opportunities. *IEEE Network, 30*(2), 92–100.

AT&T, Inc. (2014). AT&T Adds High-Quality Spectrum to Support Customers' Growing Demand for Mobile Video and High-Speed Internet. Retrieved from http://about. att.com/story_att_adds_high_quality_spectrum_to_support_growing_demand_ for_mobile_video_and_high_speed_internet.html.

AT&T, Inc. (2016). ECOMP (Enhanced Control, Orchestration, Management & Policy) Architecture White Paper. Retrieved from http://about.att.com/content/dam/ snrdocs/ecomp.pdf.

Awadalla, H. (2017). Managing Innovation in the Service Sector in Emerging Markets. In V. Nadda, S. Dadwal, & R. Rahimi (Eds.), *Promotional Strategies and New Service Opportunities in Emerging Economies* (pp. 144–163). IGI Global, Hershey, PA.

Baier, P. (1994). CDMA or TDMA? CDMA for GSM? *5th IEEE International Symposium on Personal, Indoor and Mobile Radio Communications, Wireless Networks – Catching the Mobile Future, 4*, 1280–1284.

Baker, L. (2017). Exclusive: SoftBank Willing to Cede Control of Sprint to Entice T-Mobile – Sources. *Reuters*. Retrieved from http://www.reuters.com/article/ us-sprint-corp-m-a-t-mobile-us-exclusive-idUSKBN15W26E.

Best, J. (2013). 'Android before Android': The Long, Strange History of Symbian and Why It Matters for Nokia's Future. Retrieved from http://www.zdnet.com/article/android-before-android-the-long-strange-history-of-symbian-and-why-it-matters-for-nokias-future/.

Bijwaard, G. E., Janssen, M. C., & Maasland, E. (2008). Early Mover Advantages: An Empirical Analysis of European Mobile Phone Markets. *Telecommunications Policy, 32*(3), 246–261.

Blankenhorn, D. (2010, March 31). IBM puts entrepreneurship in its cloud. Smart Planet, 1–2.

Brumec, S., & Vrček, N. (2013). Cost Effectiveness of Commercial Computing Clouds. *Information Systems, 38*(4), 495–508.

Burns, E. (2017). Largest Network Merger in Open Source History Creates New ONAP Project. Retrieved from http://www.cbronline.com/news/enterprise-it/virtualisation/ largest-network-merger-open-source-history-new-onap-project/.

Chiosi, M., Clarke, D., Willis, P., Reid, A., Feger, J., Bugenhagen, M., & Benitez, J. (2012). Network Functions Virtualisation: An Introduction, Benefits, Enablers, Challenges and Call for Action. *SDN and OpenFlow World Congress*, pp. 22–24.

Chopra, M., Rohani, K., & Reed, J. (1995). Analysis of CDMA Range Extension due to Soft Handoff. *IEEE 45th Vehicular Technology Conference, 2*, 917–921.

Cisco Systems, Inc. (2015). Cisco Visual Networking Index: Forecast and Methodology, 2015–2020. Cisco White Paper. Retrieved from http://www.cisco.com/c/en/us/ solutions/collateral/service-provider/visual-networking-index-vni/complete-white-paper-c11-481360.html.

Cisco Systems, Inc. (2016). The Zettabyte Era: Trends and Analysis. Cisco White Paper. Retrieved from http://www.cisco.com/c/en/us/solutions/collateral/service-provider/ visual-networking-index-vni/vni-hyperconnectivity-wp.html.

Cisco Systems. (2017). Cisco Visual Networking Index: Global Mobile Data Traffic Forecast Update, 2016–2021 White Paper. Retrieved from http://www.cisco.com/c/ en/us/solutions/collateral/service-provider/visual-networking-index-vni/mobile-white-paper-c11-520862.html.

Cox, M., & Ellsworth, D. (1997, October). Application-controlled Demand Paging for Out-of-Core Visualization. *Proceedings of the 8th Conference on Visualization*, IEEE Computer Society Press, Salt Lake City, UT, pp. 235–267.

Curwen, P., & Whalley, J. (2017). The Evolution of US Mobile Operators within a Multi-Play World. *Digital Policy, Regulation and Governance, 19*(1), 40–57.

Dano, M. (2016). Verizon to Shut Down 2G CDMA 1X Network by the End of 2019. Retrieved from http://www.fiercewireless.com/wireless/verizon-to-shut-down-2g-cdma-1x-network-by-end-2019.

De Grimaldo, S. (2015). US Wireless Outlook: Can T-Mobile and Sprint Disrupt AT&T and Verizon Wireless? *Strategic Analytics*. Retrieved from https://www. strategyanalytics.com/access-services/networks/mobile-operators/mobile-operators/ reports/report-detail/us-wireless-outlook-can-t-mobile-and-sprint-disrupt-at-t-and-verizon-wireless#.WN_XNqIpDIV.

Demchenko, Y., De Laat, C., & Membrey, P. (2014, May). Defining Architecture Components of the Big Data Ecosystem. *Collaboration Technologies and Systems (CTS), 2014 IEEE International Conference*, May 19–23, Minneapolis, MN, pp. 104–112.

Donavan, J. (2015). How Do You Keep Pace with a 100, 000 Percent Increase in Wireless Data Traffic? Retrieved from http://www.rcrwireless.com/20160609/network-function-virtualization-nfv/att-verizon-nfv-sdn-moves-seen-industry-leading-tag2.

Ericsson Press Release. (2017). Ericsson Tapped by Verizon Enterprise Solutions to Provide Enabling Support for NFV Services. Retrieved from https://www.ericsson.com/ press-releases/2017/2/2080007-ericsson-tapped-by-verizon-enterprise-solutions-to-provide-enabling-support-for-nfv-services-.

Frost & Sullivan. (2009). Global GSM Market Analysis. Retrieved from www.frost.com/ prod/servlet/cio/180573216.

Funk, J. (2002). *Global Competition between and Within Standards: The Case of Mobile Phones*. New York: Palgrave.

Gantz, J., & Reinsel, D. (2011). Extracting Value from Chaos. *IDC Iview, 1142*(2011), 1–12.

Geng, H. (2017). *Internet of Things and Data Analytics Handbook*. Hoboken, NJ: John Wiley & Son.

Goasduff, L., & Forni, A. (2017a). Gartner Says Worldwide Sales of Smartphones Grew 7 Percent in the Fourth Quarter of 2016. Retrieved from http://www.gartner.com/ newsroom/id/3609817.

Goasduff, L., & Forni, A. (2017b). Market Share: Final PCs, Ultramobiles and Mobile Phones, All Countries, 4Q16. Retrieved from https://www.gartner.com/ document/3606031.

Gubbi, J., Buyya, R., Marusic, S., & Palaniswami, M. (2013). Internet of Things (IoT): A Vision, Architectural Elements, and Future Directions. *Future Generation Computer Systems, 29*(7), 1645–1660.

Han, B., Gopalakrishnan, V., Ji, L., & Lee, S. (2015). Network Function Virtualization: Challenges and Opportunities for Innovations. *IEEE Communications Magazine, 53*(2), 90–97.

ITU Telecommunication Standardization Sector. (2013). Overview of the Internet of Things. Recommendation, ITU-T Y.2060. Geneva, Switzerland.

Jakopin, N. M., & Klein, A. (2012). First-Mover and Incumbency Advantages in Mobile Telecommunications. *Journal of Business Research, 65*(3), 362–370.

Jones, J. (2017). US Cellular to Spend $327M on 600MHz Spectrum. Light Reading. Retrieved from http://www.lightreading.com/mobile/spectrum/us-cellular-to-spend-$327m-on-600mhz-spectrum/d/d-id/730396.

Kagan, J. (2016). Why U.S. Cellular Growth Is Stalled. RCR Wireless. Retrieved from http://www.rcrwireless.com/20160516/opinion/kagan-us-cellular-growth-stalled.

Kenney, M., & Pon, B. (2011). Structuring the Smartphone Industry: Is the Mobile Internet OS Platform the Key? *Journal of Industry, Competition and Trade, 11*(3), 239–261.

Marek, S. (2016). US Cellular Hits 9-Gig Speeds in 5G Trial in Wisconsin. SDX Central. Retrieved from https://www.sdxcentral.com/articles/news/us-cellular-hits-9-gig-speeds-in-5g-trial-in-wisconsin/2016/12/.

Marek, S. (2017). T-Mobile CTO Says Modern Core Makes SDN Less Urgent. Retrieved from https://www.sdxcentral.com/articles/news/t-mobile-cto-says-modern-core-makes-sdn-less-urgent/2017/01/.

Matsumoto, C. (2016). What Verizon Learned from Implementing SDN & NFV. *SDxCentral*. Retrieved from https://www.sdxcentral.com/articles/news/what-verizon-learned-implementing-sdn-nfv/2016/09/.

Mell, P., & Grance, T. (2011). *The NIST Definition of Cloud Computing*. National Institute of Standards and Technology Special Publication, pp. 800–145.

Meulen, R., & Petty, C. (2008). Gartner Says Worldwide Smartphone Sales Reached Its Lowest Growth Rate with 11.5 Per Cent Increase in Third Quarter of 2008. Retrieved from http://www.gartner.com/newsroom/id/827912.

Meyer, D. (2016a). AT&T and Verizon NFV and SDN Moves Seen as Industry-Leading. Retrieved from http://www.rcrwireless.com/20160609/network-function-virtualization-nfv/att-verizon-nfv-sdn-moves-seen-industry-leading-tag2.

Meyer, D. (2016b). Verizon Enterprise Solutions Unveiled its Virtual Network Service Platform Targeting SDN and NFV Technology for an 'As-a-Service' Model. Retrieved from http://www.rcrwireless.com/20160721/telecom-software/verizon-taps-sdn-nfv-plans-enterprise-focused-virtual-network-service-tag2.

Mohan, D., Yezhkova, N., Scaramella, J., & DuBois, L. (2016). Worldwide Storage for Public and Private Cloud Forecast, 2016–2020. Retrieved from http://www.idc.com/getdoc.jsp?containerId=US42059416.

Muck, J. (2012). First Mover Advantages in Mobile Telecommunications: Evidence from OECD Countries. Dusseldorf Institute for Competition Economics. *Journal of Business Research, 65*(3), 362–370.

Murray, M. (2016, August 16). Intel Lays Out Its Vision for a Fully Connected World. Retrieved January 18, 2018, from https://www.pcmag.com/news/347046/intel-lays-out-its-vision-for-a-fully-connected-world

Netmarketshare (2017). Mobile/Tablet Operating System Market Share. Retrieved from https://www.netmarketshare.com/operating-system-market-share. aspx?qprid=8&qpcustomd=1.

Nguyen, B., & Simkin, L. (2017). The Internet of Things (IoT) and Marketing: the State of Play, Future Trends and the Implications for Marketing. *Journal of Marketing Management*, *33*, 1–6.

Omnes, N., Bouillon, M., Fromentoux, G., & Le Grand, O. (2015, February). A Programmable and Virtualized Network & Its Infrastructure for the Internet of Things: How Can NFV & SDN Help for Facing the Upcoming Challenges. *18th Intelligence in Next Generation Networks (ICIN) International Conference*, February 17–19, Paris, France, pp. 64–69.

Pfeffermann, N. (2017). The Role of Communication as a Dynamic Capability in Business Model Innovation. In A. Brem & E. Viardot (Eds.), *Revolution of Innovation Management* (pp. 191–212). Palgrave Macmillan, London.

Rice, C., 2017. Opening up ECOMP: Our Network Operating System for SDN. Retrieved from http://about.att.com/innovationblog/linux_foundation.

Ried, S., Kisker, H., Matzke, P., Bartels, A., & Lisserman, M. (2011). Sizing the Cloud: Understanding and Quantifying the Future Of Cloud Computing. Retrieved from https://www.forrester.com/report/Sizing+The+Cloud/-/E-RES58161.

Risteska, B., Trivodaliev, K., & Davcev, D. (2017). *Internet of Things Framework for Home Care Systems. Wireless Communications and Mobile Computing*. Hoboken, NJ: John Wiley & Sons.

Saha, H. N., Mandal, A., & Sinha, A. (2017, January). Recent Trends in the Internet of Things. *Computing and Communication Workshop and Conference (CCWC), 7th IEEE Annual Conference*, Las Vegas, NV, January 9–11, pp. 1–4.

Sarikaya, R. (2017). The Technology Behind Personal Digital Assistants: An Overview of the System Architecture and Key Components. *IEEE Signal Processing Magazine*, *34*(1), 67–81.

Shakya, B., Tehranipoor, M. M., Bhunia, S., & Forte, D. (2017). Introduction to Hardware Obfuscation: Motivation, Methods and Evaluation. In D. Forte, S. Bhunia, & M. M. Tehranipoor (Eds.), *Hardware Protection through Obfuscation* (pp. 3–32), Springer International Publishing, Switzerland.

Thangavel, C., & Sudhaman, P. (2017). An Exploratory Case Study on Cloud ERP Implementation. *International Journal of Information and Communication Technology*, *10*(2), 148–161.

Tscha, Y., Choi, G., & Lee, K. H. (1993). A Subscriber Signaling Gateway between CDMA Mobile Station and GSM Mobile Switching Center. *Universal Personal Communications, 1993. Personal Communications: Gateway to the 21st Century. Conference Record, 2nd International Conference, 1*, 181–185.

Verizon. 2016. Verizon Network Infrastructure Planning: SDN-NFV Reference Architecture. Retrieved from http://innovation.verizon.com/content/dam/vic/PDF/Verizon_SDN-NFV_Reference_Architecture.pdf.

Vuha, C., Rajani, M., & Vineeth, J. M. (2017). Smart Health Care Monitoring Using Internet of Things and Android. *International Journal of Advanced Research in Electronics and Communication Engineering, 6*(3), 101–104.

West, J., & Mace, M. (2010). Browsing as the Killer App: Explaining the Rapid Success of Apple's iPhone. *Telecommunications Policy, 34*(5), 270–286.

Yadav, V., Borate, S., Devar, S., Gaikwad, R., & Gavali, A. B. (2017). A Review on Smart Home Automation Using Virtue of IoT. *Journal of Android and IOS Applications and Testing, 2*(1), 1–3.

Yang, Y. Y., Cheng, W. H., Yang, C. T., Chen, S. T., & Jian, F. C. (2015, November). The Implementation of Real-Time Network Traffic Monitoring Service with Network Functions Virtualization. *International Conference on Cloud Computing and Big Data (CCBD)*, November 4–6, Taipei, Taiwan, pp. 279–286.

Yeo, K. S., Chian, M. C., & Ng, T. C. W. (2014, December). Internet of Things: Trends, Challenges and Applications. *14th IEEE International Symposium on Integrated Circuits (ISIC)*, December 10–12, Marina Bay Sands, Singapore, pp. 568–571.

Zamani, A. S., Akhtar, M. M., & Ahmad, S. (2011). Emerging Cloud Computing Paradigm. *IJCSI International Journal of Computer Science Issues, 8*(4), 304–307.

Zehavi, A., & Breznitz, D. (2017). Distribution Sensitive Innovation Policies: Conceptualization and Empirical Examples. *Research Policy, 46*(1), 327–336.

Zhu, Q., Wang, R., Chen, Q., Liu, Y., & Qin, W. (2010, December). IoT Gateway: Bridging Wireless Sensor Networks into Internet of Things. *Embedded and Ubiquitous Computing (EUC), 8th IEEE/IFIP International Conference*, December 11–13, Hong Kong, China, pp. 347–352.

Zhang, Y., & Banerjee, S. (2017). Efficient and Verifiable Service Function Chaining in NFV: Current Solutions and Emerging Challenges. Optical Fiber Communication Conference, 19–23 March 2017, Los Angeles, CA, USA.

Chapter 14

Call Centers Cloud Use in Call Centers

Alonso Miller

Adapt Telephony Services

Contents

Communication as a Service

Communication as a service (CaaS) is a concept that evolved from managed services, which is nothing more than a vendor managing a few given services, if not the whole information technology infrastructure for customers and enterprises that outsource certain areas of their IT department. Rather than paying a full-time employee to become certified and learn all of the IT platforms, a prospective customer or enterprise can pay a vendor to manage these applications that enable the company to execute sales, retain customer information, or otherwise maintain their data integrity (Garai *et al.*, 2015). CaaS is sort of a hybrid of managed services; it allows customers to outsource the management of communication platforms like CIC, Avaya, or Cisco Call Center by relying on the vendor to own the premise-based equipment and the customer only using its front-end and various levels of administrative features. In some cases, an enterprise can have a managed services agreement using a CaaS implementation model where the enterprise owns zero equipment and relies on the vendor for the full administrative management of the platform as well. Today, CaaS has evolved from strictly premise-based equipment to cloud-based communications as a service equipment leveraging Amazon Web Services (AWS) to handle most of the heavy lifting. While there are still the few and far between customers that rely on managed services to perform 100% of the administrative function of their communications platform, cloud-based systems have empowered many organizations to essentially "skip the middle man" and own the deployment and management role. However, despite the fact that the convenience factor has made it easier to deploy with very little equipment, organizations still need to configure the system and have an intermediate to expert level of IT knowledge to understand the functionalities of these communications platforms (Stratoscale, 2017).

Cloud-Based Communications Platforms

The "Cloud" has been around since the Internet was birthed, we just didn't really know what we could do with it until now, as we developed more useful protocols to carry messages and data across networks. The collaborative effort of advanced networking and routing functions to carry Session Initiation (SIP) and User Datagram (UDP) Protocols, combined with Customer Relationship Management (CRM) and stack technologies that enable platforms like Five9, Purecloud, Seranova, and Oracle to offer cloud-based contact center and workforce management solutions allows enterprises and organizations to leverage their communications tools to serve their core functional needs with little administrative effort and little to no equipment needed. These platforms also offer robust integrations with other vendors like Salesforce, Zen Desk, and Microsoft allowing even more powerful tools to be integrated with their contact center platform. Bringing them to the Cloud simplifies the delivery of Omni channel communications that include voice, chat, email, video conferencing, and social media response (Frost & Sullivan, 2015).

Cons and Skepticism of Cloud-Based Communications Platforms

Even though cloud-based communications platforms have revolutionized the contact center model, there are trade-offs and limitations of cloud-based systems in comparison to premise-based. Even with a local delivery model, where some of the equipment is located at the organization's data centers, companies and enterprises still do not have full back-end access to these platforms due to security and best practices. As more features and granular control become available, there will always be restriction or limited functionality to these platforms. While some enterprises are skeptical of the backend access or control of the platform, others are more concerned with the method of how these cloud-based environments retain valuable or proprietary information on the Cloud. More importantly, these enterprises are concerned with how the data is controlled once it is on the Cloud; often times once the information is on the Cloud, it is somewhat challenging to know how the data is retained and purged under some systems. For example, the banking sector (which is heavily regulated) is very skeptical to take their communications to the cloud. Very few have made the transition to the cloud while many others have shied away from considering a cloud-based contact center platform for the simple reason of how recordings are retained in the cloud and how internal chats are saved and audited, as well as how documents are retained, stored, and purged.

The Growth of Cloud-Based Communications Platforms

The contact center sector has seen a significant growth in cloud-based platforms in the last five years that has many major vendors competing fiercely for a slice of the cloud-based contact center space in smaller markets. While large companies, like Oracle, Cisco, and Genesys, who have a large customer base in mid-market and large enterprise markets are now investing in small and medium sized businesses, and markets under 100 seats. There are several, if not many, smaller companies and even start-ups that are also competing with these large multimillion dollar vendors for a piece of the cloud-based markets (Kavick, 2014). Companies like Seranova and InContact are having immediate impact on the contact center space and competing formidably against major giants like Oracle, Cisco, and Genesys, offering their own unique cloud-based contact center platforms that also deliver on Omni channel unified communications. Cloud-based systems are meant to target smaller markets; typically (and mostly) enterprises that are less than 100 seats, but in rare cases there are a few that are above 100 seats and a very select small number of enterprises with over 500 seats (Agnew, 2016). Even in these large cloud-based contact centers with over 100–500 seats leveraging the cloud, Amazon Web Services has still been able to manage the workload and offer impressive uptime numbers with over 100% uptime more often than not. Recently in March 2017 a system administrator at Amazon made a mistake in performing a maintenance script for Amazon Simple Storage Service (AWS S3) storage that brought down nearly a third of the Internet due to a mistake made entering in a Linux-based command. Many companies using cloud-based contact centers found themselves "dead in the water"; in other words, their contact centers were down and unable to take phone calls, make outbound calls, accept chats from their websites, or otherwise accept emails or use their platforms to perform daily tasks due to this system failure that was caused by human error (Amazon.com, Inc, 2017). Even though the event caused thousands of companies to be affected for half of a day, Amazon Web Services still managed to maintain a 99.995% uptime for the month of March. The way that it was explained to customers that questioned the validity or service level of these cloud-based platforms was that this particular event was the equivalent of a construction crew cutting a fiber line outside the office, an MPLS circuit failing, or otherwise a large part of infrastructure that would traditionally be a point of failure at the carrier level in premise-based environments failing in Amazon Web Services. The AWS and Google's of the world are now the platform "carriers" sharing the carrier role with telephone carriers to deliver the data for these companies via the Cloud.

The Future of Cloud-Based Communications Platforms

Cloud-based systems are here to stay. They have a lot of promise despite their current limitations, as well as a solid infrastructure platform with a service level just as good as premise-based equipment. Their major impact is offering the opportunity of expensive technologies that are typically offered to much larger organizations at a more reasonable price point and delivery method. Automatic Call Distribution licenses typically are an expensive feature in premise-based platforms, but in cloud-based platforms ACD licenses are affordable and available for small enterprises to leverage for their contact centers. These platforms have also allowed easy offshore deployment for multinationals or other companies with foreign offices or locations around the world. The Cloud will certainly bring more opportunities to the IT and communications world. The contact center on the Cloud is certainly one of the next big things, but they will not be replacing premise equipment any time soon.

References

Agnew, H. (2016, June 20). Deloitte targets SMEs with cloud-based service. *Financial Times.* https://www.ft.com/content/ac2c8ec8-36f2-11e6-9a05-82a9b15a8ee7

Amazon.com, Inc. (2017). *Summary of the Amazon S3 Service Disruption in the Northern Virginia (US-EAST-1) Region.* Seattle: Amazon.com.

Frost & Sullivan. (2015). *Creating Better Omni-Channel Customer Experiiences in the Cloud.* Mountain View: Frost & Sullivan.

Garai, M., Rekhis, S. and Boudriga, N. (2015) Communication as a service for cloud VANETs, *2015 IEEE Symposium on Computers and Communication (ISCC)*, Larnaca, pp. 371–377.

Kavick, M. (2014, August 8). How niche cloud providers compete with AWS, Google and Microsoft. *Forbes.* https://www.forbes.com/sites/mikekavis/2014/08/08/how-niche-cloud-providers-compete-with-aws-google-and-microsoft/#9049f262febd

Stratoscale. (2017). IaaS, PaaS, and SaaS: The good, the bad and the ugly. Retrieved from Stratoscale: https://www.stratoscale.com/resources/article/iaas-paas-saas-the-good-bad-ugly/

Chapter 15

Security

Strategies for Security in the Cloud

Victoria Bishop
Burwood Group Inc.

Sophie Guetzko
Accenture PLC

Contents

With every technological invention comes security threats—cloud computing is not exempt. Cloud computing has become a dominant force in data storage and distribution among systems. As a result, it has become a target for security breaches and attacks on data. As was previously discussed, cloud computing can make operations in an organization more efficient and cost-effective, but a vulnerability in the security of these systems can be much more detrimental than a breach on company owned and operated hardware. This is due to cloud service providers' responsibility of managing large amounts of sensitive data from multiple sources making it imperative that security is made a priority. This chapter will provide understanding on how to secure these systems and measures that can be enacted to have a proactive stance. First, we must address the kinds of threats present today before we can counteract them or take measures to ensure they do not happen in the first place.

Types of Cloud Security Controls

In order to ensure the implemented security in the architecture of the Cloud is effective, the utilization of defensive mechanisms is critical. There are four types of security controls associated with securing cloud-based applications; each assist with a different piece of cloud security.

The first is the use of deterrent controls, which are employed to reduce the attacks on a cloud system. An example of a deterrent control may include appropriate banner messages in access and high-risk warning signals. Deterrent controls act the same way a "Warning: guard dog on premise" sign may discourage an intruder from stepping into unauthorized territory—its purpose is to stop intruders before they step in.

Second, preventative measures, such as the use of a proxy server, seek to eliminate vulnerabilities by strengthening the system. Employment of strong user authentication can be one of the most effective ways by which preventative measures can be employed. The user authentication structure can act as a "bouncer" between the data and those who wish to access it. If proper authentication is not provided, the person or persons wishing to gain access are not allowed inside.

Third, the use of detective controls can provide a means by which a plan of development is created to prevent possible paths for an intruder to enter. By creating what-if scenarios, a detective control can notify preventative and corrective controls to ensure a minimal amount of damage takes place. It helps to detect unlawful users and stop them before they cause a large amount of damage to the system. An example of this would to consider a game of hide-and-seek, where the person who is "it" attempts to expose those who are hiding and notify others of their hiding place.

Fourth, corrective measures are essential in times of a breach or possible breach. The purpose of corrective controls is to limit the amount of damage done, similar to detective controls; however, the corrective controls come into effect during or following an incident that has taken place. Changing passwords or usernames or creating time limits spent on cloud storage following a breach may be implemented so that information cannot be stolen again in the future.

Data Breaches

A major threat to cloud computing is a data breach. Although a data breach can also occur on a closed local system it often is harder to breach a local system, depending on the security measures taken and the protocols in place than it is to breach a cloud computing system that resides virtually on the web. Having a system that resides on the web is theoretically accessible by anyone with the proper authentication details and an Internet connection. The issue becomes more complex and significant when the user takes into account that the cloud providers offering a public cloud platform often host several companies' data all within the same hardware environment. Therefore, one security breach can be magnified exponentially as the hacker gains access to an adjacent company's information. A single breach can mean compromising several companies' data.

To work around this, cloud providers expect the company/organization/user to secure their own data or at the very least make it clear that the company/organization/user is ultimately responsible for their own data. Despite this, cloud providers do aim to help protect the data that they host. For instance, in Amazon Web Services terms and conditions it states that they will "implement reasonable and appropriate measures designed to help you secure Your Content against accidental or unlawful loss, access or disclosure" (Amazon Web Services, 2017).

Data breaches can cause companies to incur huge fines, lawsuits, or criminal charges depending on the sensitivity of the information that was compromised and the severity of the attack. Information regarding finances, health, trade secrets, and intellectual property can cause some of the biggest issues. On top of these ramifications, it can also be expensive to react to the incident and investigate what happened, as well as notify the user-base that a breach has occurred (Rashid, 2016).

A common cause of data breaches stem from poor security protocols. For instance, a data breach can occur when credentials have been improperly shared with someone or there has been an authentication error. Furthermore, data breaches can include a poor encryption key or certificate management that allow a hacker easy access into the system. An important, but difficult, responsibility for any organization is ensuring that the correct people have access to the correct permissions and resources. If this is not maintained properly or if employees are not properly trained to follow security guidelines and principles, data can be stolen or damaged quickly and easily. This is true with cloud systems as well as local systems. In a cloud environment, employees must know the relationship between their authentication information and the provider. The security measures in place on the provider side must be followed on the consumer end as well or it becomes much easier for an attacker to breach. Because of the centralization of identity into a single repository, the benefits and risks must be weighed when an organization decides whether to incorporate the ease-of-use that cloud provides or avoid it due to the risks that can come with using it.

Cloud Security: Application Programming Interfaces

Most cloud services offered today also provide some form of Application Programming Interface (API). An API can be used by Information Technology (IT) teams to manage and interact with the cloud services in use by their business. This does provide some level of interaction and some helpful tools to the IT team, but this also means that the security of the service itself is now also directly tied to the security of the API it is attached to. These APIs tend to be a more vulnerable part of the cloud system as a whole because this is the part that tends to be readily available via the Internet. In order to keep these systems safe and secure, an organization must have security-focused code review as well as extensive and ongoing penetration testing.

Cloud Security: System Vulnerabilities

System bugs and vulnerabilities are common among all types of software, most of which are fixed before they are ever released to be used at an enterprise level. While the concept of a security bug or vulnerability is not a new one, the potential of this occurring becomes multiplied based on the multi-tenancy of cloud computing. Because all of the resources within an organization are essentially now shared and converge onto one place, this creates more ways for an attacker to make their way in. The best way to ensure that an attack does not occur and to mitigate an attack that does occur is to simply follow the best practices of IT. These include constantly scanning the system for vulnerabilities, patching the system regularly and managing updates well, and following up immediately on potential threats that are found on the system (Lukan, 2014).

Cloud Security: The Human Factor

Just as with any data security plan, proper employee training regarding phishing scams, fraud, and software exploits is an important piece of avoiding data breaches. The cloud environment adds another dimension to this by constantly being online. Attackers can eavesdrop on online activities, manipulate transactions, and even modify data. The cloud environment can allow hackers to launch attacks using the cloud applications themselves. Enabling multi-factor authentication and prohibiting the sharing of credentials between users and services are helpful steps to take in avoiding stolen account credentials. It is advised to make sure that there is always a way to prove that a human is using the system and that that human is both allowed onto the system and is who they say they are. (Rashid, 2016)

The human factor of data security does not end there. For instance, individuals from within the system can also compromise the data security and even attack it themselves. Former employees who feel wronged may attempt to take revenge out on the company by releasing sensitive data such as passwords and user information. Other more calculated crimes may be committed such as data theft to be sold on the dark web. The Cloud, as it tends to do, magnifies the ramifications of these events occurring; because it is not just a single entities' data anymore, the effects encompass all of the data on the system regardless of who it belongs to. The Cloud Security Alliance (CSA) recommends organizations be in control of encryption keys and protocols and be stringent with who has access to what information. The cloud provider generally should never be the sole provider of security on the system, as this puts the entire system at even greater risk because of a single point of failure. Another important factor to consider is whether or not an activity from within the organization was genuinely malicious or if it was simply a mistake. Ultimately, proper planning and taking appropriate security measures can deal with most of the risk of an inside threat occurring (Rashid, 2016).

Cloud Security: Advanced Persistent Threats

An Advanced Persistent Threat (APT) is a form of attack that the CSA considers parasitic (Rashid, 2016). The point of an APT is to make its way into a system, establish a point of entry and implant itself, and then steal data without being detected over a long period of time. APTs tend to be good at blending in with normal network traffic and are generally very difficult to detect, but the biggest cloud providers use the most advanced techniques for detection of these threats. Despite the diligence of the provider, the consumer still must remain aware and diligent in detecting APTs to have the most secure system possible. Some common ways for APTs to make their way onto a network is via spear phishing, USB drives, and insecure third-party networks. Staying informed, diligent, and up-to-date on the latest security measures and best practice are the best ways to avoid this threat (Damballa).

Combating the Threats

Cloud computing security continues to be of the utmost importance to companies. Organizations must put in place security policies, compliance, and procedures in order to protect the intellectual property. First, a client must define their own level of risk tolerance before determining what they need in a service agreement with the cloud provider. Once these requirements are defined and stated, it is important for both parties to understand the terms and responsibilities in case an emergency does arise. The service agreement should also state notification protocols regarding any security break, even if the customer is not directly affected, as well as clearly defined practices regarding the liability of the provider (Cloud Standards Customer Council, 2015).

It would also be wise of the client to formulate an auditing process for the compliance of IT systems. When auditing a service provider there are three key points the client must consider. The first is understanding the internal control environment of the cloud provider and what controls they have in place. For instance, some key controls for cloud services include the level of isolation of customer data from other cloud tenants and minimizing the access of the provider's staff. Secondly, the customer must have access to the corporate audit trail of cloud services. Finally, the client must be aware of the security measures taken at provider's facilities. All necessary information including authentication and authorization must be properly enforced and documented. Enforcing privacy policies will also save the client and provider from malicious attacks. It is extremely important that privacy is addressed in the cloud customer service agreement and enterprises are responsible for monitoring the provider's compliance with those policies.

Ensuring proper protection of data and information is different for each type of cloud service. For instance, with Infrastructure-as-a-Service, much of the responsibility falls on the customer to encrypt the data. Alternatively, with Software-as-a-Service (SaaS), much of the responsibility falls on the provider because the customer does not directly control the data and application code. Lastly, in Platform-as-a-Service , the responsibility falls somewhere between the customer and the provider; making defining responsibility even more important.

The client and service provider must also ensure the cloud networks and connections are secure. According to the Cloud Standards Customer Council:

> A cloud service provider must allow legitimate network traffic and block malicious network traffic, just as any other Internet-connected organization does. However, unlike many other organizations, a cloud service provider will not necessarily know what network traffic its customers plan to send and receive (Cloud Standards Customer Council, 2015, p. 19).

Some of the external network requirements include traffic screening, denial of service protection, intrusion detection and prevention, logging, and notification. In internal network security, the assumption is that attackers have already passed external defenses. Virtual Local Area Networks (VLANs) can protect customers by placing their systems on different Ethernet switches, hiding the traffic of one VLAN from the others (Cloud Standards Customer Council, 2015).

Ensuring the physical infrastructure and facilities are secure is another requirement of the service provider. The security network infrastructure is crucial to the entire security network. For example, to maintain proper efficiency, an audit must include making sure that the physical infrastructure and facilities are held in secure areas, that there is protection against external and environmental threats, and that there is control of personnel working in the secure areas. The facilities should be equipped with proper cabling, maintenance, disposal of equipment, and failure backup plans.

The final step to ensure security success within the cloud is understanding the security requirements of the exit process. For the sake of security, once a business has chosen to exit the relationship with the cloud provider, it must be clearly defined that none of the information should stick with the provider unless a law specifies a retention period. There must be a smooth process put in place that benefits both sides so that the customer has the data and the provider does not become susceptible to a data breach (Cloud Standards Customer Council, 2015).

Internal and External Security

Organizations have placed emphasis on their investment in cloud due to the cost savings, scalability, and flexibility involved with the storing of data. However, organizations are now turning to cloud for the purpose of security, especially in public cloud services. This shift is taking place under the realization that cloud providers have the capacity to invest more in security and deliver higher-end security than the private sector does. Traditional security measures have been adapted for the purpose of securing data moving in and out of the Cloud. Use of data encryptions, firewalls, and types of control are outlined as internal and external factors associated with the Cloud.

Data Encryption

Data encryption is a process that takes place through technological transmission of data from one device to another. While there are a variety of different aspects of data encryption, its main purpose is to protect the privacy of data being transmitted through a channel. The process, cryptology, and aspects of data encryption are outlined to decode the use and implications of data encryption in the safety of data in a network (Stine & Dang, 2011, pp. 44–46).

Purpose of Data Encryption

Encryption of data in network security is a crucial part of maintaining the safety of a network. The use of data encryption uses the "scrambling" of data so that it is inaccessible by unintended parties (McDowell, 2016). The purpose of the data "scrambling" has different intentions, which include the preservation of data integrity, confidentiality of data, and user authentication.

The first purpose of encryption is to preserve data integrity. Although data integrity can also be supplemented by using both backup and archiving systems, the use of encryption is another means by which data can maintain its integrity on the original device. With the history of data growth expanding exponentially, it is important to pursue the use of data encryption in order secure the data owned by individuals (Elovici, Waisenberg, Shumeli, & Gudes, n.d., p. 5).

A second purpose of encryption is to increase confidentiality. The secrecy of data is important, especially in the sending of classified information. With the use of cloud computing on the rise, there is a new need for data encryption and the capacity to maintain privacy in data when it is stored outside of the device and inside of a server that may or may not be in the same place as the organization or individual putting the cloud to use. Achieved through the use of cryptology, or the "scrambling" of data, the transmitted information is kept private through algorithms. In traditional and general data encryption, confidentiality is also important, especially in the transmission of passwords, financial numbers, and other private information (Soofi, Khan, & Fazal-e-Amin, 2014, pp. 11–17).

The third purpose of encryption deals with user authentication. User authentication is actualized through an easy-to-use interface often known as a "login," or the use of an individualized username and password configuration. It maintains data security and does not allow access to any person, system, or server of which the information does not belong. It requires that the individual attempting to retrieve data provides credentials by which it can be proven that the accessible information belongs to him or her. Other means of providing user authentication may be through a certificate that the server provides to an individual accessing information. If a certificate is not accessible and the device believes one should be, a user may receive a notification that a certificate from the server is not available and ask if the user wishes to proceed. At that time, a user must determine whether or not they would like to proceed. The use of the certificate is often determined by the firewall installed on the computer, used in accessing the Internet (Boston University, n.d.)

Process of Data Encryption

Data encryption begins in one device, which then employs the use of an algorithm to encode a message. The use of this algorithm reorganizes the message so that it is not easily accessible to hackers who may attempt to infiltrate the channel. The message then travels through the channel into the second device, which decodes the algorithm and it is then readily available to the receiver to determine how to respond to the message (Stein & Dang, 2011, pp. 44–46).

When a packet is traveling through a network and is not encrypted, it runs a risk of a hacker accessing the data and then corrupting the data. In a normal packet, the header and data are stacked on top of one another. It begins at user one's computer and when it travels through the firewall and across the Internet it may be intercepted by a hacker who then corrupts and/or accesses the data before it is sent toward the firewall to the computer of user two. The implication of this corruption can include the following:

- Financial information or stolen identity
- Exploitation of other information
- Compromised data sent to the second device

The significance of black hat hacking in encryption can lead to serious danger, especially if confidential information is accessed through the hacking experience (Jones, 2016).

Hackers and Encrypted Packets

Encryptions place a protection around the packet being transferred. Therefore, when a packet leaves user one's computer, it travels through the firewall and into the Internet, where it is then transferred through another firewall to user two's computer. The difference between an encrypted packet is that it disallows the high risk of a hacker corrupting the data. As noted under ciphertext, encryption of packets is present in secure wireless network connections (Jones, 2016).

Firewalls

A firewall is a piece of technology that assists in the filtering of threats that attempt to gain access to private information.

Packet filtering is used to validate packets of information such as protocol, time range, source and/or destination Internet Protocol (IP) addresses, source and/or destination port numbers, Differentiated Services Code Point, type of service, and others.

Routers, switches, wireless access points, Virtual Private Network concentrators, and many others all have the ability to contain packet-filtering, and due to its accessibility on devices, it is an advantage to a network.

Switches may use Routed Access-Control Lists, which provide the capacity to control the traffic flow on a routed interface; Port Access Control Lists, which are assigned to a switched interface; and Virtual Local Area Network (VLAN) Access Control Lists, which have the capability to control switched and/or routed packets on a VLAN. The access control lists have predetermined criteria that must be met based on IP addressing in order to allow or deny the traffic to flow through it (Blair & Durai, 2009).

Cloud-based firewalls are used primarily in businesses and other entities, and implement SaaS. Provided as an option for businesses, there is no longer a need for a company to purchase software or hardware in order to protect their information. These types of firewalls are called Web-Application Firewalls (WAFs). Use of WAF through SaaS has become more viable for businesses and individuals to implement. It also allows the client to rapidly receive updates for innovative and new features (D'Hoinne, Hils, & Neiva, 2016).

Firewalls, in conjunction with data encryption, can be assistive technology in securing a network. While data encryption is concerned with protecting authenticity of the data, a firewall assists in protecting the network itself.

Social Engineering

What is social engineering and what role does it play in data security? Social engineering is defined as the art of manipulating people so they give up confidential information (Criddle, n.d). Social engineering attacks differ from "hacks" because these attacks rely on the human factor of susceptibility to be manipulated into an action. This is due to humans having a natural inclination to want to trust and help people. Consequently, individuals are fooled into believing that others will always have their best interests in mind. Individuals believe that if someone seems genuine, then they are. Social engineers prey on these types of individuals to gain unauthorized access to private information such as bank account information, data on enterprise servers, and other information that is protected.

The major differences between computer hacks and social engineer attacks are that computer hackers attempt to breach the network from the outside while most social engineering attacks will breach the system from the inside. Although both pose serious threats to security, social engineering threats are especially dangerous due to how easily a whole system can be compromised in a short amount of time with very little difficulty. The seriousness of these types of attacks are simple: network defenses are set up to protect from the outside threat (against hackers) but remain vulnerable to the inside threat (social engineering attacks). Human error can circumvent all security measures put in place by an enterprise in a matter of moments.

Social Engineering: Types of Attacks

Social engineering attacks can be broken down into two common types: computer-based and human-based (Warlock, 2013). Computer-based attacks use software to attempt to gain desired information. Some attacks of this type include phishing, baiting, pretexting, and quid pro quo (Bisson, 2015).

Human-based social engineering attacks are completely different from computer based attacks. The difference is human interaction; the person to person engagement to retrieve data. What makes this type of attack difficult to defend against is the fact that no one wants to believe the person in front of them is trying to be deceptive. These attacks instill a false sense of trust in the attacker, which allows the target to be manipulated. According to Info Sec Institute, an expert of information security training, the major human based attacks are: Impersonation, posing as an important user, third party attack, desktop support staff, shoulder surfing, dumpster diving, and reverse social engineering (Warlock, 2013).

Computer-Based Social Engineering: Phishing

Phishing is one of the most common forms of computer-based scams present on the Internet today. Phishing email messages, websites, and phone calls are all designed to steal money. Cybercriminals can do this by installing malicious software on a computer or by stealing personal information off a computer (Microsoft, n.d.). Phishing attacks work because they make the target (the individual being manipulated) believe that they are receiving legitimate information. The target may receive an email that looks like it is from a legitimate source (a banking institution, a contracted vendor, someone from the IT department within the company, etc.) all with the goal to trick that person into trusting them to do what the attacker asks. Phishing attacks usually involve a hacker sending out a mass email to many individuals with the hope that a few will believe that the communication is real and follow the hacker's commands. There are also attacks that target specific individuals or groups which is known as spear phishing (FBI, 2009). As mentioned previously, these attacks prey on a person's need to trust and believe something that looks and feels genuine. Most phishing emails usually contain something that makes the target absolutely believe it's true and immediately trust the source. Furthermore, phishing scams demonstrate the following characteristics: they seek to obtain personal information such as names, addresses, and social security numbers; they use link shorteners or embed links that redirect users to suspicious websites in URLs that appear legitimate while also incorporating threats, fear, and a sense of urgency in an attempt to manipulate the user into acting promptly (Bisson, 2015).

Computer-Based Social Engineering: Baiting

Baiting is another form of computer based social engineering. While there are similarities to phishing, baiting is different because there is usually an offer to entice the victims to click on links or to give up their log-in credentials (Bisson, 2015). These offers usually promise a free movie or music download in exchange for a certain action. What also separates baiting from phishing is that baiting attacks are not limited to just web based schemes. Many hackers and social engineers use physical media to break into systems as well. According to Dara Security, an award-winning data-security-based company, a social engineer with the end goal of infiltrating a company's network may distribute malware-infected flash drives or similar devices to employees hoping that this hardware will be inserted into network-connected computers as the means to spread malicious code (Dara, Social Engineering - Would You Take the Bait?, 2015). Hackers can distribute these while impersonating a member of the IT department or by placing these in a high traffic area and allow people passing by to pick them up by believing they are free gifts. These schemes also prey off a person's natural curiosity which leads them to want to find out what is on the USB drive or other infected media.

Computer-Based Social Engineering: Pretexting

In a pretexting scheme, a social engineer focuses on creating a good pretext, or a fabricated scenario, that they can use to try and steal their victims' personal information (Bisson, 2015). With this scheme, a social engineer will pretend to be someone they are not, typically an IT professional or representative from a relative company, to gather information from the target. What makes this attack so successful, and therefore very concerning, is the amount of research that is involved with this scheme. For example, in October 2014, a group of scammers posed as representatives from modeling agencies and escort services, invented fake background stories and interview questions in order to have women, including teenage girls, send them nude pictures of themselves (Bisson, 2015). For pretexting to work, the target must believe that the social engineer is indeed the person that they are pretending to be. If a social engineer pretends to be a company representative from a company that the actual enterprise does not partner with then the social engineer's story will not work.

Computer-Based Social Engineering: Quid Pro Quo

Quid pro quo is another major form of computer based social engineering. Latin for "this for that," quid pro quo is a classic social engineering scheme that relies on an individual's naiveté to allow a criminal to access sensitive information (Dara, Quid Pro Quo—What's the Cost of a Free Gift?, 2015). With this attack, the attacker can impersonate someone and gain information in exchange for something in return. While an attacker can use many different angles to attack from, most often they impersonate IT personnel and use their "expertise" to help solve problems. An example of this would be when an attacker calls every line of a company in search of the one person who is in actual need of assistance. Upon finding this person, the attacker ensures the target that they can help resolve their problem but before they can even begin to help them, the target will have to surrender their log-in information. Now the attacker has obtained the information and is in the system. Other less sophisticated schemes for obtaining critical information include: strongest password contest and surveys that requested credentials that would lead to receiving free items upon completion (Dara, Quid Pro Quo - What's the Cost of a Free Gift?, 2015).

Human-Based Social Engineering: Impersonation

Impersonation is when an attacker "impersonates" or pretends to be an authorized user to gain access to any area or data that they are not allowed to access. This allows an attacker to work their way through established security measures without much resistance. An attacker can impersonate an employee, an IT professional or even a janitor to gain unauthorized access to the network and the computers on it.

Attackers can also get into restricted areas by posing as an important person. In this scheme, the attacker poses as someone high up in the company or someone who should have access to these areas. The attacker might use fear and intimidation to make the person comply with their requests to let them into certain areas or the attacker might make the person believe that they are supposed to have access, and as such, the target will not question the attacker.

Human-Based Social Engineering: Third Party and Other Methods

An attacker using a third-party approach pretends to have gained permission from another person to use the system. The person being attacked in this case is unable to verify that the attacker has the authorization that they claim to have. For instance, by contacting desktop support, an attacker could pretend to be an authorized user who is locked out of an account or have currently misplaced their login information. Due to the nature of helpdesk support being trained to help, they typically fall prey to these attacks; this attack is a classic social-engineering technique (Warlock, 2013).

Another method is shoulder surfing. This involves an attacker watching the target, entering their credentials, and remembering them for later use. With this attack, the attacker uses minimal manipulation so that the target will put their guard down and enter the information without noticing that the attacker is observing. The target is completely oblivious to the fact that the attacker is looking nor is the target worried enough to try to conceal the credentials.

A similar approach that feeds on users' carelessness about concealing credentials is dumpster diving. In this method, the attacker finds sensitive information that has been discarded by a company, usually in the trash, that allows them to gather sensitive information. Since trash is often overlooked, it can be a major source of intelligence gathering (Granger, 2001).

Furthermore, piggybacking is the art of gaining entrance to an area without authorization by entering the area behind or with someone who does have access. An example of this is when a delivery driver gains entrance into a building that requires key card access by entering the building when an employee swipes their badge and asks them to hold the door open for them.

Human-Based Social Engineering: Reverse Social Engineering

A more advanced method of gaining illicit information is known as reverse social engineering. Using this technique, a hacker creates a persona that appears to be in a position of authority so that employees ask the hacker for information, rather than the other way around. For example, a hacker can impersonate a help desk employee and get the user to give them information such as a password (Granger, 2001). Again, being aware of current employees is vital to keeping information secure.

References

Bisson, D. (2015, March 23). 5 social engineering attacks to watch out for. Retrieved from http://www.tripwire.com/state-of-security/security-awareness/5-social-engineering-attacks-to-watch-out-for/.

Blair, R., & Durai, A. (2009, May 21). Chapter 1: Types of firewalls. Retrieved from http://www.networkworld.com/article/2255950/lan-wan/chapter-1--types-of-firewalls.html.

Boston University. (n.d.) Understanding authentication, authorization, and encryption. Retrieved from https://www.bu.edu/tech/about/security-resources/bestpractice/auth/.

Criddle, L. (n.d.). What is social engineering? Retrieved from Webroot: https://www.webroot.com/us/en/home/resources/tips/online-shopping-banking/secure-what-is-social-engineering.

Dara. (2015, February 3). Social engineering—Would you take the bait? Retrieved from Dara Security: https://www.darasecurity.com/article.php?id=32.

Dara. (2015, May 1). Quid pro quo—What's the cost of a free gift? Retrieved from Dara Security: https://www.darasecurity.com/article.php?id=38.

D'Hoinne, J., Hils, A., & Neiva, C. (2016, July 19). Magic quadrant for web application firewalls. Retrieved October 5, 2016, from https://www.imperva.com/ld/web-application-firewall-magic-quadrant-2017.asp.

Elovici, Y., Waisenberg, R., Shumeli, E., & Gudes, E. (n.d). A structure preserving database encryption scheme. Ben-Gurion University of the Negev, 5. Retrieved from http://www.ics.uci.edu/~ronen/papers/structurePreservingDBMSEnc.pdf.

FBI. (2009). Spear phishers: Angling to steal your financial info. Retrieved from FBI: https://archives.fbi.gov/archives/news/stories/2009/april/spearphishing_040109.

Granger, S. (2001, December 18). Social engineering fundamentals, part I: Hacker tactics. Retrieved from Symantec: https://www.symantec.com/connect/articles/social-engineering-fundamentals-part-i-hacker-tactics.

Jones, S. (Fall 2016). Discussion. Retrieved from Ball State University Blackboard, ICS620-01.

Mahesh. (2016, September). Data security and security controls in cloud computing. Retrieved from http://www.iraj.in/journal/journal_file/journal_pdf/12-295-147547115711-13.pdf.

McDowell, M. (2016, October 1). Understanding encryption. U.S. CERT. Retrieved from https://www.us-cert.gov/ncas/tips/ST04-019.

Microsoft. (n.d.). How to recognize phishing email messages, links, or phone calls. Retrieved from Microsoft: https://www.microsoft.com/en-us/safety/online-privacy/phishing-symptoms.aspx.

Rashid, F. Y. (2016, March 14). The dirty dozen: 12 cloud security threats. Retrieved from https://mis-asia.com/resource/cloud-computing/the-dirty-dozen-12-cloud-security-threats/?page=1

Soofi, A. A., Khan, M. I., & Fazal-e-Amin. (2014). Encryption techniques for cloud data confidentiality. *International Journal of Grid Distribution Computing*, *7*(4), 11–17. Retrieved from http://www.sersc.org/journals/IJGDC/vol7_no4/2.pdf.

Stine, K., & Dang, Q. (2011, September). Encryption basics. *Journal of AHIMA*, *82*(5), 44–46. Retrieved from http://library.ahima.org/doc?oid=104090#.WD4hW_krKM8.

Warlock. (2013, September 23). Social engineering: A hacking story. Retrieved from Infosec Institute: http://resources.infosecinstitute.com/social-engineering-a-hacking-story/.

Further Reading

Kirkham, "For-profit college executives make much more than their higher education counterparts [INFOGRAPHIC]."

"For-profit college students less likely to be employed after...." 21 Feb. 2012, https://capseecenter.org/for-profit-college-students-less-likely-to-be-employed-after-graduation-and-have-lower-earnings-new-study-finds/.

"Top 10 most influential tech advances of the decade." PCMag.com. 4 Jan. 2011, http://www.pcmag.com/article2/0, 2817, 2374825, 00.asp.

"K-12 edtech trends." https://www.edsurge.com/research/special-reports/state-of-edtech 2016/k12_edtech_trends.

"ECAR study of undergraduate students and...." EDUCAUSE Library. https://library.educause.edu/resources/2016/6/~/media/files/library/2016/10/ers1605.pdf.

"Butler University sees success leveraging ClearScholar student...." 6 Mar. 2017, https://clearscholar.com/butler-university-sees-success-leveraging-clearscholar-student-engagement-platform/.

"ECAR study of undergraduate students and information technology...." https://library.educause.edu/resources/2016/6/~/media/files/library/2016/10/ers1605.pdf.

"Higher ed cloud adoption on the rise." Campus Technology. 22 Sep. 2016, https://campustechnology.com/articles/2016/09/22/higher-ed-cloud-adoption-on-the-rise.aspx.

"Trends in cloud computing in higher education." eSchool Media. http://eschoolmedia.com/wp-content/uploads/2016/06/vion0622.pdf.

http://patft.uspto.gov/netacgi/nph-Parser?Sect1=PTO1&Sect2=HITOFF&d=PALL&p=1&u=%2Fnetahtml%2FPTO%2Fsrchnum.htm&r=1&f=G&l=50&s1=6,397,242.PN.&OS=PN/6,397,242&RS=PN/6,397,242

http://www.brianmadden.com/opinion/A-brief-history-of-Xen-and-XenSource

http://perspectives.mvdirona.com/2016/03/a-decade-of-innovation/

https://www.channele2e.com/2017/02/09/cloud-market-share-2017-amazon-microsoft-ibm-google/

http://www.docker.com

Chapter 16

Ontario Cloud
Contact Savvy—Launching A Multi-Cloud Solution

Kevin Keathley

Ontario Systems LLC

Contents

Ontario Systems and Contact Management

Ontario Systems is the leader in the U.S. accounts receivable (AR) and revenue management software market, with over 75,000 seats across the accounts receivable management, healthcare, and government segments. Their market dominance was extended further when Ontario Systems purchased the second largest AR software firm in mid-2016. As you might expect, consumer and patient 'contact' is a key element of systems that serve this space, and Ontario Systems has always had a fully integrated contact management platform as part of their service offerings. Historically, these have been hardware devices designed to use the legacy time-division multiplexing (TDM) telephone networks; but these are increasingly becoming Voice over IP (VoIP) solutions served from a Software-as-a-Service (SaaS) platform.

Goodbye TDM, Hello VOIP

Through the late 1990s and early 2000s, the transition from traditional TDM telephony service to VoIP was in full swing. It started as specific services that could be offered via packet switching versus the circuit switching technology that had dominated 20th-century telephony. As time has passed, Session Initiation Protocol and VoIP are garnering an increasing share of telecommunications spend and offer greater efficiency, flexibility, and cost saving potential. Ontario Systems started offering Version 1 of their fully integrated SaaS-based contact platform in 2013, Contact Savvy. This solution includes automated and manual dialing, Interactive Voice Response, Automated Call Distribution, Automated Messaging, and voice recording which provide a compliant solution for driving agent efficiency. Almost immediately following, and building on what was learned from the V1 product, work started on developing the next generation of the contact management platform – what would be the first service in their new Ontario Cloud offering.

Compliance and Load Optimized Instances

The revenue management industry is one driven by operational efficiency and a high level of compliance. The data that resides in these enterprise applications almost always contains Personally Identifiable Information, account numbers, commercial and credit account numbers, Private Health Information, and all manner of data requiring systems compliance with Payment Card Industry, Health Information and Portability Act, Federal Information Security Management Act (FISMA), and other data security standards. The Ontario Systems Contact Management application must also comply with the Telephone Consumer Protection Act and related state regulations.

Ontario Systems Contact Management application architecture utilizes microservices running in Docker containers which are spread across a variety of load optimized infrastructure instances. Some services require high compute capability, others high memory usage, and some need particularly high input/output (I/O) to support media recording and other real time back-end processes.

These factors led Ontario Systems to Amazon Web Services (AWS) as their infrastructure provider, where the underlying instances offer both high compliance and an extensive menu of configurations to suit the resource needs. They were especially attracted to the security rigor in the AWS east region for commercial business, and the FISMA compliant GovCloud located in the west region to support plans to expand their presence in the government space.

Real-Time Transport Protocol— Bare Metal Solution

While the Contact Savvy Service in AWS provides all the logic and signaling control of the contact platform, Ontario Systems has a partner that provides the switching and common carrier services. Anyone who has worked with real time, two-way communication applications know these platforms like to have direct access to the actual hardware. While Real-Time Transport Protocol services can run in a virtualized environment, high workload systems that operate at large scale need to run on physical hardware with direct access to those resources to ensure optimal user experience with minimal latency. For this reason, IBM SoftLayer was selected as the infrastructure provider for the real-time telephony portion of the contact management platform. Softlayer is one of the few cloud providers that offer bare metal 'physical' servers in a quickly expandable infrastructure; they were a great fit for this use case.

Two Clouds—One Solution

Ontario Systems had optimized their V2 contact management platform using the best cloud infrastructure providers available, based on the business needs and technical requirements. This left the task of creating a solution for the optimal network architecture that has the signal and control logic running in AWS, fully integrated (via Representational State Transfer Application Programming Interface [REST API]) with the real-time media processing in SoftLayer. Complicating this further, many of their larger clients require private connectivity to the solution. This normally involves connecting at least one (sometimes several) contact center(s) with agents, and their AR enterprise application to the contact management platform.

Tying It All Together—Clients and Clouds

The solution calculus began in 2015 as the team set out to create the network architecture to support the vision. Ontario Systems had been using DataPipe for several years to help with infrastructure management and running their ever-expanding regulatory and compliance programs. When the application is real time and has a relatively low tolerance for latency, physical geography is a key determinant. Ontario found two locations where AWS, Softlayer, and DataPipe all had a point of presence presenting in the same data center—they were Equinix data centers in

Ashburn Virginia and San Jose California. This also fit well with the strategy to launch in the east region, and eventually expand to the West where they could take advantage of AWS GovCloud for government sector compliance needs.

Equinix has a history of building carrier neutral data centers that provide prime locations for public and private interconnections. The Ashburn location, for example, is famous for having become the de facto replacement of the original Mae East—one of the largest Internet peering points on the planet that at one point was thought to carry more than half of the traffic traversing the Internet. The Equinix Cloud Exchange offering is designed to provide interconnects between network service providers (NSP) and cloud providers, much the same way as their Ethernet Exchange facilitated Internet peering. High speed and highly redundant Ethernet fabric connects over 600 carriers across a dozen data centers on the Ashburn campus.

This provided Ontario Systems with a key element of the network design, a unifying component of the network architecture that supports a multi-cloud solution, as well as private connections from clients in a carrier-neutral facility. The team ended 2015 with agreements in place to support the Alpha and Beta phases through 2016.

Multi-Cloud—From Theory to Deployment

Ontario Systems spent the first quarter of 2016 refining the deployment automation for their stack in AWS, and developing and testing the deep integration with their telephony partner. By the end of the quarter, Ontario had deployed their switch stack in Ashburn DC10 and provisioned two 10 Gbps ports to the Cloud Exchange. Ontario's telephony provider, Ampersand, had their Cloud Exchange ports delivered from SoftLayer as well, so they were then able to build the virtual circuits (VCs), decommission the test virtual private networks, and start traversing the Cloud Exchange to exercise the final state 'production plumbing.'

The results have been very impressive. During several months of Alpha testing over the network and the exchange, they observed very consistent 2 ms ping times with absolutely no loss. The fact that a multi-cloud solution that lives within different cloud infrastructure providers still has latency rivaling the best internal LAN is an outcome that was better than expected. Subsequent testing with the first private circuit customers connecting to the solution has also shown solid low latency results as well.

Other Upsides for the Enterprise

A connection to the Cloud Exchange offers flexibility as well as other long-term benefits to Ontario customers. Besides Ontario Systems, there are many other cloud service providers that present on the exchange, including: AWS, SoftLayer, Google,

Microsoft Azure, Office 365, Oracle Cloud, Rackspace, and others. A client may order their Cloud Exchange connection to support connectivity to Ontario's cloud and contact platform, but they may also leverage that same connection to provide private high-speed connectivity to other cloud service providers. In the future, Ontario believes it will be common for their clients to have their own AWS account for long term storage of their voice recordings, which are a component of all customer interactions required for compliance. Many clients may also leverage the connection to include direct access to Office 365 for their corporate use or other advanced cloud services. This connection is not exclusive to any one provider and the Ashburn endpoint can be virtually connected to many cloud providers via software networking VCs—it is quite literally 'multi-cloud.'

Best of Breed Partners

Ontario Systems made some good partner decisions for the launch of their V2 contact platform. They are positioned well for the future and have a solid strategy for their products as well as their cloud infrastructure, architecture, and vision. They may be a little 'ahead of the curve' in some ways, but are confident in the strategy. The only issue reported so far, is that the NSPs are very slow to change their ordering and provisioning systems, and seem to be viewing the Exchange as a "product" decision more than an interconnect solution. As more and more carriers understand the footprint, Ontario Systems is confident the NSP carrier options will continue to grow.

Index